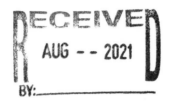

THE
TIGHTENING
DARK

THE
TIGHTENING
DARK

AN AMERICAN HOSTAGE IN YEMEN

SAM FARRAN
AND BENJAMIN BUCHHOLZ

hachette
BOOKS

NEW YORK

Copyright © 2021 by Sam Farran and Benjamin Buchholz

Cover design by Terri Sirma

Cover photograph © D-Keine / Getty Images

Cover copyright © 2021 by Hachette Book Group, Inc.

Translation of Quran 2:286 verse from *The Quran: Translated to English by Talal Itani*. ClearQuran, Beirut. 2012.

Hachette Books
Hachette Book Group
1290 Avenue of the Americas
New York, NY 10104
HachetteBooks.com
Twitter.com/HachetteBooks
Instagram.com/HachetteBooks

First Edition: July 2021

Published by Hachette Books, an imprint of Perseus Books, LLC, a subsidiary of Hachette Book Group, Inc. The Hachette Books name and logo is a trademark of the Hachette Book Group.

The Hachette Speakers Bureau provides a wide range of authors for speaking events. To find out more, go to www.hachettespeakersbureau.com or call (866) 376-6591.

The publisher is not responsible for websites (or their content) that are not owned by the publisher.

Library of Congress Control Number: 2021938259

ISBNs: 978-0-306-92271-8 (hardcover); 978-0-306-92272-5 (ebook)

Printed in the United States of America

LSC-C

Printing 1, 2021

For those who have served

CONTENTS

Yemen and the Houthi Advance

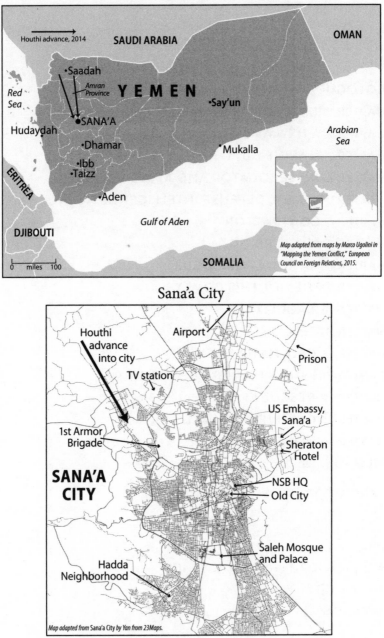

Sana'a City

Map adapted from maps by Marco Ugolini in "Mapping the Yemen Conflict," European Council on Foreign Relations, 2015.

Map adapted from Sana'a City by Yan from 23Maps.

PROLOGUE

I HAD PASSED THROUGH Sana'a International Airport so many times that part of me, a big part, tried not to pay attention to the changes, tried not to be worried about the things I saw that were so markedly different from all the other times I had entered through the airport's gates. This part of me kept me calm. This part of me knew the smells of Sana'a: the thin, cool air infused with dust wafting up 7,000 feet into the mountains from the emptiness of the Rub al-Khali desert below. This part of me didn't worry about mongrel dogs scurrying around. It didn't worry about sirens or the occasional celebratory gunfire from a wedding down the street. It didn't care about squalor. It noticed human suffering, people in the shadows, in every shadow, watching, hungry, threadbare, but it did so not in a state of panic or despair but more as a matter of contrast between rich, clean Dubai—where I now lived—and the Middle East's poorest country. My bravado and my experience of Yemen allowed me to step forward, one

1

foot in front of the other, despite all these things. It allowed me to smile at the baggage handlers, the workers in the ratty airport café, the passport inspectors, and even the multitude of guards and armed military personnel who hadn't always been so prevalent—lounging about on the fringes of the runway, laughing in the baggage hall, leering at us passengers in the passport lane, watching us from the taxi stand outside on the curb in front of the airport.

Sure, I could be cool. I could come and go and pretend like everything was okay.

But another part of me itched.

This part knew something had changed. It knew something was different and wrong.

In one corner of my mind, I heard the voices of my friends, Yemenis and others who had fled and had been telling me not to come back. I also heard the voices of my friends inside the country, calls I had made to them before getting on the plane this time. These people who had stayed—highly placed in Yemeni military or intelligence posts or just businessmen who knew what was what—warned me it wasn't wise to come back to Yemen, not right now, not even for the savviest American, not even for an American who had grown up like me: Lebanese, fluent in the culture, fluent in the Arabic language, of course, and an ex-Marine too.

CHAPTER 1

IDYLLS OF A LEBANESE CHILDHOOD

LEBANON

I was born in a small village called Tebnine in the far south of Lebanon, just on the other side of the border from what is now Israel. My village is an ancient and beautiful one, situated in the mountains on the road between Tyre and Damascus. The Crusaders built a fort here. Saladin, first sultan of Egypt and Syria and founder of the Ayyubid dynasty, took it over. The Ottomans ruled us. The French too. And a lot of the worst fighting in the Lebanese Civil War throughout the 1970s and 1980s happened right around us, there in the south near and in my village. But I left before those latest calamities and remember only good things from Tebnine. The first seven years of my life come back to me wrapped in this sense of goodness, as if enveloped in a golden mist.

As a youngster back in the 1960s, I had the run of the whole place, from one grandfather's house in the Hayy Harra, the Hill

3

Neighborhood, down to my other grandfather's house in the valley, or Hayy Tahta, the Low Neighborhood, as we called it. I roamed the Christian area freely too, perched on its hill with its church bells. We hardly knew there was any difference back then, Christian or Muslim, as every day we heard both the muezzin crier in the minaret of our mosque and those deep bronze bells in the church tower. They filled the air in a way I always thought of as beautiful, haunting almost in its contrast and cacophony, though most people would find it odd, I think now, those two sounds together at intervals or overlapping.

The gang I ran with were all kids related to me. In fact, most of the townspeople were relatives of some sort since, as I said, Tebnine was and is just a village—1,500 or 2,000 people back then, probably no more than 3,000 now—and almost everyone belonged to one of two families, the Fawaz or the Berri. My mother was a Fawaz, the dominant family. The Berris were the rich ones, though everyone got along just fine, and even the Berris were friendly people. Nabih Berri, the current head of that clan, is now the most powerful man in Lebanon as the Speaker of Parliament. His sister Nabiha married my mother's brother in a match that has probably been repeated a thousand times over the centuries, someone from Fawaz marrying into Berri and vice versa. We're all family in Tebnine.

I knew of these things as a kid, history and marriages and war, but they weren't my world. They were only peripheral subjects that grownups talked about and that seemed somewhat unreal to me. My world involved running through the streets with my friends, cousin Hussein and cousin Ahmed, both of whom were just a little bit younger than me, with a parcel of even younger siblings—Hisham and Ibtissam—trying to keep up with us whenever they could.

Lebanon

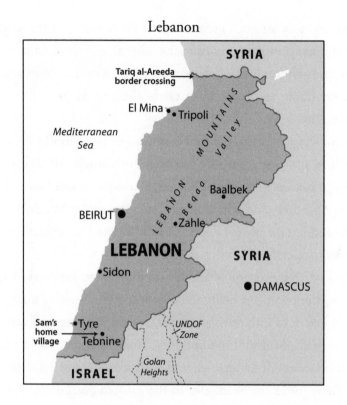

We played a lot of war games, did a lot of hunting. We were experts with slingshots like Tom Sawyer, searching out the perfect Y-shaped branches in our grandmother's fig or olive trees, cutting them (which got us scolded or smacked), and then stretching lengths of bicycle tire so that we could heave fist-sized cobblestones with enough accuracy and power to kill birds. We'd bring the birds home to my mom for dinner, especially the tasty little *asafeer*, which were like sparrows. Or sometimes we'd bring them to grandmother to repay her for the branches we'd swiped. We'd often also shoot each other with pebbles, starting little wars between ourselves or bullying the little ones so that always, it seemed, one or another of us would need to run away, down the hillside, through the narrow stone streets, to take refuge at the house or in the neighborhood of some cousin or aunt from the other side of the family.

This was typical life in Lebanon for a kid. Free rein. Sunshine. The best mountains and climate on earth. Everything grew like weeds, including us.

There was work too, but that I remember most fondly of all.

"Wake up, sleepy head," I remember my uncle Ali saying many mornings before first light. He'd steal into the room where I slept with my brothers and sisters around me and shake me, only me, by one shoulder until my eyes opened. I didn't need to be told what was going to happen.

Uncle Ali owned one of the few cars in town. He'd take me and Hussein, the two of us being the oldest and strongest of our generation, and pack us into the backseat of that car to bring us down to his tobacco fields. Still rubbing our eyes, Hussein and I would grasp at old oil lanterns Ali handed us, and we'd stumble out into the darkness. There, once the headlights of the car had been doused and our eyes had adjusted to the dimmer but warmer glow of the lamp light, we'd see other figures in the fields adjacent to us, in our own field too, some of them moving, their lamps swaying slowly, some walking through puddled light from lanterns placed on the ground so that their shadows loomed and receded, blending with the shadows of the waist-high plants. Each field held a constellation of such lanterns. The shadowed figures moved around them, bending, picking, stuffing big canvas sacks with tobacco leaves, maybe fifty people in each field all busy at once. Hushed voices. Quiet and simple hearts. Tebnine was famous for tobacco. Best in the world. Our families, our own hands, picked it on those cold, quiet mornings, all of us like ghosts as the sun shivered up from beneath the mountain ridges.

We'd make a few cents from this enterprise, so we loved it. We loved the money, a big privilege to have some for ourselves, but we also loved the camaraderie. We loved being singled out by Ali as his helpers. I remember that Hussein and I were paid most often to string the tobacco, taking a nine-inch needle and a long thread and sewing the leaves onto a line that we stretched between makeshift sawhorses that had been brought out to the field. The leaves were left like this to dry. And we'd get five cents a string, usually completing two or three strings in a morning.

This money we would save up for the Friday market (Souk Al Jumma), which was a fixture of our childhood: that time after prayers at the mosque when all the vendors set up their little tented shops and we could buy sweets, popguns, knickknacks, all the things kids crave. On outings to the market, and elsewhere too, Hussein and I led our little gang, which also included my younger sister Ibtissam and Hussein's sister Fatimah, as well as my baby brother Hisham.

■ ■ ■

ONE THURSDAY NIGHT, after we had been tucked into our beds, sleep came with difficulty, as I didn't know whether Hussein and I had earned enough in the tobacco fields to supply everyone with goodies for the market that coming morning. As our mother blew out the candle in our room, Ibtissam asked me for the tenth time what flavors of ice cream I thought the Friday market might have that week. I didn't know. But I had a lot of fun making up strange concoctions and imagining her face in the darkness as it registered disbelief and worry: pumpkin, mulberry, goat cheese, grass, all kinds of strange things.

Truthfully, I felt a little sick to my stomach about sharing the money I'd earned. I really didn't want to spend those coins. I'd worked hard for them. But we always treated things more communally. Ibtissam, in my mind and heart, had earned a share of my tobacco proceeds just by being my sister. It really wasn't a choice; it was more a lifestyle, or a culture, but even then I already knew it was a good one, though it required me to put aside some of my personal desire for riches (and sweets) in order to share with my "tribe."

Morning came at last, and with it the Friday market.

It turned out to be everything we expected. The Friday market was, and still is, an institution in Tebnine, as in many other villages throughout Lebanon. Vendors come from all over. Awnings are set up. Wares are spread gleaming in the sun. Musicians and singers find shady places in the town square or walk from place to place strumming their *ouds* or trilling their *mijwiz* flutes.

We kids knew the market. We frequented it every Friday. We hung around the edges, listened to the music, ogled the shops. But never before did we have anything nearly as much as two whole *lira* to spend.

We got our ice cream, a couple popguns, a few other doodads, a ribbon Fatimah twisted into her hair. We were as happy as we'd ever been, close-knit, picking our way among the crowds of adults who filled their bags with fresh produce or sat in one of the cafés on the square, smoking shisha, that mainstay of Arab and Turkish cafés, also sometimes called a hookah, while also drinking little cups of Turkish coffee.

Under the big tree in the square center, a storyteller had gathered a small crowd around him, all of them sitting cross-legged on the ground. We were pulled toward him, as if by magic, or by an attractor beam, but just as we came near enough to hear his words, I saw my grandfather, the one from the High Neighborhood. He wasn't Hussein or Ahmed's grandfather, but they knew him—101 years old, wizened, ancient, and nearly blind too. They saw him approaching the storyteller, striding forward in his insistent but shriveled way, and they pulled us forward even though Ibtissam and I tried to turn away.

"C'mon," said Hussein. "This'll be classic."

I couldn't say anything. I feared it would be a train wreck. My grandfather could be a very agreeable person, tender and full of attention to us kids. But he could also be argumentative. And this looked like an argumentative moment.

The storyteller stopped speaking as my grandfather stepped right into the middle of his cross-legged crowd.

"You want a story?" grandfather said. "I'll give you a story..."

Everyone had heard my grandfather's stories a hundred million times. He was, justifiably, famous for them. But he couldn't stand someone else stealing center stage. The situation felt combustible. I didn't know what might happen, with my grandfather such an institution in town and this storyteller, obviously, foreign—swarthier than anyone in town but also strangely fluent in not only our language but also our accent, our voice, our way of saying things in Tebnine. Lebanon was like this back then, still is to some extent. Just by how we speak you can tell who is a big-city person, who is a village person, who is from the north or the south or the Beqaa Valley. You can tell who is from your village or from the village next door through small little signs, some of them secret, some not, like passwords in pronunciation. This storyteller must have been an adept at voice, I thought, because he nailed it. He sounded just like one of us despite being, quite obviously, from somewhere else.

"Story!" my grandfather said again. "A young man like you, what can you know about stories!"

The storyteller simply stood and held his ground against my grandfather's approach.

More quietly but still quite clearly, the man said, "And what would you give us to keep these people entertained, *hajji*? Will it be a story of how you escaped from the Turkish army? How you had been kidnapped and then 'recruited,' brought north to the war to fight the British at Gallipoli or the peasants in Armenia or wherever, and how you escaped not once, not twice, not three times, but four— ditching your uniform and walking back in a potato sack or dressed like a Sufi, wandering months and months across all of Turkey's wilderness until you came home, only to get 'recruited' again the next time the Basha's troops came to town?"

This was no storyteller. This was a mind reader, a magus, a wizard. He'd called my grandfather's bluff. He'd spoken just as if he had pulled the words from my grandfather's mouth, a sweet and perfect summary of exactly what grandfather's stories always focused on: his long-ago exploits evading service with the Ottoman army.

My grandfather's mouth fell open for a moment. He took a half step backward. But then a twinkle filled his rheumy eyes. He squinted. And then he held his arms out wide.

"Son," he said.

I looked from my grandfather to the storyteller and back again. I couldn't figure out what was going on.

"Son..."

The two men clasped each other, not in a handshake or in the semiformal embrace of long-lost friends, but in a hug much more tender and endearing. My grandfather's body shook a little. It crossed my mind that he might be crying.

Ibtissam grabbed my hand. "What's happening with grandpa?"

"I don't—" *No. No. I knew. I knew what was happening.*

"Dad? Pappa?" I said, and I pulled Ibtissam with me toward the two men.

People started to stand from their cross-legged places of comfort. They started to clap, to whistle. A woman ululated, that trilling noise Arab women make with their lips and forefingers when they're overcome by emotion. Ibtissam and I pushed our way through and joined in the hug. Hussein and Ahmed and Fatimah hugged too, though they seemed a bit more confused. We were all hugging.

Ahmed was asking me what was going on. I remember telling him, the words forming almost in disbelief, that it was my dad, my father, returned home.

As the dark-skinned man broke his grip on grandfather, he picked up Ibtissam and held her in front of him, far in front, at arm's length, so he could see her well. "You've grown so much!"

"And me?" I asked.

"You?" he joked. "Who are you? I don't know any teenagers."

"I'm not a teenager. I'm seven. It's me, Papa. It's Haisam."

"Of course," he said, pretending to wipe away a cloud from in front of his eyes and see me more clearly. He shook my hand, as if I were a man, then pulled me closer. His skin was tanned from working construction in the burgeoning economies of the Gulf, under the unceasing sun there. He hardly appeared to be Lebanese, more Egyptian, or even Saudi. But he certainly sounded Lebanese. He sounded Tebnini. He sounded just as I remembered him, funny and serious all at once, though perhaps a bit more gravelly voiced and tired.

Dad led us all home, and we repeated—or tried to repeat—the same scene for the benefit of grandmother and mom. We tried to make it a surprise, a charade. But my mom and grandmother smoked it right away. Perhaps they heard us laughing as we walked up the hill toward the olive grove. Perhaps they identified him by more than just his face or hands. Maybe his eyes hadn't changed. Likely his two-year absence didn't dim their recollections as completely as they blinded our young and cloistered minds. The women rushed in. Ibtissam and I and the other kids were pushed away, but not far, only to the dancing, jittering perimeter, grabbing at the hems of the adults' robes, their elbows, their hands. Everything was chaos. The noon bells of the church and the *dhuhr* call to prayer crisscrossed in the air around us, a wingless and bodiless flight. Kisses seemed to fall from the sky. And just as suddenly as that, the women turned to practicalities: *What would we eat? How would we rearrange the rooms? When would we have a party to celebrate father's return and our reunion? How long was he staying and how had he traveled here and how was he feeling and wouldn't he like to have a seat inside for a minute, maybe some tea, some figs?*

Dad hardly let those questions hit the air.

"We're moving to Libya," he said. "I've got a new job there."

LIBYA

My dad believed in hard work. How could he not? He'd earned his money through hard work, and most of that money during his Kuwait construction days he sent home to take care of me, and mom, and Hisham, and Ibtissam, and little baby Bassem, who was still not weaned, as well as having some to spare and distribute among parents and brothers and sisters.

I remember my father telling me, when I first started working for him—not in those idyllic tobacco fields with Uncle Ali, which was lovely work, but later, working in a restaurant he opened—that I had it easy. As a kid my age he had walked a day or two south each week to the Israeli port of Haifa. There he wandered the streets with a wooden tray slung from a rope around his neck. He sold odds and ends from that tray: condiments, razor blades, shaving cream. When he'd dispensed with all his supplies, he would walk back to Tebnine, another two days' journey but this time uphill, back into the Lebanese mountains that kept us safe and sheltered.

That was my dad. Great sense of humor but also as serious as serious can be, and quite a traveler too. He told us we needed to go to Libya to work, but really this was 1968, and the Arabs had just suffered a mighty defeat at the hands of Israel. My dad knew bad things were in store for Lebanon, and he wanted us to get away before they started.

We couldn't afford tickets for the whole family, so Ibtissam and Hisham remained behind in Tebnine with grandmother, while dad and mom and baby Bassem and I boarded a passenger ship in Beirut and sailed for Alexandria. While Alexandria doesn't seem too far from Beirut, the weather was nasty that year, and I remember most from the journey the empty, stormy sea, no land anywhere to be seen, and my own constant, hourly rush up narrow, cold stairs from our berth to the railing, where my seasickness gave me plenty of time to watch the Mediterranean's wine-dark waves roil in the ship's wake.

Egypt still smacked of embarrassment and a bit of panic after its failure in the Six Days' War against Israel. The Israelis had been stopped at the Suez Canal more by diplomatic effort than Egyptian forces. To try to build back his country's confidence, Egypt's president, Gamal Abdel Nasser, could be seen and heard everywhere: posters, broadcasts, speaking and putting out policy among the other

Arab nations. He was a big man, for sure, but also a man who had just lost and lost badly. So our passage from Alexandria south to Cairo occurred amid a backdrop of propaganda, with us being foreigners, though foreigners of the most unnoticeable sort, fellow Arabs—a bit different, obviously Lebanese, but largely unthreatening.

We spent a few days in Cairo getting our paperwork in order. There we saw, of course, the pyramids but also the Khan al-Khalili Souq, which made my eyes go wide with its richness and the storied, colorful, winding streets. Everything looked like a Friday market, except instead of sun and country greenery and laughter, the Khan al-Khalili was filled with strange scents of spice and glittering bits of glass and bronze and old *mashrabiya* windows with their deeply latticed shutters, behind which, in my young boy's mind, a million eyes were watching me from the buildings above. I'd never been somewhere so big, so overflowing with people. Compared to Cairo, even Beirut felt like a village.

When we'd walked through most of the souq, my father turned to me and took my hand. We left mother and Bassem on the street corner, and father led me forward, across a bit of park. There we stopped in front of the great mosque of Hussein.

"Have you prayed before as a man?" he asked me.

"Yes, I have," I said.

"Good, then you will come with me."

We took off our shoes and entered the mosque, which is one of the holiest places in the world for Shi'a, because we believe the head of Prophet Muhammad's grandson, Hussein, is buried there. Truthfully, I had prayed now and again, but in Tebnine it wasn't a major thing for me. I was still young then. Hills and streets, tobacco picking and slingshots figured much more prominently in my life than prayer or going to the mosque. And also my father had been gone, so I was left to my own devices much more than I should have been, at least when it came to something like prayer. But there, in Cairo with my father, in that huge and holy space, I caught myself just staring about me, taking in the vastness of it, the quietness, how the barefooted men assumed such reverence and how, together, we all took our places and performed the *rukaa'a*, the prescribed sequence of kneeling, praying, kneeling, rising, and praying, all facing toward Mecca, over and over. It stirred a chord in me, one of belonging and rightness, but also like a whisper in my blood or a connection to something in the air, something more than human: I *felt* it. For the first time I felt it. This experience, praying in the Hussein Mosque, still remains the most vivid and impactful memory I carry with me of my father. I spent the rest of the day, and maybe longer, maybe even the next few weeks of our new life, in a state of awe and inner quiet.

From Cairo we went overland in a hired car. This was a bit like a bus, except it was just a car into which our four family members, all our luggage, and a whole additional family and its luggage were crammed. I sat on my father's lap most of the way, with my mom having to deal with baby Bassem, who was still breast-feeding then.

We first spent a year in the eastern city of Derna, right on the water in the only really green and forested part of Libya. Here the mountains spill down to the sea, so the place looks and feels a bit like Lebanon. This helped remove some of the shock of leaving home, though I remember not making many friends, at least not right away.

My dad worked a construction project in Derna for a year, until Libya also stirred with unrest as Muamar Qadafi came into power. Again, and almost as suddenly, father announced we would move—this time to Benghazi, a little further down the Libyan coast, and this time not for a construction job. Dad and mom had decided to open a restaurant.

We lived behind the restaurant in an unfinished apartment building, without even concrete on the floors yet, just dirt. For a bathroom we used the one in the restaurant. And I was put to work, really put to work, for the first time in my life, washing dishes, cleaning, and waiting tables. Our living conditions were harsh, nothing as sweet as the mountains around Tebnine, but otherwise the restaurant turned out to be a resounding success. We were the first to provide Lebanese cooking in Benghazi, a big deal right then because a whole bunch of people had just moved from Syria and Lebanon and Palestine and Jordan. My parents made money hand over fist, enough to allow us not only to travel back to Tebnine a couple times but also to bring back with us to Libya my siblings Hisham and Ibtissam, reuniting all of us.

For my first trip back, my mom dressed me. New clothes, starchy. I was jumping out of my skin with excitement, and the last thing I wanted was to be bound up in fancy clothes. But when my father called me into his bedroom, I understood better the reason why I had to wear not only a shirt and tie but also a tailored jacket.

He handed me a belt that looked strangely lumpy. I didn't have too much experience with belts, with formal clothes. But still something looked wrong.

"What is it?" I asked.

"A belt."

"I know," I said, taking it and trying to put its fat end through the loops at my waist. The belt wouldn't fit, not easily. "But what's on it?"

"Packages."

He explained that Qadafi wouldn't let more than one hundred lira leave the country at any one time and that he wouldn't let Lebanese people keep their savings in a bank either. So we had no choice but to smuggle it out of the country, back to our family in Lebanon. It was just a larger version of Hussein and me sharing our tobacco-stringing money with our siblings.

The scheme worked perfectly. I passed through customs with hardly a glance, both in Tripoli's airport and in Beirut. I should have been nervous, but I wasn't. I just felt fortunate not to have to take a boat back to Lebanon and risk seasickness again. And also the idea of all that money just made me think of the Friday market and how, instead of buying a few ice creams and popguns, I'd be able to set up as a merchant myself, selling rubies and diamonds and all the best spices, opening my own Khan al-Khalili. Of course, I would be the hero all over again, quick to resume my place at the head of the gang.

Though Tebnine has always remained in my heart (and even now I've bought my cousin Khalil's old house and am refurbishing it for my retirement), my story only rarely intersects with it again. Sure, I made those trips back, and many more even during the bad parts of Lebanon's civil war in the 1980s, but my life went a different direction. I hit a fork in the road almost immediately on my return to Libya from that first money-laden trip, for I realized then why my parent's restaurant had done so well: the Palestine Liberation Organization (PLO).

Black September that year had seen King Hussein of Jordan kick the PLO leadership out of his country. They fled to Lebanon and Syria, reestablishing headquarters there. But they also set up a training camp in Benghazi. After the regular rush on Fridays, my parents would close the restaurant down to our normal customers, and a couple of big buses of young men—hungry young men, polite young men—would come. I served them their food. They ate, and they joked, and they did all the normal things done by normal twenty-something kids. I liked them.

"How old are you, boy?" one of them asked, putting his hand on my shoulder when I delivered a big bowl of tabbouleh to his table.

"Ten."

"What do you think of Palestine?"

"I love it."

"Good boy."

The chatter of the other PLO trainees had not stopped. But this man and I seemed frozen in place, with everything else eddying around us. I could see my mom out of the corner of my eye, beckoning to my father from the kitchen, not looking at me, not worried. Everything was normal. But I was stuck there, mesmerized. The man had green eyes, nothing abnormal for a Palestinian or a Syrian, but he did not blink. And he had a line on his face like he had been cut by a very fine razor blade. It made me think of my father when he was a child, selling those razors on foot in Haifa port.

"Would you like to learn to shoot?"

"I know how to shoot." I pantomimed the action of my slingshot, a bird falling from the sky.

The man laughed. "No," he said. "Guns."

I shook my head no, but then, ever so slowly, the side-to-side no motion changed to an up-and-down nod, like I was spinning, dazed.

"Next week then," he said. "I'll come for you on Thursday night, and we'll bring you back when we come here Friday after prayers. An overnight adventure!"

I got nervous then. I stood a bit straighter, didn't answer him directly, turned away, and half-ran back into the kitchen. I didn't say anything to anyone about this encounter, but, as I sat on a sack of rice, I saw my mother look from me to the young fedayeen member, and then back again. Her eyes were filled with worry.

CHAPTER 2

A NEW AMERICAN

T HE NEXT DAY we unpacked the jar where my parents stored the spare money, rented another car (this time not shared), and drove around the long bay that connects Benghazi with Tripoli, the capital of Libya, several hours away. My parents barely spoke the whole way. They just said we were going on a vacation. And that's exactly how it seemed: off to the biggest city in Libya, off—maybe—to the beach. Indeed, we checked into a hotel in a nice part of Tripoli and had a good dinner, and we children felt our hopes rise in expectation of enjoying the coming day.

However, the following morning we were all—Hisham, Ibtissam, me, mom, dad, and Bassem—hustled into our very best clothes before daybreak. We left the hotel without eating breakfast and went to stand on the street, five or six people ahead of us, in a line that grew and grew as dawn started to shed a honey-colored light over the faces of Tripoli's white-washed facades.

I asked where we were. My mom avoided the question, just telling me that we were in line. She meant for me to drop the question, but I persisted. She waved a hand at me, demanding silence, and we kept our places, queuing along the street.

"Where are we?" I asked.

"We're in line," mom said.

"But where?"

"Hush."

When the line had grown to half a hundred people, a window opened, and a guard came out from a door I hadn't noticed in the high, spike-topped wall. This guard was the biggest human I'd ever seen, seven feet tall I thought. He had blonde hair and very white horselike teeth. He was dressed in an immaculate, deep blue uniform with red stripes on the legs as well as medals and insignia everywhere on his chest and along his high starched collar. The sun shone on him, and the medals and insignia caught its light, reflecting it back at me in a blinding kaleidoscope. This man held a rifle over one shoulder, smartly and confidently, and he squared his corners, turning at right angles, sharp in all his movements as he stepped into position beside the doorway, there to bring the rifle's buttstock crashing down beside his foot before he seemed to freeze in place, standing there statue still.

Just like in the Hussein Mosque, I found myself transfixed, not wanting to enter the gate in the wall as the line crept forward and my father pulled me into the US Embassy. This was my first sight of a US Marine, this guard at the embassy in Tripoli, and—not surprising at all for a boy my age, though certainly a unique thing for a Lebanese boy—the experience of him, his regal bearing, his professionalism, stood out to me as something aspirational. The mosque had been

spiritual and profound. The young man from the Palestine Liberation Organization (PLO) had felt more like home, like a friend. But
the Marine—though he did nothing in particular, nothing different
from what he had been trained to do, nothing different from the
things a thousand other Marines do at embassies every day, even now,
the world over—my ten-year-old brain fixated on him. I had a first
inkling not of the person I was *meant* to become (all my heritage and
upbringing should have predisposed me to life as a harvester of tobacco or, if I yearned for something exotic, to follow the beckoning
of that fedayeen) but of something even more special—the freedom
to imagine a different and better future.

We'd all heard plenty about America. Who hadn't? But this first
direct experience, at the very moment when I was ripest to be influ-
enced, changed me completely.

AMERICA

The rest of that visit to the embassy and to Tripoli blurs together in
my mind. Overwhelmed by the image of that Marine beside the gate,
all other memories seem dim and washed out. Only that tall figure in
his uniform remains clear. And I can trace one of the most fateful
moments in my life back to that experience, the outcome of a hundred little decisions adding up over decades and bringing me back to
that place, there by the embassy gate.

We got our visas to America within a few short days. This was
made easier and smoother because our history in America goes back
to 1916, with my great-grandfather Ahmed Hamzey Fawaz, who arrived in 1916. He was part of the first wave of Lebanese immigrants
to America, the same batch that included the poet Kahlil Gibran.

Then my mother's father, Fares Ahmed Fawaz, arrived in 1924 and went to high school here, later marrying my step-grandmother, Najla. So, in fact, my family had been American for two generations already, and we had contacts there, a history, a landing pad to help us adjust. This was the key that opened the door for us. My uncle, Robert Hamzey, son of Fares Ahmed Fawaz and Najla, sponsored my mother's immigration.

In 1971 we took a Scandinavian Airlines flight to New York City. To a ten-year-old this flight seemed to take forever, but unlike when we moved to Libya, our whole family remained together. My mother and father had been able to save the equivalent of somewhere between $50,000 and $60,000 from the restaurant, squirreling it away in pots and mattresses back in Lebanon after smuggling it out of Libya any way we could. This was a good amount of money back in the 1970s. It gave us a head start and allowed us to begin our time in America with a house, a car, and some of the essentials we kids needed for school or that my parents needed for work.

■ ■ ■

OUR PLANE TOUCHED down in New York City, but we didn't spend any time there. We caught sight of the Statue of Liberty out the plane windows, misty and green against the gray, choppy waters of the harbor below us. Then we transferred planes and headed right to Michigan, where we stayed at my great-grandfather's house in Highland Park before using some of that hard-earned restaurant money to buy a house a week later in Dearborn. The month was February, and not the sort of February we had grown up with in Lebanon or Libya: Michigan was frigid. First order of business, we all got winter clothes. Second order of business: school. We started right away, on either the second or third day we landed. Knowing one word, "hello," and pretty much shell-shocked from the change in country, culture, weather, time zone, and home, I sat in the back of an almost-normal US elementary school classroom wondering how the heck I would survive.

I say "almost normal" because Dearborn, Michigan—even at that time—was a different place than "normal" America. We had such a high population of Arab families, fathers who had come to work in the automotive industry after other family members settled there, that this school, Salina Intermediate School, had one of the nation's first English as a second language (ESL) programs. ESL helped me immensely, allowing me not only to work on learning how to communicate in my new country but also to continue my studies of math, science, history, and geography, while transitioning to English. ESL bridged the time between when I arrived and when I could undertake those other subjects in English by providing dedicated resources to ensure I did not lag behind. It allowed me to continue learning in Arabic while I learned English. This, along with the overall quality of the education, really motivated me to come to school and take advantage of the wonders of America.

But it wasn't just ESL that helped me transition. About 40 percent of the other kids in my classes hailed originally from Lebanon and Palestine, some of them even from Tebnine, so I felt right at home, could talk with them, could make friends and find support. A kid from Lebanon, from a village near mine, Mohamed Ajrouch, who had only arrived a month before me, took me under his wing. We went to ESL together, and he helped me with my English as we sat in the back of the classroom.

Two days into my time at Salina, I experienced my first real culture shock. This happened in gym class, during a swimming lesson. I stepped into the locker room, and all the boys started taking off their clothes.

This never happens in Lebanon.

It's taboo across most of the Middle East. You have to make sure the bathroom door is locked ten times before you ever do your business.

There in that locker room I was stunned, staring and frozen in place, no idea what was going on and refusing to get naked myself. The gym teacher, Mr. Costia, who wasn't Arab at all, still had taught himself a few words of Arabic.

He said, "*Habibi*, what's the matter?"

Everyone liked Mr. Costia. He was not only the gym teacher but also the football coach. He had a heart of gold, and as his attempts at Arabic showed, he really took an interest in us as kids. But his phrasing here turned out to be especially unfortunate: *habibi* means "my love." Everyone had gotten naked already. Some had already run out of the locker room and jumped into the big pool. As I stood there with Mr. Costia calling me his "boy love" and waiting for me to strip, I felt more and more isolated as the other kids went out to the pool. I thought the worst rumors about America might actually be true! What sort of depraved situation would this become? What would happen if I took off my clothes?

I clammed up, refused.

I wouldn't take off my shoes, let alone my shirt.

I absolutely refused to take my pants off.

So, of course, Mr. Costia had no choice. He sent me to the principal's office.

In Lebanese culture this is also a big no-no—to dishonor yourself, to cause your parents stress and make them get involved in your shortcomings at school. Needless to say, the whole experience turned out to be traumatic for me. Even after the principal patiently explained, through one of the several interpreters on staff at the school, the purpose of the swim class, the cultural norms of locker room etiquette, and the requirement for me to get changed in order to not fail the course, I still didn't want to do it. But my parents had a stern discussion with me over the kitchen table that night, and at the next gym class, I bucked up, stripped down (blushing all the way), put on my swimsuit, and jumped into the water.

Which wasn't the end of the problem.

I didn't know how to swim! But I sure wasn't going to resist and have my parents called to the principal's office again.

That episode almost killed me twice over—once from sheer embarrassment at my nakedness and then again as I sank to the bottom of the heavily chlorinated deep end, only to be dragged spluttering up to the surface by Mr. Costia, who had to jump in to rescue me.

Although gym class frightened and nearly killed me, I've got to say again that school in America overall turned out to be a dream. Free milk. Free lunch. And every day during lunchbreak we were given the choice to pay a nickel to watch a movie. All these things amazed me, so different were they from school in Libya or in Lebanon, which was rudimentary and sometimes even cruel, with headmasters not averse to whacking our fingers with a stick and with twenty or thirty kids of all ages crowded into a single dingy, undersupplied classroom.

I did not take the benefits around me in my new city and country for granted. The movies were fun, sure, but like the ESL classes, they served a purpose in helping me improve my English. And the lunches and milk, well, perhaps I was a little skinny—not malnourished because my parents ran a restaurant, but certainly skinny. There seemed to be nothing as effective at putting on pounds as good American milk and a hot lunch at an American school!

My parents used the last of their savings from Libya to open another restaurant in Dearborn. They bought a Coney Island Diner, which was a popular chain in the 1970s—vinyl upholstered booths along one wall, a few stools at a coffee bar, a cash register with a glass-topped cooler beside it to display pies and other deserts. Their concept was to remake it in Lebanese fashion, serving hummus, tabbouleh, shawarma, kibbeh, and all the great things that made their Benghazi restaurant such a hit. Problem was, they opened it up on the wrong end of town. East Dearborn was still predominantly white, Italian, and Irish, and under the notorious administration of Mayor Orville Hubbard, it was known as one of the most segregated communities north of the Mason-Dixon Line. We got about twelve customers a day, a few Poles or Italians who came in and then a few brave Arabs who drove the whopping four miles across town to patronize us. Obviously, the restaurant failed pretty quickly. But my dad wasn't daunted.

In addition to my father's working the assembly lines, first at Chrysler for a few months and then at Ford for a number of years, we bought another restaurant, this one on the South End of town and fated to have a much longer life. I worked there, as well as at a convenience store my family bought soon after, for most of my middle and high school years, busing dishes, waiting tables, and even cooking on the night shift.

Amid all this, our family took on yet another American trait within the first year or two after landing: we started to go on annual family vacations. While that trip from Benghazi to Tripoli felt a little bit like a vacation, at least in hindsight—with all of us loaded into that hired car, basically fleeing willy-nilly to avoid the recruitment efforts of the PLO—we now got to experience the true joys of the annual car trip.

Our trips didn't focus on Disneyland. We didn't trek out west to Yosemite or Yellowstone or even to Mount Rushmore. We didn't do the kitschy stops along Route 66.

My dad had a favorite, though, and it was his choice, for something like ten years running, to pack the whole family up and sojourn to Niagara Falls.

What did this look like for a Lebanese family newly arrived in America? Not too different from what most people remember from those days before cell phones, video games, and LCD screens mounted on the backseats of shiny SUVs sank their pixelated claws into the scrum of our kid brains and kid energy to anesthetize the whole experience. Although my dad's trophy car, purchased after his first few years of hard work on the assembly line and in the restaurants, was a red '77 Cadillac Eldorado, he didn't ever take us to Niagara in that. No, we piled everyone into a conversion van: plush seats, tinted windows, upholstery, cheap venetian blinds making the inside always a bit like a cave or a bordello. Four kids, mom, dad, sometimes a random assortment of aunts, cousins, or friends added to the mix: this whole gaggle crossed via the Detroit-Windsor Tunnel or the Ambassador Bridge, traffic depending, and took Highway 401 along the north shore of Lake Erie toward the falls.

The trip involved all the normal threats to pull over and sort out the fighting, maybe to blister a behind or two, as well as the constant questions (by this time in a mix of Arabic and English) about how much farther we had to go and when we'd get there. Kids got carsick.

Parents came up with games to divert our attention from beating and poking one another—games like "I Spy" and song singing and searching for all fifty states' license plates. All of that is, I think, roughly the same experience every kid and parent from the 1950s through the early 1990s had on American highways.

The main difference, on this four- or five-hour journey across a bit of American-ish Canadian territory, was that when we stopped midway at a park or roadside turnout, my mom would get out an assortment of decidedly Lebanese food, usually breakfast because dad liked to get going before daybreak on these vacations. We'd have *ful* (beans) and *lebnah* (Lebanese sour cream) and cheeses and flatbread, as well as tea, not a breakfast most Americans would ever eat, though we loved it.

When we finally arrived in the afternoon at the falls, my father's eyes would go wide, just the same on his tenth visit as on our first. We'd tour around the falls. We'd hike a little. And then we'd do just what any other American family would do, albeit with Lebanese force and passion: we'd fight over where to stay for the few nights of our visit, which restaurants to eat at, who got to sleep in what bed, and what things to do and see.

Overall these vacations were as exhausting as they were enjoyable, but we did them as a family, together, and that counted for a lot. No one was ever allowed to beg off, to skip, to have other obligations. Dad set the date of the vacation, and come hell or highwater, all of us found ourselves bundled into that dark conversion van, chugging down the road toward the falls.

Although so much more happened during these middle and high school years, so many things that helped shape me as a man and form my identity as an American, the really important thing I still need to mention from this period is how I met and wooed my first love, Zainab.

In high school the idea of becoming a Marine really started to take hold in my heart. I kept it to myself for my middle and early high school years. But when I was a junior, I began to visit recruiters. I couldn't shake the image of that Marine at the embassy gate. When I thought of myself growing up into manhood, there was nothing I wanted or envisioned for myself more than that, no higher aim I could imagine. When I went to those recruiters the first few times, they shooed me away, telling me I was still too young. But I'd get their promotional stickers, bright red- and gold-colored emblems emblazoned with the eagle, globe, and anchor. These stickers I not only collected but also began to display in a sort of weird and funny way by putting them on my silver polyester warm-up jacket. That kind of jacket was a cool guy thing back then, though the richer kids sewed patches onto the sleeves and back, rather than just applying stickers. I would have loved patches, sure, but I didn't hesitate to use the stickers, and I was pretty proud of that Marine-emblazoned jacket as I walked the Fordson High School halls with my big Afro Sheen hair.

Oh, how awesome those days were, back in the late 1970s. And just imagine what a work of art I was when I first met Zainab around about that time.

Here's how we met: I took a class my senior year called community service, which sent me to elementary, junior high, or other high schools to serve as a teacher's aide. So, I was somewhat official, an older, wiser authority figure (with that hair, that jacket, that teenage self-assurance). That's how I met Zainab. She was a student in one of the classes I helped with. She'd just come to America that year, which was 1978, and I met her fresh off the boat.

At first we didn't say much to each other, but I noticed her. And she noticed me. Over the coming few days we began to communicate more and more as I went about my duties in the class. I helped her with small things, with new words and American expressions, and also with the classwork. She asked me questions, both about schoolwork and about myself. We started to get to know each other. Then we realized our fathers knew each other too. That pretty much sealed the deal, like we'd been fated to meet on this far shore, fated to reenact the traditional sort of village courtship that began with two young people discovering each other and then continued through long periods of suffering and uncertainty as the families weighed in on the suitability of the relationship. Our families both came from Tebnine, though her father had moved her family away when I was very young and Zainab had not yet even been born. Zainab herself had hardly ever visited Tebnine, spending all her childhood in Beirut. She knew of Tebnine though. It formed part of her identity, just as it formed part of mine. That's a big thing about Lebanon: no matter where you are in the world, your village, your Lebanese home, is part of you. Tebnine was part of me, and it was part of her in just that way.

Eventually I told Zainab I liked her, and I started walking her home with her little brother Farouk as our chaperone. We kept our growing fondness for one another pretty much secret for a while, being traditionally minded like that. I would walk her most of the way before she got to the corner of her street, and then I'd say goodbye as her brother walked ahead. I never turned that corner or took her any closer to her house during those first weeks and months.

Secrecy like that probably fooled no one, but it kept the aunts and moms and relatives from beginning any sort of more official dialogue. It kept the pressure off all of us, and as kids, we thought we were the first ever to have such a secret crush.

Zainab and I stayed together throughout the whole of my senior year. A few times I would skip class and pick her up. We'd go have lunch, nothing too forward, still keeping it pretty traditional and being chicken about doing much else. After a few repetitions of this though, I upped the ante. Showing off, I "borrowed" my dad's car, that red '77 Eldorado. Usually I drove a '71 Maverick, which was nothing more than a souped-up Pinto, definitely nothing to impress the love of my life. But the big new Eldorado, boy, that thing clocked in about twenty feet long. When we skipped class that day, we went for lunch like usual but then drove around a bit too. With my palms sweaty on the wheel, I parked behind the Dearborn Civic Center. No other cars were in the lot. No one came in or out of the civic center. Everyone else still sat in their stupid classes.

Zainab was too shy to try much, so I planted the first kiss on her cheek, very tenderly. She sprang back, a little surprised, maybe a little offended even. Perhaps I had read things the wrong way? Perhaps she wasn't interested in me as anything more than a friend?

I sat in my seat, very still, and noticed that my hand was starting to shake. I wondered if I had made a big mistake. I wondered if I had botched everything. I imagined Zainab's father storming over to see my father, having a confrontation about his daughter's honor. I imagined myself grounded forever, probably with a bruised backside. But then Zainab put all those fears to rest. She leaned over and took my hand in hers. She pulled it toward her, and I was like putty, boneless, spineless, falling all over myself as I curved my torso toward her over the central console again. She put my hand on her shoulder. She took my other hand and guided it around her lower back. And then she lifted her chin and brought her lips close to mine so that all I had to do was move another inch before we met lip to lip in that first, magical, real kiss.

This, to me, was America.

This was the John Cougar Mellencamp "Jack and Diane" fairy tale, but done up with me, Haisam Farran, as Jack, and Zainab as Diane. It didn't have quite the same ring, our names in place of those American names, but it worked. It worked perfectly for me. I bought into it just like I bought into the silver windbreaker, just like I bought into the eagle, globe, and anchor, just like I bought into family vacations in the conversion van, lunchbreak movies, and free milk in paper cartons.

Perhaps the one thing that should have given me pause was my parents' new restaurant, successful as it was. Still, it served mostly Lebanese, Palestinians, and Yemenis, the people who had come here to work hard on the assembly lines at Ford, Chrysler, and GM. I should have thought about this restaurant and why it was successful when the first one, in East Dearborn, wasn't. As a teenager, it's not easy to see one's life from the outside, to understand how Dearborn could be both fully American and also something different, a separate and intermediary place with segregation and discrimination woven into its societal fabric. Back then I wasn't aware of the way that so many other ethnicities and nationalities (like we Arabs) had come here—the Irish, Africans, Italians, Latinos of every sort—and how they had gone through the same slow process of discrimination and then, to varying degrees, assimilation. I could not see such things then; nor could I foresee how, even in my lifetime, the acceptance and slow process of merging into America would receive a terrible jolt, one that I would help combat as a Marine.

No, all I could see then was my dad's big red Eldorado, how it had worked wonders in impressing my girl. I didn't want to stop there with impressing her either. Zainab had a few more years left of school. So I followed through on the most manly and amazing thing I could think of, upping the ante once more and keeping myself (I thought) firmly bedazzling in Zainab's eyes: I took myself down to that Marine recruiter's office and signed up to devote my life to Uncle Sam.

CHAPTER 3

MARINE DUTY

O NE AFTERNOON DURING my senior year at Fordson High School, I walked into my parents' restaurant, not alone this time, not coming to work to bus tables or wash dishes or cook through the long hours of the night shift. I brought company with me that afternoon, a new friend, the local Marine recruiter. I'd been visiting the recruiting center pretty regularly for the past month, comparing the deals I could get with the Army, Navy, Air Force, and Marines. At that time, I thought I wanted to start as a jet mechanic and later parlay my experience into becoming a pilot, which meant the Army was more or less out as an option. And the more I investigated, the more I kept coming back in my mind to the Marines, to the image of that first Marine guard at the embassy in Tripoli, to his immaculate uniform, to the esprit de corps I'd started to absorb and respect, all reinforced by the stickers I'd been collecting on my silver jacket.

When I brought that recruiter with me to the restaurant, my parents thought at first that I'd gotten in trouble and was being escorted by a police officer. But, in truth, I was still only seventeen years old and needed at least one of my legal guardians to sign my enlistment papers. The recruiter had come with me to cinch the deal, even though it had been one of my best and lifelong friends, Faisal Salamey, who, having joined up a few months earlier and already returned from boot camp to serve a stint as a recruiting assistant, convinced me at last to take the big leap.

Faisal, as much as I love him, got me what must have been the worst-ever deal for joining the Marine Corps—a three-year "open contract," with my exact military job dependent on how I scored on the Armed Services Vocational Aptitude Battery Test (ASVAB). When Faisal convinced me to take this deal—though in hindsight, the term "indentured servitude" seems more appropriate—all I could see was his crisp uniform, the goal and object of all my thoughts since Tripoli. I lost sight of my plan to become a pilot, and I didn't even care that this open contract meant that the Marines could decide what specialty I got, allowing them to put me into the worst sorts of jobs if they so wanted or needed. I could easily become just a normal infantry man, what we call a "grunt" or "cannon fodder." Worse, they could make me a cook, and it would be like I was back in the restaurant all over again, only without my family or friends around me. (Things didn't turn out quite that bad. I scored well enough on the ASVAB to become a heavy equipment operator in the Engineers, which at least gave me some meaningful, skill-based training.)

Anyway, I sat down in one of the booths, and when my parents came over to see what was happening, I introduced them to the recruiter, who wore the chevron stripes of a staff sergeant on his uniform. I also boldly proclaimed my intention to join the Marine Corps.

My father's back straightened a little. He seemed about to speak, but my mother, whose tongue was always faster, cut him off.

"What!" she said. "No way."

Her voice rose to a dangerous pitch. She began to wag her finger at me, then at the recruiter. "No way, no way, no way."

All hell broke loose then as my father took my mother by the arm and my mother wrenched herself away from him, breathing fire and wagging that finger still. Father then did something dramatic, grabbing her around the waist in a giant bear hug, picking her up, throwing her over one shoulder, and carrying her, still screaming, "No way," through the carousel doors to the kitchen.

All this happened in front of about twenty astonished guests.

One man, a family friend just like most of the diners, began to clap a little, first in the direction of my parents, whose squabbling could be heard over the normal racket of pots and pans, then toward me and the staff sergeant in the booth across from me. The staff sergeant took this all in stride. Maybe he hadn't seen quite this level of Lebanese passion. Maybe he hadn't seen a protesting mother picked up bodily and carted off to the kitchen of a restaurant. But he'd been through plenty of iterations of the same sort of argument, the mother often resisting and the father a bit sad, maybe shocked, but also proud. He took a sip of his coffee and was ready, more ready than me, to meet my father's gaze when he came back into the dining area.

"We need to discuss this," my father said, though I knew from the look in his eyes that he was ready to sign. Anything additional, all the talking and cajoling that evening and the next day, he did just to ease my mother's mind, to convince her, and to make me demonstrate that I, myself, was committed enough to stand up in front of my mom and face her.

I did that. I succeeded.

I think it was my first real venture into manhood, more so than stealing my dad's Eldorado to impress Zainab. This was about me. This was about my choices for my life. And I wasn't going to back down.

So on November 2, 1978, I officially enlisted in the United States Marine Corps, with a scheduled "ship date" to boot camp immediately following the end of my senior year. Thus, on June 15, three days after graduating, I was on my way, along with another one of my Dearborn friends, Moussa Sareini, to the Marine Corps Recruiting Depot (MCRD) in San Diego for "Boot."

Moussa and I arrived in San Diego at 0100 in the morning.

As we stepped down from the bus that took us from the airport to the MCRD, we were immediately surrounded by yelling, screaming, spitting drill instructors (DIs). Leading from the bus, the famous yellow footsteps painted onto the pavement and followed by a million other recruits brought us front and center toward those waiting DIs. In my mind, over and over, I remember repeating just a single phrase, as if my thoughts got stuck in a loop and just couldn't break free: *What the f@!% did I get myself into?*

They shaved our heads, a process that took less than a minute each and turned us into skinheads.

They gave us big camo-green duffle bags, our seabags, and loaded them with gear, linens, uniforms, and boots.

Each of these things happened at a different station.

And each time, between stations, we returned to the yellow footsteps where the DIs waited, yelling and cussing at us, making us stand straighter, keep our eyes glued forward, and requiring us to answer in short, precise blasts of "Yes, sir!" or "No, sir!" I remember looking for Moussa during this time but not being able to turn my head an inch side to side or to distinguish him, with his newly shaved head, from anyone else. He might have been right next to me, toeing the line on a nearby set of footsteps. He might have been somewhere else, in one of the other lines, or getting yelled at, or already quitting— I didn't know. I didn't have time to ponder it. It seemed like all the world had dropped out from under my feet. And all my mind could say, over and over, was *What the f@!% did I get myself into?*

This continued for about three hours.

Then we were marched off to the barracks for less than two hours of sleep, before being awakened suddenly and loudly by the sound of trash cans being thrown across the open squad bay and our new drill instructors beating the lids with sticks. They yelled and screamed for us to get out of the rack and gave us two minutes—and two minutes only—to dress in our new uniforms, which none of us knew how to wear right, and get into formation outside the barracks. And God help the last man out of the bay!

Disheveled, mind foggy from short sleep, body tired from the long flight the previous day as well as all the activity of getting our heads shaved and our seabags filled, we stood in our first platoon formation, about eighty of us. Our DIs stood out in front of us, pacing like angry tigers.

"I have never seen such fucking lowlife maggots in my life," said senior drill instructor Staff Sergeant Boxely. He was spitting mad. He talked for two, three, maybe five minutes. It felt like forever, and in the predawn chill—even in June in San Diego—my fingers started to go numb at my sides. He told us, among many other things, how unfit we were to be part of His. Beloved. Marine. Corps. He didn't promise to whip us into shape. No, he said nothing so positive as that. He threatened us, saying he'd run any lily-livered weakling out of the platoon as fast as he could. Then, looking weary, he turned to the other two instructors, Gunnery Sergeant Steffek and DI Sergeant Garbowski, and asked, rhetorically, "Whatever have we done to deserve such trash as new recruits?"

Steffek and Garbowski informed us they'd collectively be our "mommy" and our "daddy" for the next thirteen weeks. Both Boxely and Steffek were Vietnam veterans, and you could just see it in their eyes: a deadness and coldness demonstrating, more than words could ever say, that they'd been to hell and back.

It was the mission of these three instructors, over the coming weeks, to break Fox Company, Series 2061, Platoon 2064 down completely and then build us back up, systematically, via routine, physical exhaustion, and a thorough reprogramming of our formerly lily-livered brains. All of it was designed not just to teach us what it meant to be a Marine but to mold every reflex into the automatic, expected, mandated Marine response. To make us act and think together as one single machine. To ensure, no matter how hard the physical work might be, that the mental part would start to flow as we lost our earlier identities and adapted to, then adopted and came to live, the expectations and patterns of Marine life.

I think all the major training events during Boot—the marksmanship, the ruck marches, the obstacle courses, the physical training, the medical first aid, the KP duty, the work with radios—all of that stuff mattered, but less than the overall mission of molding us into Marines. That was the first and most important aspect of Boot. All the rest was just the means, the icing on the cake, necessary stuff but wholly without value if it wasn't done to build up the core identity and distinction of this new mindset.

We got through it.

And we learned, almost, to love it. Certainly looking back on it, I can remember the pain of it, the challenge. But all the bad parts tend to fade, and what remains is pride and camaraderie and even humor, dark humor, that helped bond us one to another and get us through the worst of our shared experience. Every time I want to remember boot camp, I simply watch *Full Metal Jacket*.

September 12, 1979, was the proudest day of my life as I marched on the parade deck for the first time in my green uniform with the eagle, globe, and anchor on my chest. I had earned the title of United States Marine, and the only thing I could picture at that moment was the Marine security guard at the embassy gate in Tripoli, high and tight in his dress blues with the very same eagle, globe, and anchor on his collar. *What would he think*, I wondered, *if only he knew what a difference he had made in one little Lebanese boy's life.* Semper Fi, I say, whoever and wherever you are.

From MCRD in San Diego, I went to Fort Leonard Wood, Missouri—which we affectionately call Fort Lost-in-the-Woods—for engineer school. This lasted several weeks and qualified me to handle the heavy machinery my "open contract" specialty required me to operate. Then, after Boot and engineer school, I got ten days of leave to visit my family in Dearborn in December 1979.

My dad made me wear my uniform every day. In my green Alphas (I hadn't been issued Blues yet, so didn't look exactly like the Marine security guard from my memory), dad took me everywhere, to see friends and family, to show me off to relatives.

Of course, I got to see Zainab too.

While I was gone, my father, who knew Zainab's father from Teb-nine, talked to Zainab's uncle. He said, "Talk to your brother. When Haisam returns from Marine training, we want to come and ask for Zainab's hand the old-fashioned way."

So things were organized for this major event while I was gone. I returned to find that I had a very special occasion to wear my Alphas for: the visit—along with all of my family—to Zainab's father's house, where all her family gathered in the living room. Mother, father, aunts, uncles, brothers, sisters, all these people crammed around me in my hot uniform and around Zainab, who sat on the far side of the room in a demure dress with her eyes cast down. Even my Uncle Ali, the tobacco farmer, happened to be visiting. He came along to lend support.

The discussion focused on the future, what it would look like for Zainab and me.

After a while, in the normal fashion for these formal gatherings, the conversation was put to an end. "Let the girl think on it," said Zainab's father.

"We'll get back to you," Zainab's mother added.

Turns out, this was a bit of subterfuge. I was flying to Japan the next day for my first assignment in the Marine Corps. Zainab's family knew this.

"We'll wait until he's back from Japan," Zainab's mother said.

But the following summer she secretly flew Zainab to Lebanon, took her to her own family's village of Shahoor, and forced her to marry one of her cousins.

This was, and still sometimes is, the way of things in Lebanon.

In Iwakuni, Japan, I received a Dear John letter informing me not only that I would not be marrying Zainab but that she had already married another man. A man she had not previously known. A man chosen for her by her family.

■ ■ ■

THE NEXT FEW YEARS went by in somewhat of a blur for me. But one incident in 1982 remains a painful memory and goes a long way to explaining why I would eventually leave the active-duty Marine Corps.

Lebanon was restless in 1982, just before the bombing of the US Embassy. Leaders in the military could tell that something was brewing, and so a call went out for anyone, anyone at all in the Marine Corps, with Arabic language skills. I had come back from Iwakuni and was stationed at Camp Pendleton north of San Diego then. I saw the announcement requesting Arabic speakers and volunteered.

There weren't many of us then, really just a few random enlistees like me and Moussa and Faisal Salamey from Dearborn, so we were offered reenlistment bonuses six times greater than normal to join the linguist program. The Marines (and other services) had a long history of sending people without perfect language skills but with proven aptitude or desire to the Defense Language Institute (DLI) in Monterey, California. There they would study intensely, eight to ten hours a day, every day, for six months, a year, and even eighteen months for more difficult languages like Arabic or Chinese. This was the linguist program. Only problem: I already spoke Arabic.

At Pendleton I was made to take a battery of language tests, even though I told them I was fluent. The Marines have their rules. I'd learned it isn't wise or a good use of energy to fight those rules. So I took the test. I was even prepared, if required, to go to DLI. Maybe they would train me in another dialect or in Farsi or Russian or something cool. I was pretty interested in seeing what the future had in store for me along this new career path, and so I went into the test trying my best at it.

Out of about one hundred questions, I missed two. This less-than-perfect result pissed me off. I should not have missed a single answer.

I was a sergeant then. A staff sergeant was in charge at the testing center for the intelligence branch. This staff sergeant looked at my result and immediately accused me of cheating.

"You're accusing me of cheating," I said, laughing, "but I'm mad at myself for missing these two questions...I'm a native speaker, not a DLI graduate."

But the staff sergeant wouldn't let it drop. "Where did you get the answers from?" he said.

"What do you mean, where did I get the answers from?"

"Nobody scores this high."

"Are you actually accusing me of cheating?" I asked, ice creeping into my voice.

"No," he said. "But I've never seen a score like this, so you must have known the answers."

I told him to keep the test. We exchanged a few more words, less and less pleasant ones. I left and walked out, went back to my command, and dropped the subject, never saying a word to anyone about my decision.

The Marine career planner kept calling me, but I only put him off, now uninterested. My battalion commander, a lieutenant colonel, summoned me to his office because he was receiving a lot of pressure to find people to go to Lebanon as translators and interrogators. But I was really pissed off, more pissed off than I'd ever been at the Marine Corps. That staff sergeant questioning my honor cut to the very center of my identity, my respect for what the uniform represented.

Not only did I thumb my nose at the call for translators, but I actually started thinking about getting out of active duty altogether—that's how sour a taste the episode left in my mouth.

Events between that moment and Desert Storm in 1991 conspired to bring me full circle, and in the meantime I had bigger things to worry about.

■ ■ ■

I CAME OFF ACTIVE duty in 1984 and went with my family for a visit to Lebanon. There, just like for Zainab, it was somehow arranged for me to marry one of my cousins, Wafa', who was eight years younger than me. She moved back to Dearborn with me. We had a son in 1986, Mohammad, whom we call "Mo." And then another child, Ali, two years later.

But Wafa' and I—though close, though family—never felt the flames. We were in love but love of a different sort.

I worked in my family's businesses again. I kept my military affiliation by enlisting in the local Engineer Reserve Unit, drilling with them once a month for a weekend and then for a couple weeks in the summer. And I went to school to get a job as a social worker with the state of Michigan. This was a fateful decision on a couple levels. First, it meant that I got a degree, later enabling me to qualify to become a warrant officer (WO) in the Reserves. Second, and more immediately, I had health insurance for the first time, and just in the nick of time because I had developed one heck of a toothache.

That seems trivial, I guess, at least on the surface.

But when I walked into the dentist's office that first week of having health insurance, the receptionist behind the desk froze cold. Our eyes locked together. Neither of us moved.

It was Zainab.

After about a minute of utter speechlessness, one of her coworkers came into the room. Zainab stood up and, without saying a word, put her hand to her mouth and fled to some back room in the office.

I didn't know what to do.

I didn't know what to think. I was a little mad still. It had been six years, but the Dear John letter from her still hurt, like a wound that somehow always stayed raw.

I filled out the normal dental paperwork and sat in the lobby, waiting to be called to have my tooth examined.

Zainab came back in.

"I'm sorry," she said.

"Are you?" I asked.

"Yes," she said. "It wasn't my idea."

"It's the way of things."

"Yes."

I could tell she wanted to say more, but she didn't have a chance. I got called back just then and had to sit there, chair tilted back, jaws open, blinded by the dentist's overhead light, my mind stunned, blinded just like my eyes, by seeing Zainab again. I could feel my anger in the way I gripped the armrest of the dental chair. I could feel my sadness every time I blinked under that harsh light. It felt like sand had gotten caught in my eyelashes or like I'd spent a long time, a really long time—maybe even six whole years—crying. That's not an easy thing for a Marine to say. And really, the crying part, the part of me that was deeply and forever hurt by Zainab's being married off to another man so suddenly and without explanation, that part had hidden for six years under veils of anger and indifference. I'd gone about my life, but it was a life that lacked flavor and spark. It was a normal life. A life expected of me.

I got up from the chair feeling woozy, unable to speak clearly. I walked from the dental room to the lobby again.

Zainab was waiting. We were alone.

"If you would like to talk to me, call," she said. "Just call the number here at the office."

Those days we didn't have cell phones. And calling her at home was, obviously, not going to be allowed. I didn't know what to say to this. She was married. I was married. I had two children. Mo was two years old then, and Ali had just been born.

I had no words, and with my mouth numb I couldn't pronounce words anyway.

But she said the only thing that I needed to hear right then: "I still love you, Sam."

The numbness in my mouth seemed to shoot down my arms and then sparkle from the tips of my fingers and toes.

"What?"

"I love you," she said again, just a whisper. Then she added, "I'm getting a divorce."

It took me about a week to call her.

A year later we were married.

I'd like to say that there was an affair or that something illicit occurred. That might be easier to explain. But that's not what happened. We were too good to each other and too traditional.

We started to see each other, having lunches and dinners, driving around in the car. Just like high school all over again.

And then we got married, the traditional Muslim way. Muslim men are allowed four wives. And I'll admit both Zainab and Wafa' were victims of our cultural marriage practices.

I didn't ask for a divorce, and I wasn't about to have an affair.

I got married to Zainab and then brought Wafa' to Zainab's house.

Wafa' was surprisingly okay, at least at first. She said, "You're married to her, fine. You're married to her. That's your right."

The two women, my wives, seemed—at least on the surface—alright with this arrangement.

Wafa' at least endured the situation, but before long her family got involved. They gave me an ultimatum: "Either divorce Zainab or divorce Wafa'."

Wafa' had been a good wife to me. I had no issues with her. But facing this decision and feeling, with Zainab, a spark and a fire I had never felt with Wafa', I made my choice.

That's when Wafa' went crazy.

We were in my father's house. She screamed, "How can you do this to me?"

The fight moved from the living room to the kitchen, from the kitchen to the bedroom we used at my father's house. It wasn't a hot fight. But it was words, lots of words, torrents of words. I stayed the course. I'd made my decision. If I had to choose between the two of them, the choice was easy.

That day in 1989 we went to the mosque, to the sheik, and divorced in the traditional way, following it up thereafter with the paperwork required in Michigan. It was Zainab then, Zainab alone for me, just like it should have been from the beginning.

■ ■ ■

IN 1990 I BECAME a warrant officer, an unusual rank structure used mostly for people with special technical skills. Pilots are often warrant officers. A lot of maintenance supervisors for heavy equipment hold the WO rank. That's what I became with my Engineer Reserve Unit. But the military often employs the WO structure with one other specialty: intelligence.

Also in 1990, six months before Desert Storm, my father died of a sudden stroke.

We were able to conduct traditional Muslim funeral rituals for him, praying over him, reading the Quran, bathing him in a manner similar to how we perform *wudu* before prayers. After that we wrapped him in a burial shroud called the *kafan*. Then we laid him to rest in a special section of the cemetery in Plymouth, Michigan, designated for Muslim burials, all the graves facing Mecca. I performed the bathing ritual myself, with one assistant, washing his body for the last time.

My mother was a new widow.

I was the head of the family, running the family business and thinking occasionally about the few lira I had shared with my cousins and siblings back in Tebnine. Our way of running the gas station and the convenience store followed that same mentality. It was a true family business. Six months later, when I was called to do my duty and fight in Desert Storm, everyone in the family came together to support me, so leaving wasn't as hard as it could have been, even though my father had so recently passed, and even though, by this time, Zainab and I had brought a daughter, Marcelle, into the world. Having spread the wealth of the convenience store and the gas station around, as I had spread my tobacco earnings around my friends at the Friday market, I now had plenty of hands to help and allow me to concentrate on getting ready to fight for the USA.

My colleagues at the Social Services Department were all supportive as well. I was the only reservist on staff, so my departure was hailed as patriotic, and the staff supported me with kind words and extra help as I prepared to leave, transferring my cases. The mood of the country had certainly changed since Vietnam too. People still protested the war. They protested the policy. But they managed to separate the men and women serving America from that policy. No more were Marines and soldiers, corpsmen and ensigns and airmen subjected to taunts and humiliation for conflicts they had not started.

■ ■ ■

IN THE ARAB COMMUNITY in Dearborn, because America was preparing to go to war against an Arab nation, the mood was a little tenser.

"How can you go and fight against a person who everyone thinks"—at least back then—"is a hero?" some would ask.

"Saddam is just sticking it to selfish Kuwait," others would say. "Kuwait has been stealing oil by drilling under Iraqi land."

My standard answer was that I was a Marine and had signed up to serve and obey the commands of the president of the United States. That was pretty high-flying for some people, though, so occasionally I'd give more rationale. And this, combined with my commitment to serve and to honor my oath, is what I really thought of Desert Storm: "Iraq invaded a country that it had no right to. Doesn't matter whether Arab or non-Arab, and the country that was invaded pleaded for help from the United States and Gulf countries."

People respected that. Most everyone respected that.

For the ones who didn't, and for my family, in private moments, when I had time to really think and express myself more fully, I would recall the way our village, Tebnine, behaved during the difficult years of the Lebanese Civil War, years my family thankfully had missed while we were making our new home in Dearborn, but incidents and issues of which we followed very closely.

"You know," I said, to no one and everyone in particular, at least once or twice during this time when I was preparing to go to war, "in Tebnine some of our neighbors are Christian, some are Shi'a, some Sunni. And it doesn't matter. All of the neighbors behind my grandmother's house, on the hill, only a five-minute walk from my grandfather's house, are Christian. We lived together, never had any problems. In fact, if you recall, a militia came to behead the Christians, but the village, the whole village, took up arms and defended them. Church bells rang whenever there was a death in the village, and the mosque would start reciting the Quran at the same time, no matter whether the person was Christian or Muslim." What I meant by this: It didn't matter. Religion wasn't the definition of a person. It wasn't the reason, the sole reason, to go to war or stay out of war. I had learned religion as a personal endeavor, a private endeavor, and one that didn't affect my outward allegiances.

I drew on my roots, on Tebnine, when getting ready to fight for America and against Saddam.

When my engineering unit got the call, we mobilized to a staging base in Yuma, Arizona.

My roommate, Captain Bill Black (now a retired colonel), who was the officer in charge, went into the headquarters of Marine Wing Support Group 17 (MWSG17) one day. This was the group we had been assigned to support.

Captain Bill Black ratted on me.

Just like in 1982, messages were coming out daily looking for Arabic speakers. The colonel in charge of MWSG17 called me into his office and said, "Well, Gunner, pack your bags. You're flying out." "Gunner" is what we call warrant officers in the Marines. After my unit returned to Michigan, I was tapped by the Defense Intelligence Agency to join them, so I left without my unit and went on to become a translator/interrogator working out of Kuwait and Iraq for the six months it took us to build up our forces and then win the war.

■ ■ ■

I RETURNED TO DEARBORN in the fall of 1991.

Coming back we were treated to a hero's welcome. By that time the "support the troops" mentality was so strong that anybody who did not was looked upon as a traitor. This tamped down the voices of people opposed to the policies of the war, but it meant our welcome home was wholehearted, in terms of both tickertape and parades and also more substantial things, like how our community accepted us, even the Arab community in Dearborn. It is tough to be sour about success, and most people in Dearborn, regardless of race or religion, identified strongly as American and celebrated together as Americans. I didn't experience any resistance after the war from within Dearborn. Nobody dared to speak up, if they did have such feelings, because of that strong swell of patriotism at the time. Nobody really wanted to be that person.

For the next couple years, I went back to work for the Engineer Reserve Unit. I also restarted my social work position with the state of Michigan and continued managing the family store and our gas station. Zainab and I had another daughter too, Amira, bringing my brood of children to four: Mohammad, Ali, Marcelle, and the new baby. I certainly enjoyed that time and look back on it fondly as a period of domestic quiet, a calm before the storm that the rest of my life became, for the Marines and the Middle East weren't done with me yet. Not by a long shot.

CHAPTER 4

INTERROGATOR AND ATTACHÉ

A BOUT A YEAR AFTER Amira's birth, I happened to be reading the Marine Corps Reserve Officers Association magazine and stumbled on an advertisement for Arabic-speaking personnel to apply for work with the Defense Intelligence Agency (DIA) as interrogators. My previous work with DIA during Desert Storm had been rewarding, and while I loved being an engineer, I'd done that for quite a while. I thought I might finally put my language skills and cultural background to better use. The sting of my first attempt at using my language to help the Marines—and being called a liar because of that native skill—had never completely faded, but it had faded enough. I was ready to help in a new and more specific way.

I applied. DIA flew me out to Washington, DC, for a single interview and hired me on the spot. From that moment on, instead of spending my one weekend a month drilling with a local engineer unit in Michigan, I traveled wherever DIA needed me. Some of the work happened in DC. Often, though, I'd be sent to substations around the country and around the world to work on active interrogations. In the mid-1990s, we had a lot of former Ba'athist personnel who had taken refuge from Saddam's retribution after the First Gulf War. These people—especially when spoken to cordially and in Arabic—provided us with reams of useful information that helped us better understand (and plan against) Saddam's communication, leadership, and military capabilities in the future, for a war none of us knew was coming.

Although working with and interrogating these asylum-seeking Iraqi personnel formed the bulk of my duties during this time, it's important to step back just a bit and discuss the real catalyst for this call by the Marine Corps (and many other agencies) for Arabic-speaking personnel: the first bombing of the World Trade Center in New York City in 1993, less spectacular than the 9/11 attacks and less successful, but a harbinger of things to come.

I was in Michigan then, attending to my family, my businesses, and my work with the state, as well as doing weekend duty with the engineer unit, when a truck loaded with explosives detonated beneath the World Trade Center's North Tower. The explosion was meant to cause the North Tower to collapse into the South Tower. It didn't work but did end up blowing a hole through several layers of the parking garage, killing six people and injuring thousands.

This attack was financed by the radical Muslim cleric Khalid Sheikh Mohammed—who continued to finance terror, including the 9/11 bombings of the World Trade Center. It was carried out by a group of al-Qaeda operatives, including Ramzi Yousef, Khalid Sheikh

Mohammed's nephew. During his trial for the bombing, Ramzi Yousef justified the legitimacy of targeting the United States by stating that it had introduced terrorism to the world by killing innocent people with the atomic bomb, by using Agent Orange in Vietnam, by imposing economic embargoes on various locations, including Cuba and parts of the Middle East, and, of course, by supporting Israel. Ramzi Yousef even provided forewarning of future attacks, like 9/11, in a letter he sent to the *New York Times*: "If our demands are not met, all of our functional groups…will continue to execute our missions against the military and civilian targets in and outside of the United States."

In Dearborn, 90 percent of the Arab community was very upset about the bombing. Everyone had been working hard to assimilate and become part of the American community. It was, and is, felt that every event, big or little, associated with al-Qaeda or other militant groups results in a backlash against Arabs and the Muslim community in general, even though the vast majority of us denounce these crimes and many of us actively work to prevent them. The results of this showed up tangibly in our community: guys like me and some of the friends I have mentioned by name, among many others left nameless here, volunteered to serve in the military, in the government, and in our communities. Just like other American communities, Dearborn gave, and still gives, back to the United States.

But, on the other end of the spectrum, even back then, we had demonstrators come up from down south, mainly Christian evangelicals. They'd protest in Dearborn against the Islamic population. They've got a right to protest—a right protected by the Constitution—but we also have rights, to our religion and to our membership in the idea and the community of America, rights directly attacked by these demonstrators. We were aware that their chants of "Go back to your country" were wrong because America had become our country, and so those types of insults just sounded stupid to us. But we took it less well when they'd throw around pejorative phrases, based on hate and misunderstanding. Their favorite phrase from that time, no doubt— I heard it a million times, I think—was "camel jockey."

I could laugh at that a little since camels were no part of my experience in Lebanon. But still I felt the menace of these groups. They'd set up all over Dearborn—in parking lots, in front of stores, in front of the city hall—as was their right. But when they hurled racial and religious epithets at us, they showed their true colors: their belief in a false and dangerous idea of America as a place for white, Christian evangelicals only, which I believe was never the intent of our Founding Fathers. Though discrimination of this sort has sometimes been legalized in misguided laws, I believe the moral arc of the United States toward greater inclusion and freedom for all people truly makes this country a beacon for the world.

So I overcame, or at least ignored, those insults. And my work as an interrogator provided me with more proof of the good intentions of Arabs who came to America (despite the horrible actions of a radical, militant minority).

Doing this work reinforced for me the balance of what was happening. Yes, every once in a while, we'd catch someone with bad intentions, or at least with suspicious indicators and associations. But for every one or two of these individuals, who mostly proved harmless after more thorough vetting by our sister agencies, we'd screen hundreds and even thousands of normal people without a blip, people coming from all over the Arab world (and all over the world as a whole). The percentage of wrongdoers or even of people with unfortunately coincidental names or weird connections in their families or backgrounds was infinitesimal. It made the search for nefarious intent akin to the proverbial search for the needle in a haystack, but one in which, if you did find a needle among all that innocent hay, you also had to spend some serious time looking into the needle's soul (or at least deeply into its history). Otherwise how could you tell whether it might prove harmful?

After a few years working as an interrogator, an even more interesting opportunity with DIA presented itself to me: to become a defense attaché. Despite the fact that attachés are almost always normal commissioned officers rather than warrant officers, a good friend of mine, Ahmed Habib, who had worked for DIA for a long time, recommended me.

Military attachés work out of US embassies around the world. In addition to being the ambassador's local military experts, these personnel conduct intense liaison with host-nation military personnel and with the attachés of other nations, who, like them, are stationed in the host country's capital. Additionally attachés run programs facilitating the transfer of US-manufactured arms and military technology to other countries, while monitoring those sales to ensure compliance with terms, conditions, and humanitarian restrictions. Stateside, military attachés can be found in a number of billets too, helping provide cultural context to planning and strategy discussions at the senior staff level.

Because of the nuanced, often sensitive nature of this work, the attaché training program usually includes intensive language training at the Defense Language Institute (DLI), a stint in the Advanced Civil Schooling program to pick up a relevant graduate-level degree in international relations, and in-country time polishing language and diplomatic skills. It's an intense but rewarding training program and an even more rewarding career path.

Because of my language and cultural aptitude, the Marines did not need to send me to the Defense Language Institute; nor did they need to give me extra schooling or a year of in-country immersion. So I was a bargain for them, ready to go directly to the final stop in the military attaché training program: Joint Military Attaché School at Bolling Air Force Base, across the Anacostia River from the Capitol in DC.

Colonel Dan Cronin was in charge of the Middle East program for attachés at this time. He called me up after I interviewed and said, "Sam, since you're doing a real good job, I am going to recommend you for the attaché course. You know we've never had warrant officers in this course, so from what I know you'll be the first."

A month later the course started at Bolling. I still had my credentials and entrance badge from my work as an interrogator, so unlike the other officers, at least some of whom were coming into the building for the first time and walking around in a bit of a daze, I strode right into the class where I belonged, wearing my Marine uniform with my warrant officer rank clear on my collar.

The lead instructor for our course, a lieutenant colonel who had just come back from Israel, where he worked as the Army attaché, said, "Chief, I think you're in the wrong classroom. The operations coordinator course is in the room next door." This course is for enlisted personnel who run the attaché office but not for the attachés themselves.

I said, "Thank you sir, but two things." Everyone in the class had turned to look at me, on this first day, the lowest rank among them being a major. I needed to be careful but also firm so that I set the tone that I wasn't going to be pushed around. "First, don't ever call me 'chief.' Second, is this the attaché course?"

"Yes," he said.

"Then I'm in the right place."

I sat down and started out that day not only as an attaché in training but also as somewhat more of an equal despite the rank difference. Of course I had to explain to the Army and Air Force officers in the room that in the Marine Corps, warrant officers are called gunners, not chiefs. In the Navy, chiefs are senior enlisted personnel. So I told them to call me gunner or, more formally, warrant officer, but not chief.

We hit it off after that, especially once they learned that my language skills weren't a product of the Defense Language Institute but instead reflected a native fluency. The instructor went so far as to recommend that I didn't need country orientation but could go straight into the field, a situation that worked out extremely well because Morocco had an open position for an attaché at that time, and Morocco, if you don't know, like Lebanon, is a jewel of a country, green and cultured and easygoing.

My gig there for the next few years was still a Reserve job. I stacked drills so that instead of flying all that way for one weekend a month, just to be jet-lagged and ineffective while there, I consolidated those weekends into a larger block of time. I also still belonged to a Marine Corps unit too, so I had to do some drills at Marine Corps HQ C4I, right there in DC. Mostly these were administrative requirements to keep me current and approved for overseas duty. Technically I still belonged to C4I and just did my DIA work on loan. In any given year I'd end up spending two to three months in Morocco, much more time than typical reservists spend on their weekends and summer training, but funds were available, and there was certainly plenty of mission to accomplish, especially after the king of Morocco died in 1999 and everyone, from the president on down, came to visit for the funeral and to reaffirm with the new king our existing long-term relationship. (Morocco was the very first country to recognize the fledgling United States, and so our embassy there was the oldest as well.)

I liked attaché work so much that I considered going back to full-time active duty, but I had my businesses and my job with the state, and—truthfully—this level of involvement suited me just fine. It allowed me to do something productive and interesting as a break from job and family and business stress, a getaway to live in another world and another time.

While most of my attaché work supported the US Embassy in Morocco, I occasionally also supported the US embassies in Algeria and a few other places like Bahrain and Qatar, countries very different from Morocco. The work in Algeria, for example, was much more locked down, much more confined to just our embassy. And Bahrain and Qatar had much larger Navy missions. In Morocco, on the other hand, things were very free, and we could play fast and loose a bit. One of my main responsibilities, because all the other full-time attachés in the US Embassy at Rabat were either Army or Air Force, was to provide the liaison for US Navy ships calling at Moroccan ports. Some of this involved helping orient the sailors and crews to the country, briefing them on dos and don'ts. But it also entailed facilitating training and events, as was the case with the very first ship I helped host in Morocco, a US Coast Guard cutter coming in to conduct law enforcement training at the port in Casablanca.

Sometimes I handled ship visits. Sometimes I helped man and staff embassy parties, for which I'd get the call back in Michigan and jump on a plane with my dress uniform, arriving to organize and chat up other attachés from other foreign embassies, do the liaison thing with the security and the gendarmerie in charge of the ports, secure everything, and help with etiquette for receptions onboard ship or on the embassy grounds or in the ambassador's house. At one such event down at our consulate in Casablanca (the embassy is, of course, in the capital, Rabat), two of our consular officers saw how I was chatting up people from different countries, especially the Arabic countries, speaking fluent Arabic. They asked if I'd been to DLI. I told them I was a native speaker, from Lebanon. They looked at each other knowingly and said, "Uh oh, sounds like a conspiracy."

"What do you mean a conspiracy?"

"You Lebanese are all over the place."

I smiled, knowing this was true after watching my parents start businesses in Libya and Dearborn and knowing Lebanese the world over were doing just the same. We'd formed quite a diaspora.

I started to say something about that, but one of the officers interrupted me.

"No, no," she said, "of course your people are taking over the world one restaurant and delicious bowl of tabbouleh at a time." Then she went on to explain. Little did I know, but the new US ambassador in Morocco, Gabriel Edwards, was himself of Lebanese descent, as was the consul general, Nabil Khouri. Both were in Casablanca and rose to ambassador status and even higher positions in the State Department.

While most of the time my interactions with staff at the embassies was of this sort—humorous, good-natured, and accepting—all kinds of folks came through with different viewpoints and backgrounds. A lot of congressional delegations (CODELs) made it a point to visit Marrakech, Agadier, and Fez. So I escorted them, often giving them their first taste of Arab culture in the process.

Most of these interactions were good, but every once in a while I'd get a more difficult one. In particular I remember hosting two desk analysts from DIA who scheduled their "country-orientation trip" to Morocco at the worst possible time, right when King Hassan's funeral was going on, with two presidential escort missions (both Bushes and Clinton) and a large number of CODELs sapping the manpower of the attaché office and the embassy as a whole.

My boss, the chief of attaché operations at the embassy, tried to reschedule the visiting analysts for a later date, but for whatever reason headquarters overrode him.

"Sam," he said, "I need you to take one for the team. I want these analysts out of my hair. They wanna come do country orientation. You get them way out in the sticks, okay?"

So I took them all around, a really fantastic trip up into the mountains, to little villages, waterfalls, and hidden spots and even out to the magnificent village of Ouarzazate, the door to the desert, the Sahara, a place not many Americans got to see back then.

After ten days of this, we made our way back to Casablanca and were having dinner when one of the two, a woman named Deborah, posed what seemed like a hypothetical question: "What country do you think has the highest standard of living?"

I said, "Based on my travel and experience, with the Marine Corps having sent me to live and work all over the Far East, Okinawa, the Philippines, Korea, the Near East, and all the European countries, living in Lebanon, Libya, I think the best country and best standard of living is the United States."

Leon, the senior analyst, nodded his head in agreement but gave me a strange look. I wasn't sure why. His eyes flicked toward Deborah.

On her face I saw a surprising look of scorn. "I beg to differ," she said.

"Beg all you want. Which do you think has the best?"

"Israel."

Then she turned around and said, "Even here they have a good standard of living. Even Morocco is better than America."

That's when I lost it. "Excuse me. You think they have a good standard? What are you basing that on, one week of travel? Do you not remember the kid Mohammed who came to shine my shoes in Ouarzazate for one dirham? A single dirham! That's like a dime. And that was his summer job. He told us if he doesn't collect enough money to buy his books for school next year, he won't be able to go. You felt so bad you gave him ten dirhams, a whole dollar! My son Mohammad, sitting back home, playing Atari, has not a worry in the world that the bus will come, pick him up, take him to school, and that his books, pencils, papers, lunch, all the things he needs will be provided for him. My Mohammad doesn't have a worry in the world. You said the standard is here, Morocco, or Israel. Here they have to travel twenty to thirty kilometers to the nearest hospital. If something happens to my son in Detroit, it's an ambulance in two to three minutes, a hospital in two miles. What do you have that tops that?"

"How about all the people sitting out here at this beautiful café?" she answered.

"Debbie," I said, "look at these people. There are seven or eight people sitting at a table, and they take turns buying a single drink each night so they can sit here. Just because what you earn in per diem for one day is a month's salary here. Don't confuse your well-being with theirs."

I finished by reiterating that the United States had the best standard of living and that I loved it. Everything else might look good from afar, but her romanticism, or her lack of experience, prevented her from seeing what America stood for or wouldn't allow her to see the truth. Despite our differences, Debbie and I became good friends.

And perhaps that same feeling underpinned the experiences of a lot of the delegations I took around Morocco. They were enchanted by the beauty, even by the rundown corners, the aged and cracked facades from better days, the mystery and the waft of danger. It all perhaps seemed magical to these congressmen and staffers and analysts. But it wasn't real. Real was that kid, Mohammed, fighting to pull himself up by his bootstraps. Real was being born in a tobacco-farming village and never having the permission, let alone the freedom, to dream of having or of being something more, something better.

Perhaps a few of the wiser visitors understood this and went back to America more grateful for our society, more accepting that they might have to pay a few dollars in taxes or sacrifice with a bit of service to the country to keep things running, to oil the machine of liberty. But I think most just came to Morocco and were dazzled, unable to see themselves and their position of privilege through the eyes of the kids who watched them from the alleys and would have switched places with any of them in half a heartbeat.

I could tell stories about Morocco forever.

And I could have kept working there forever too. I loved it. I loved how it refreshed me and offered the perfect balance between participating in that world and coming home to Zainab and our growing children.

But things were about to change, less so in Morocco than in America and the rest of the Middle East. A change for the worse, for sure.

■ ■ ■

KHALID SHEIKH MOHAMMED and Ramzi Yousef's attempt to blow up the North Tower of the World Trade Center with a truck bomb had been the first indication.

The second happened in Yemen, on October 12, 2000, when the USS *Cole* pulled into Aden for a port visit just like those I had helped organize time and again in Casablanca and Rabat. Al-Qaeda struck, with two suicide bombers ramming the side of the destroyer with a smaller vessel packed with C4 explosive and blowing a forty-by-sixty-foot hole in the *Cole*'s side. Seventeen sailors died.

I happened to be in Lebanon visiting my mother, who had taken to spending part of each year in her home country, at the time when I saw it on the news. I called DIA right away and said, "Hey, if you guys need me, I'm here in Beirut, ready to jump in."

Colonel Dan Cronin told me to stand by and be ready.

I stood by, and I stood by.

Two weeks later, I headed back to the United States. I could sense Yemen calling. It felt almost fated at that moment. I didn't feel frustrated. I totally understood when Colonel Cronin explained that the Yemeni government was throwing up roadblocks to any request to bring more people, more investigators or linguists or bomb experts, into the country. I had a little taste of Yemen then, reading about how the country's ungoverned and ungovernable interior had become an al-Qaeda sanctuary and hotbed. Something in me knew that my path would take me there, but apparently not right then.

Before I'd get that call, another thing happened, a much bigger milestone in the fight against radical Islam. It took all our attention for the next few years, so that Yemen's connection to al-Qaeda receded. Even Khalid Sheikh Mohammed's connection faded as another name rose: Osama bin Laden.

In truth, we were witnessing one and the same issue: Ramzi Yousef and the *Cole* bombers. This was Ramzi Yousef's threat being played out in real time, just as he wrote in his letter to the *New York Times*, promising to "continue to execute...missions against the military and civilian targets in and outside of the United States."

Yemen and the *Cole* bombing. Exporting terror and pursuing the masterminds of that terror deep into Yemen's tribal heartlands.

All that would happen.

And so, too, 9/11—that world-changing day, like John F. Kennedy's assassination. Members of my generation, perhaps especially those of us who are Arab Americans, know exactly where we were, what we were doing, and how we experienced the horror of those two smoking towers collapsing in New York.

I was in Lansing, Michigan, taking a course in quality control for investigative training so that I could assume a new role as an auditor for the state's Social Services Department. Perhaps twenty-five to thirty people from all around Michigan had come for this training conference. We were staying together in a hotel, and the seminar was being held in the hotel's conference room. We'd taken a break, just like a hundred other coffee breaks, with a smattering of attendees gathered together in the breakroom, watching the news and chatting, when the first images of the burning tower came in. We didn't go back to the conference. Everyone just stood together in shock.

At that time I didn't analyze it; I could only form the thought *What the hell is going on?* Even for me, with my training and background, trying to make sense of it proved too much. At the beginning I had a notion that an airline pilot had made a mistake, a simple but horrible mistake, and accidentally crashed into the building. But as we stood there, we watched in real time on the monitor of the breakroom TV as the second plane flew into the second tower. The lights went on for me. I knew I was watching an attack on America. We all did. My colleagues knew who I worked for and what I did in the military, so they looked to me for answers. I just shook my head and said, "This is hell."

The phone rang less than an hour later. Wearing the same clothes I had put on that morning for the conference and unable to fly with all planes grounded, I got into my car and drove to DC. The world had changed, and I knew, deep down, that I had a part to play.

CHAPTER 5

YEMEN, DEFENSE INTELLIGENCE AGENCY

THE DAYS RIGHTS after 9/11 were filled with frantic activity. America had just been attacked on its own soil for the first time since Pearl Harbor. This shocked all our systems, on an individual and personal level, so that we were all walking or running around somewhat dazed and grief-stricken. Personally we were all wrecked. But the same thing also happened on an institutional level. The blame game hadn't yet started. Within the walls of Marine Corps Headquarters, the Pentagon, the CIA and FBI, and all the other agencies, we were still reassessing vulnerabilities, trying to figure out if another attack was planned, and if so, where it might come, when, and how. The system had been shocked. It was now starting to recover, but that recovery wasn't smooth, not by any means.

Dissecting the why and how of this first attack was best left to the pundits on the news. For us at Marine Corps HQ, the mission was clear: make sure another attack would be anticipated and prevented. As an organization, even while we mourned individually, we set about to do our part to prevent what many feared would be a follow-up attack in this emerging war of terror.

To this end I began my call-up in those first days after 9/11 as one of the personnel manning what the Marine Corps calls the "critical desk" at its headquarters' C4I cell, its command, control, communications, computers, and intelligence node—much like mission control at NASA but with more of a warfighting flavor: maps and graphics, live streams, generals coming and going, lots of coffee, underlings scurrying around preparing reports and briefings, chasing down inane details or responding to the latest crises. I performed this duty for about two weeks, necessary duty, an integral cog in the machine, but—strangely enough—history almost repeated itself at this time, at least for me and for my linguistic and cultural usefulness.

The officer stationed next to me, manning another of the "critical desk" stations, got tasked to call around throughout the Marine Corps to find Arabic speakers and get them enrolled in Marine units that anticipated having need of such skills. I suppose I had gained some wisdom over the decade or two since first trying to raise my hand as an Arabic speaker for the Marine Corps and didn't try to do so this time. Still, I was flabbergasted that this man could sit next to me every day, even complaining to me about how hard it was to find Arabic speakers, without thinking at all about my accent, my name, or even the fact that I'd told him I grew up in Lebanon. I shook my head at the fact that this man was striking out in his assignment to find people just like me, when I was right there in front of him. I didn't push it though. Like I said, maybe I'd gotten wiser over the years.

I still wanted to serve. And still wanted to put my language skills to use. But this episode really made me shift my focus away from trying to do that with the Marine Corps.

Fortunately, I knew where my skills were better understood and better appreciated. I picked up the phone, the very phone in my "critical desk" cubicle, and called the Defense Intelligence Agency (DIA).

I connected right to my desk officer and said, "Hey, I'm here at HQ Marine Corps, and you guys still get first dibs on me. If you want me, pull me in."

They didn't know I'd been called up on emergency orders. But because of the attaché training they'd put me through, they still had an arrangement in place to get me reassigned, if needed, from Marine Corps HQ to their offices.

■ ■ ■

TWO DAYS LATER I had orders reassigning me to DIA headquarters, where I worked through the logistics necessary to get sent down range, this time to the defense attaché office in the US Embassy in Cairo. These orders came through not as a generic emergency call-up with generic language but chock full of verbiage stating that I had been selected for presidential recall to active duty for the War on Terror. This meant I was no longer a reservist but a mobilized active-duty Marine.*

---

* I still have those orders (as do many soldiers and sailors activated at that time for the same reason) because the wording, that presidential activation, and the start of the War on Terror, even then, seemed weighty and worth holding on to, a unique thing in our country's history, a turning point, for better or worse.

Once I got all the details straightened out for my impending assignment to Cairo, I slipped away for two days to Dearborn and put my personal affairs in order: packed my things, saw everyone, had a nice home-cooked meal—though no farewell party. There just wasn't enough time for a party, and—perhaps more importantly—the whole nation was still in too much shock, feeling too somber, too much in mourning, especially our Arab community in Dearborn as we began to catch the first whispers of blowback, the anti-Arab and especially anti-Muslim rhetoric that has become such a staple of public debate nowadays. All of us were too stunned and too sad to organize, let alone to feel like celebrating, a party in honor of a military deployment.

Around October 10, after I had returned from Dearborn, my desk officer again called me up. I had airline tickets for Cairo booked for October 12, so I anticipated this might be just a last-minute briefing or perhaps a review of my travel plans, contingency preparations, and other precautions I needed to rehearse, normal activities in the intelligence world.

But rather than going down such a routine path, the desk officer said, "You need to come in. Colonel Cronin wants to see you."

Colonel Dan Cronin had risen to become the division chief, in charge of all attaché affairs in the Middle East. He was waiting for me in his office when I arrived at the DIA headquarters annex in Clarendon, Virginia, right across the river from DC. The building wasn't anything special, standard 1980s government construction, though different from government buildings nowadays because none of the security procedures or barricades that went into place after 9/11 had been mandated yet. So it had just basic security, mall cops and badging controls at the elevator entrance. The culture at DIA, especially compared to Marine Corps Headquarters, was much less military and much more like a corporate or federal civilian environment: men in suits, women in heels and smart dresses, notebooks and briefcases and nerdy glasses, all much more in vogue than camouflage or spit and polish, though occasionally a person or two scurried down the hall in uniform. I came in wearing a suit but no tie, clean shaven, and fully caffeinated from the Starbucks down the street. I was ready and braced but not especially nervous.

Colonel Cronin's station in this building consisted of a corner office on one of the higher floors, a big desk beneath which an even bigger Kashmiri carpet spread, a piece he'd likely collected during his own days as an attaché in the field. The carpet lent the room a touch of flair that contrasted markedly with the somber grays and blues of the government construction. Maps of every regional hot spot covered the office walls, also adding color but giving the space a stronger feeling of purpose and usefulness than the normal supervisory sterility. Real decisions happened there. I imagined Colonel Cronin lecturing from those maps or holding them up (some of the fancier maps were framed, but some were actually pinned or taped up and had been marked with Post-it notes or covered with arrows and circles in various hasty colors by intemperate hands).

Behind and under these maps, not exactly forgotten but subsumed, lay souvenirs from every single country in North Africa, the Gulf, and the whole Middle East: ceremonial daggers, camel hobbles and riding crops, plaques from various Middle East schools, a copper tea set, a chess board in mother of pearl, plaques with elaborate thank-yous, expressions of gratitude, graduation certificates from schools and training programs, photos of Cronin shaking the hands of famous people in formal settings. All of these were deposited on the walls and shelves, gathering dust under this fresh new whirlwind of maps.

Beyond this interior scene, a wire mesh obscured the outsides of wide, regular windows. I knew this mesh was a technical counter-surveillance measure rather than a sunscreen or antiblast shielding (like later iterations of these headquarters buildings often have). DIA was, and is, an intelligence command after all. Electronic methods of eavesdropping and old-fashioned telephoto lenses had to be taken into account. No one could sit in an office building across the street and tune in to our conversations or watch Colonel Cronin and his staff scribbling on those maps. The facility had a corporate feel, coupled with serious precautions, given a bit of flair in this one office by the colonel's own personal memorabilia.

The last two items of note were two uncomfortable-looking office chairs opposite the room's big desk. I didn't sit in either but entered and reported to my boss, military style, despite the fact that neither of us wore our uniforms right then.

He tried to joke around with me a bit, but I wasn't in the mood, remembering that the last time he called me into the office he reassigned me from Morocco and sent me on a much more difficult and austere mission to Algeria. Nowadays the hotbeds of conflict seemed to be Afghanistan and Yemen. I didn't think they'd send me to Afghanistan, as I didn't possess the language skills, and the war hadn't quite kicked off there yet. So I took a stab at an explanation.

"I'm going to Yemen?" I asked.

"You're going to Yemen."

"Sir, with all due respect, my orders are for Egypt. I'm ready to go. I've done my prep. I've got my plane ticket and I'm leaving in"—I looked at my watch—"thirty hours."

"Well, things have changed. Sit down, we really need to discuss this."

He took one of the pinned maps from his wall and spread it on the desk in front of me.

Together we looked at the map: Yemen like a cup or sickle curving around the lowest point of the Arabian Peninsula, a wicked mountain chain leading up its western side and not stopping at the border between Yemen and its northern neighbor, Saudi Arabia, but rolling along the whole length of the peninsula, right to the holy cities of Mecca and Medina. Then, eastward, a vast expanse of desert, the Rub al-Khali, or Empty Quarter, which had no border at all really, just a line in the sand drawn on a map, a no-man's-land with nary a road, river, or important feature to it, all sand dunes, *sabkha*, and scrub connecting the interiors of Saudi Arabia, Yemen, Oman, Qatar, and the United Arab Emirates. Other than the big eastern mountain range and the empty desert, the one remaining geographical feature seemed paltry, a chain of mountains and plateaus, separated by deep valleys, all along the southern edge of the peninsula, spanning Yemen and Oman both. This range received just enough rain during the *khareef* monsoon season to allow a smattering of villages and farms to shelter there. It was the backcountry, the forgotten part of Yemen, and really the place where groups like al-Qaeda held the most sway.

Colonel Cronin pointed all this out to me. I knew much of it already, though in truth my experience—and my interests, personally and professionally—didn't really include any of Arabia, except for the constant prayerful focus on Mecca and Medina. Given my background in the region, the culture, and the language, I started way ahead of most other Americans, most other Marines, and even most other attachés, but Arabia just hadn't been my jam. North Africa, sure. The Levant, of course. I knew Dearborn better than I knew Yemen. I knew DC better than I knew Yemen.

But sitting there, a warrant officer being lectured by a full colonel, I knew I didn't have a fighting chance. My cushy assignment in Cairo had been blown away. I couldn't *not go* to the place where DIA most desperately needed people. I couldn't *not go* to this strange and isolated land where the bin Laden family had its ancestral home before emigrating to Saudi Arabia and making their millions. I couldn't *not go* to the hotbed.

"Look, Sam," Colonel Cronin said, "you know as well as I do that we tried to get you into Yemen for the *Cole* bombing. Now we have 9/11, and al-Qaeda is there, and we need someone on the ground to assist both with what's going on with al-Qaeda and to help tie up the *Cole*'s loose ends. You're the best person for this. You're mine. And you're going."

He said this last bit with extra emphasis. I knew the scene might get ugly, but I wasn't going down without a fight, wasn't going to take this hellish assignment without wringing some sort of concession from him. So, I took a chance and said, "Alright sir, you want me to turn in my orders for Cairo and go work in godforsaken Yemen for six months, fine. But let's make a deal."

He said, "Alright, what do you want Sam?"

"Give me temporary duty orders for two months, and if I like it, I'll stay there the full six."

He must have been desperate. Without even pausing, he said, "Deal."

No handshake. Nothing formal. Just his word. I trusted it.

But he had one last zinger left for me. As I stood and prepared to leave his office, he said, "By the way, you leave in five days. Go home.

Wrap up your affairs and be back on the fourteenth. You fly on the fifteenth. Here are your tickets."

He picked up an envelope on his desk. Everything done already: orders, plane tickets, diplomatic passport, the whole thing. He'd had his staff working overtime, and all of this negotiating with me was just for show. The decision had been made, and he'd merely been playing nice guy to smooth my feathers. This made me laugh. I respected this kind of strength: self-assured but also concerned enough with the *person*, with me, to put in place these little precautions and niceties.

As I was walking out the door, he had some last words of encouragement. "Sam?" he said.

"Sir?"

"I know you're going to do a very good job over there, and I bet you lunch that you're going to love it."

Truth be told, that son of a bitch collected his lunch in Yemen the following year when he came out to do his annual visit. I was still there, still working away, seriously overstaying not just the two-month promise I'd made but also the six-month tour they'd wanted me to do, leaving Yemen three years later. Yemen hooked me. Without a doubt I owed Colonel Cronin lunch—I was there, in the thick of it, loving every minute.

■ ■ ■

BEFORE LEAVING DC I had the opportunity to sit down with one of our previous defense attachés from Yemen. He gave me a good, thorough briefing and ended with an admonishment: "Whatever you do, don't fly Yemenia."

I whipped out my ticket and saw the word "Lufthansa" written across the top. I showed it to my colleague, and he said, "Yeah, that's good. But remember, never do Yemenia. And also remember that Yemenia is the *better* of Yemen's two airlines. Never, ever, under any circumstances, fly their smaller airline, which mostly just goes between domestic locations and Djibouti. That one is called Sa'ida or Happy Airlines, and it's literally chickens in the overhead compartments and qat chewing in the aisles."

I didn't yet know much about qat, the mild narcotic leaf that almost all Yemenis chew in big wads in their cheeks, though I was to learn. But the upfront warning about these airlines certainly rang true and was driven home later that week.

On October 15, I arrived at the airport in DC with a one-way ticket to Yemen (remember: right after 9/11!). I didn't think anything of it, but that was a mistake. What could go wrong with a Lebanese man trying to get to Yemen right then?

The woman at the check-in counter looked at me, then at my ticket, and said, "Hold on a second, sir."

She picked up the phone, called a number, turned around, and smiled at me while acting like she was continuing to process my ticket. In my mind I knew exactly what she was doing, since I'd been involved in similar screening processes at the border in Michigan and elsewhere over the last several years. I swallowed my pride and braced for what would happen next.

About thirty seconds later two FBI agents showed up at the counter.

"Excuse me, sir," they said. "Can you step aside and come this way with us?"

Then, once we'd moved to a private room out of view of the main passenger area, they said, "Can we see your ID?"

Something perverse and pugnacious in me wanted to extend this moment, to toy with these earnest agents a bit, nothing too aggressive, just playing the system: I gave them my Michigan driver's license rather than my military ID or my diplomatic passport. I wanted them to have to do a little digging. I wanted to see what their process was like. After all, I was going to Yemen, leaving lovely America, and so I wasn't exactly in a rush to board the plane! There's a quality admired in the Middle East and actually all throughout the Mediterranean world that's a little different from normal American straight-shooting behavior. Perhaps Odysseus best exemplifies it: clever and bold navigation of a difficult situation through a combination of mental gamesmanship and physical audacity. I think this incident—in which I behaved in a semielusive, semicombative manner when I easily could have explained myself—is an early example of a trait that served me well later, in Yemen and elsewhere, as I used it to get things done and gain respect in non-Western cultures.

At that particular moment, though, I'd gotten myself into what looked like a pickle. Still, I was calm, knowing I held an ace in the hole.

The agents started firing questions fast and furious. They thought they'd caught a big one.

"Where are you heading?"

"Yemen, the capital, Sana'a," I said.

They made furious notes.

They asked a number of other questions. I provided truthful but perhaps veiled answers, never mentioning the embassy or my role there. I didn't want to give away my little game yet.

Finally, one of them asked the thousand-dollar question: "What is your purpose traveling there?"

I wasn't going to lie outright, so I had to come clean. Handing them my diplomatic passport, military ID, and military orders, I said, "You know what I am now, right?"

"Yes," they said, visibly deflated. They didn't laugh—they had very little sense of humor—though I was chuckling inside.

They took me back to the luggage counter and told the woman there that she was clear to process me for boarding. Poor lady, she probably wasn't told anything more and just had to send me through. She likely never knew what was going on and likely got home that night to her family with a strange story about busting someone headed for Yemen on a one-way ticket, only to have the feds send him through without even a decent roughing up.

My flight on Lufthansa took me to Frankfurt for a layover, and there, much to my chagrin, I had timed things badly. Lufthansa and its risk management and security people decided it would be best to cancel all future flights to Yemen. The second half of my ticket instantly became worthless. I had to find a new way to get to the country. The only carrier available? Yep, Yemenia.

No chickens in the overhead compartment, but a six-hour delay on the runway. A stop in Rome for additional passengers. Another delay, three or four hours there. A lot of praying by the passengers on the plane, probably by the flight crew too. And then we landed in Sana'a at last, coming in low and fast over the terraced green mountains just in case anyone decided to test a surface-to-air missile or an old Soviet-era ZPU antiaircraft gun. All was peaceful and fairly smooth, though somehow in the eastern distance the whole world seemed to dissolve away, the terraced green slopes giving way to jagged, burnt-looking hillsides and then to the haze of sandstorms and sinuous dunes where the Rub al-Khali desert bumped up against Yemen's backbone of mountains.

Sana'a itself lies cupped in a bowl-shaped valley amid some of these mountains, a bowl tilted toward the north, which is the direction our plane came in from. As we approached the more populated "suburbs" around Sana'a, houses began to loom up amid the fields, connected by twisted mountain roads and pasture spread out on the plateau tops. Most of the houses were white and square or brown and squat, compounds with gardens and generators and single light poles. Then things got more and more urban, more closely packed, with better roads connecting the denser villages and intersections, a profusion of power lines, bigger buildings, all patterned on what seemed to be a single square, white, blocky architectural plan. I saw a wastewater plant, then the airport: civilian planes parked on the sides of the runway as we touched down, also military planes, a few rows of dusty MiGs and a couple very old American F-5 jets, a pod of helicopters, everything haphazardly placed, though the military equipment was generally pulled out, parade style, in front of deep bunkers, as if the whole country had learned from Saddam Hussein's experience of having his air force destroyed on his runways a decade earlier.

It was about sunset when my Yemenia flight finally touched down. Sana'a airport has no direct boarding or deboarding from planes into the airport; instead travelers descend a set of mobile stairs on the tarmac, then hop on to the several buses lined up, waiting to ferry them to the terminal. This was my first step into, and taste of, Yemen. And when I say "taste," I literally mean *taste*: the wind was blowing at just such an angle that it brought the stench of that nearby wastewater plant full upon us. I covered my face. I wasn't too squeamish and knew such plants were necessities, but still the odor overpowered the better scents of Yemen, the scents I would learn to love and identify as part of my new home: the wafting up of sand and heat from the Rub al-Khali, the cooking smells of *salta* and *bint as-sahin*, the wetter greenery watered by small pipes or fountain channels. All of this was there in that moment, though smothered by that thick, sickly sweet wastewater breeze.

Passage through the airport occurred without incident or delay: customs, passport, baggage pickup. The airport had been built in the 1960s and boasted the best of stucco, tile, and arched white plaster and alabaster; a poor attempt had been made to replicate in midmodern fashion some of the *qamaria* windows so famous in Sana'a's Old City. A *qamaria* is a half-moon shape, beautiful when done right. The cheaper airport version just made things look dingy, tacky, and a bit dark.

Two members of the defense attaché office, Sergeant First Class Jeff Healy and Major Mark Conroe, met me at the baggage claim. They brought a security detail of local Yemenis whose members lounged outside at the back of the diplomatic vehicles in the parking lot. None of them were kitted up. They probably had weapons in the car but weren't wearing flak vests or ammo holders; however, they were packing concealed handguns. These were early days. Sure, 9/11 had us on edge, but Yemen was still a functioning country at that time, with police and military forces keeping things in order (albeit third-world style) and a government well accustomed to the idiosyncrasies and balancing acts of long-time president Ali Abdullah Saleh. We all wore civilian clothes: polo shirts, khakis. That would be our everyday attire, except when big meetings or events induced us to wear a suit and tie or, even less fun, our military regalia.

To start, I was housed in a spare bedroom in Lieutenant Colonel Paul Newman's house. He was the defense attaché, the head of the office over Sergeant First Class Healy, Major Conroe, and a few others of us, and so his place was biggest, a cavernous, tiled mansion behind fifteen-foot-high fences situated in the heart of Sana'a's ritzy Hadda neighborhood. No one thought I was going to be there too long, given my two-month orders, so it seemed easier and more expedient to put me in a temporary place, where no one had to do extra paperwork, take extra security precautions, do a site survey, contract for a new place, or take any other extraordinary measures.

After my first temporary duty assignment and my decision to sign up for another few months, they moved me out of the temporary bedroom in Lieutenant Colonel Newman's place to a room in the Sheraton Hotel, much nearer to our embassy but still a temporary solution.

Of course, the Sheraton later became something of a ground zero, when Yemen really heated up after the Arab Spring. The embassy leased the whole hotel and fortified it, moving all its permanent personnel out of the nice houses in Hadda and into the hotel compound. But that was much later, so the atmosphere at this time was no different from that of a hundred other hotels in the Middle East—I was on my own, with a few other short-term embassy employees, a sprinkling of semipermanent expatriates, and a ton of normal businessmen and tourists coming and going. The hotel had a bar on the roof with karaoke and a dance band, a big pool, tennis courts, waiters, a shisha smoking lounge, a couple of restaurants, and a weight room. Not too terrible a place to be. Best of all, it was right next to the embassy, which cut my commute through Sana'a's horrendous traffic down to almost nothing each day. Furthermore it was located high up on the flanks of one of the mountains, looking down over the bowl of the valley and the bulk of the city, right across the minarets and frosted mudbrick skyscrapers of the Old City toward distant Hadda tucked behind the rising shell of President Saleh's new mosque.

We worked. We worked hard, and we played hard. These were wild times in Yemen because of the combination of freedom and danger. I got to go all over the country. And the party scene was absolutely crazy down there in Hadda and across the rest of the city.

Right away, on the second or third night after my arrival, Mark Conroe took me to meet one of his best contacts in Sana'a, Abdulghani Jamil. At that time Abdulghani was still the assistant to the chief of customs or some such thing. Over the next year or two, he became the head of Yemen's countersmuggling unit and then the mayor of Sana'a. Already at that time he drove a big white Land Cruiser and sported fancy suits and sunglasses. I remember—not too long after this first meeting, when he'd climbed the totem pole from assistant to countersmuggling chief to mayor—how he would openly boast of being the youngest mayor in the world at only thirty-five. All this he owed not only to his affable and gregarious personality but, more importantly, to his status as the scion of one of the major tribes on the northeastern approaches to Sana'a, critical terrain opposite President Saleh's own power base south and east of the city in and around the village of Sanhan. President Saleh needed Abdulghani's tribe to shore up power in that region, and so Abdulghani found the way before him paved in gold, all doors open, all wishes fulfilled. He knew it. And he knew how to use it to his best advantage.

That first night Abdulghani Jamil and Mark and I chewed qat together, Mark stripping a few fresh leaves from a branch and chewing them lightly, almost suspiciously, while young Abdulghani filled his cheek to the point that the skin became almost translucent as it stretched around the baseball-sized mass he'd created. I took something between the two, my first go at it—I wanted to try the stuff, to get the full effect, perhaps to impress my Yemeni host. He and I were chattering away in Arabic, becoming fast friends, while Mark—with his more rudimentary Arabic, learned at the Defense Language Institute—hung with us.

Mark leaned over at one point, motioned to the qat, and said, "Hey, take it easy on that."

I was feeling a bit light-headed, a bit carefree, but nothing terrible. In fact, I felt quite good. I shrugged and gave him a green-gummed grin.

"I'm Arab," I said. "I can handle it."

"But remember," said Mark, "this kid"—for in truth Abdulghani was perhaps twenty years old—"is going to be someone someday."

Mark was right about that, but not right about making me slow down with the qat. I handled it just fine and soon realized it isn't addictive; instead it's a great mood enhancer, an enabler for the four-, and five-, and even six-hour world-problem-solving conversations that would become our bread and butter in forming deep relationships with trusted individuals in Yemen.

Mark wasn't right about the qat, but he was right about Abdulghani—not just in those first stages of his career progression but even now, as our dear friend has risen in these last frantic years of Yemen's civil war to serve as minister of state. Abdulghani has proven adept at navigating the different demands of tribe, nation, family, and foreign relationships, even though (and even in Yemen's darkest days) he sometimes still reverts to being a bit of a big kid. He was just the sort of person with whom we, in the defense attaché office, needed to build a strong relationship.

I was thrown right into the fire with Abdulghani. But the rest of the office was as slammed as you can imagine during these critical post-9/11 days. We had one Naval Criminal Investigative Service officer on loan with us, one Force Protection Detachment officer (to mind our security), a couple other attachés, our boss Lieutenant Colonel Newman, and myself. Not a large crew.

I found myself traveling far and wide all over Yemen, going right away to the Red Sea port of Hudaydah, humid and malarial compared to Sana'a, even in mid-October. There I did the advance work—site security setup, local liaison, and various other organizational tasks—for a visit from the US deputy secretary of state to President Saleh, who happened to be conducting his government business in Hudaydah at that time rather than in Sana'a. Likewise, I found myself in the far south, in Aden, site of the *Cole* bombing, helping there about every week or every other week. Aden had once been the second-busiest port in the world by volume, as British steamships stopped there in transit to India to resupply with coal and water. The city retained a mixed British and Arab feel, with significant Indian and African influences too; it was a real cultural melting pot and a fun place to be right on the water. I went to the Hadramawt Valley, way out in the hinterlands, where the bin Laden family had its roots. I went to the port of Mukulla in the far east of the country, where the commerce from the Hadramawt Valley flows over a last escarpment and out to the sea, a strange place because it has no real value of its own other than being the connector between the Hadramawt and the rest of the world. And, perhaps strangest of all, I went to the eco-logically pristine and totally weird island of Socotra, which looked more like Ireland than the Middle East, with its green, chalky cliffs, plants like the dragon's blood tree that can be found nowhere else in the world, and a population subsisting off the land.

I even went to Saadah a couple times, in the northern mountains near the border with Saudi Arabia. Saadah is the base of power for the Houthi, at that time only a moderately influential tribe from among many other Zaydi Shi'a tribes that held sway throughout most of northern and central Yemen. The Houthis would rise in power over the coming years as they clung to their mountain fast-nesses and battled back against Saleh's government over the course of a decade of civil war.

I went there, right to their center of power, not once but a couple times during these first years in Yemen—and the place didn't really seem bad, threatening, or out of the ordinary to me. I'm Shi'a after all. In some ways the Houthis, and the Zaydis more generally, were closer culturally to my Lebanese roots than Americans or even than the Sunnis among whom I'd lived and worked in other places such as Dearborn, Morocco, Algeria, and Libya.

Upon completion of each set of temporary orders, DIA would talk to me about taking other assignments, but each time they just ended up sending me right back to continue the work I was doing in Yemen. At long last, after the first year or so, I got assigned a house of my own in Hadda.

In part DIA kept sending me back because I'd taken on a signifi-cant role training Yemeni military units. Usually this role was han-dled by another group that exists in most of our embassies, variously called the Office of Military Cooperation (OMC) or the Office of

Defense Cooperation. This office would be stocked with similar personnel as the attaché office, but instead of liaison and relationship work, the OMC focused on training and supplying—via military sales programs—our allies with excess or outdated US equipment, a process that augments these partner forces, strengthens the relationships and interreliances between the countries, and provides ongoing economic benefit to US-based manufacturers. Basically, the joke runs, the OMC represents our team of legal arms dealers.

The OMC in Sana'a had been shut down after the First Gulf War, when Yemen sided with Saddam Hussein. We could no longer pretend that sales of arms and provision of training to the Yemenis would be a good strategic move when they were the one country in the Arab world siding against us and our allies.

President Saleh stood by that position for a very short time. He realized soon who would win that war and the extent of the equipment he was foregoing and the training value that came with it. The shuttering of our OMC was a bad thing for him. When 9/11 happened, ten years later, the training had been restarted but the OMC not yet officially reconstituted; our attaché office ran the training. I became the guy tabbed to honcho that program, with a first big success during my time represented in the signing of a memorandum of understanding between the Yemeni Ministry of Defense, our military, and our embassy to authorize this official training relationship.

That's a bit of inside boringness, really, the military talk, the discussion of those memorandums and training programs. But it gives a flavor of the work being performed. It accounts for why I kept going back, kept getting reassigned. And it also helps explain why I eventually got that house in Hadda rather than ghosting through the halls of the Sheraton as a card-carrying member of the hotel expatriate crowd.

I loved the work in Yemen. But I also loved the people and formed a number of really close, critical relationships that have continued to give back to me, both personally and professionally.

One relationship formed during this time serves as a good example: I befriended the family of a young man who did some work on my car, not only repairing it when the need arose but also washing it regularly—just showing up with a bucket, rags, and soap, ready to do whatever needed to be done. We struck up a friendship in addition to this side-hustle business arrangement, and he invited me to dinner at his family's house, the type of formal bonding that one doesn't say no to in this culture.

Their house, as I imagined, proved no bigger than a midsized hotel room, divided up into a bedroom, kitchen, *majlis* sitting area, and bathroom, shared between three daughters, three sons, and the mother and father of the family. Of the children, the youngest, a girl named Yasmine, had a real spark intellectually—a passion for life and a curiosity that I found incredibly hopeful and also sad, given her family's financial situation. I knew she wouldn't have the opportunity to get much schooling, to realize any of the potential I saw, which, quite frankly, her family saw too. They'd already banded together— the work her brother did washing and repairing my car was one example—to scrounge whatever money they could to send her to a good elementary school.

I ended up chipping in, making sure she had books, materials, that sort of thing. And by the time I left Yemen a few years later, I'd formalized the situation even further, paying regular visits to the family and becoming something of her sponsor and adopted godfather.

Throughout the coming years, even after I left DIA and undertook other work, I stayed in touch with the family and continued to support Yasmine, paying for vocational school after she completed high school at only fifteen years of age.

■ ■ ■

ONE MORE IMPORTANT PART of the mission in those days: parties.

Embassy parties. Private parties. Planned parties around holidays and commemorations. Impromptu parties.

Lunch meetings that spun into afternoon qat chews and then diverged into trips to someone else's house, a meeting with a dignitary or well-connected person we just had to get to know, a session smoking shisha in a parlor, drinking coffee at 2 a.m. outside the zoo or the parade grounds or at a swanky café in Hadda beneath the shadow of Saleh's huge and ever-growing new mosque.

We were making the critical connections that would facilitate the work we'd been sent to do: government connections, business connections, connections with influential private citizens and NGOs doing humanitarian work in remote places or right there in the tougher-to-reach corners of Sana'a's Old City.

Sometime during that first year of our operations, Sergeant First Class Healy got a follow-on assignment and left our office. He was replaced by a new operations coordinator, Sergeant First Class Henry Grant, who loved throwing parties. His place in Hadda became the new hot spot in town. All the diplomats and attachés from other embassies joined us nightly, or at least several times a week, with the regulars being our counterparts from the British, French, Dutch, and German embassies. To the Germans we quickly learned to extend qualified invitations—"You have to bring your own drinks"—because, wow, those guys could down a lot of beer. Of course, a lot of girls would also show up, especially Ethiopians, a lot of them maids, and a lot of Yemenis from the top classes of Yemeni society.

One night we had a bigger party than usual. I think this one was sort of a welcome party for a group of Special Operations Forces (SOF) soldiers who'd come in specifically to augment, and eventually take over, the training portfolio I'd been tasked with in the interim. At this event we probably pushed our attendance at Grant's house up to the max, 100, maybe 150 people. It was a zoo. One young State Department guy got so drunk, he started puking all over, and as a nondrinking Muslim, I was the sober one and had to drive him back home.

By the time I got back, the party was raging even more maniacally and had started to attract attention. I sort of switched modes then, from participating to trying to make sure we kept on the right side of things. As the sober one, I felt a bit responsible.

Outside the front gate of the house, we'd started to collect a representative smattering of Yemen's law enforcement and intelligence services, all peering into the courtyard, trying to see what was happening in the house itself through the windows and the opening and shutting front door, watching people come and go from the balconies and the roof. They were interested not only in the noise and ruckus of the party but also in tracking which guests were showing up, how they were behaving, and perhaps who was leaving with whom.

In this gaggle I saw members of the National Security Bureau (NSB), the Political Security Organization (PSO), the Sana'a city police, and the Department of Military Intelligence (DMI). The DMI was represented at that time by young Captain Ahmed Yafa'i—a man who, like

Abdulghani Jamil, became a good friend and a good contact for our office as he quickly rose to the rank of general and chief of DMI. Also, like the family of Abdulghani Jamil, Ahmed's family, the Yafa'i, were favored by President Saleh because their lands straddle the main route south to Aden. All these security and intelligence personnel were gathered together in a huddle, with various nameless lackeys around them, recording who was coming in and going out. I almost had no choice but to approach and start chatting them up, to try to diffuse any rumors they were hearing or calm whatever other fears had taken hold in their minds and at least to listen in and understand their concerns and agendas.

Unfortunately, right then Sergeant First Class Grant ran out of the house and made a beeline right for me, pulling me away from the intelligence officials.

"Sam," he said, a bit too loudly, "get in here and hurry up."

I rushed into the dining room, where the table had been pushed aside and a space had been cleared for a dance floor.

Blood covered the ground and was splattered across one of the walls, like a modern art painting.

Sergeant First Class Grant wouldn't let me stop there, among the drunk but oddly quiet people. He rushed me through that room and into one of the ground-floor bedrooms.

"Get in here," he said, shoving his way through a posse blocking the door.

There, around the bed, five or six of those newly arrived Special Forces guys stood over the body of a little Ethiopian girl in a short black dress.

"What the hell happened?" I asked.

One of the SOF guys was a medic and had brought his kit, which he had strewn over the bed. He was removing the air bubbles from a big syringe, squirting a fine jet of fluid into the air above the bed. He bent down and jabbed the needle into the Ethiopian girl's arm, which made her stop wailing almost instantly.

Pulling the needle from her arm, he bent the tip of it down and then, with his other, obviously very practiced hand, whipped out some thread already laced through the eye of suturing needle. He sat beside the quiet girl, her dark eyes rolling back in her head, parted her hair down the side of her head, and began to sew shut a several-inch-long gash in her scalp.

The biggest of the SOF guys around the bed, maybe six foot four, muscular, the sort you never want to mess with but who often turn out to be the milder, more empathetic types among that lot, was shaking like a tree in the wind. "Sir," he said, "we fucked up. I fucked up."

He told me what had happened in pieces that didn't all make sense, fractured little bits of a story from which I eventually deduced that he had been dancing with this girl, having a great time, and decided to do the "*Dirty Dancing* scene," lifting her over his head to spin her around. Only problem: the ceiling fan. It had clipped her head in the middle of one of these twirls.

This was deep doo-doo.

Especially with the PSO, NSB, and DMI out front. Not to mention the police.

We ended up dressing her in an *abaya*, the traditional head-to-toe covering some Muslim women wear, with full face covering, though we still had her head wrapped beneath it. She was woozy from the painkiller the medic had given her, so we propped her between us and got her into one of the cars in the courtyard to take her to the Yemen German Hospital in Hadda. For a moment, passing through the gate and beyond the group of baffled Yemeni intelligence officials, we thought we'd made a clean escape. But the PSO officer caught on, jumped in his car with some of his men, and followed us.

We got her into the hospital and kept the PSO at bay long enough to sequester her in an examining room. We'd washed off most of the blood, but her head was still wrapped up with a kitchen towel that now looked like a bandage from World War II.

I told the hospital staff that she was our maid and that we'd had a party. She was working the party when someone spilled on the tile floor, and she'd slipped and hit her head on one of the counters, a good enough story. And the girl didn't offer any sort of counterexplanation because, by this time, she was unconscious. She was okay; the painkillers and all the excitement had just been a bit much for her. They gave her an MRI. We did the paperwork and wrote down the story, and everyone stuck with it, even when the PSO finally nosed in and alleged, based on rumors, that someone had hit her.

"We want to investigate," they started to say.

But I cut that notion off right away, saying, "Hey, we're all diplomats here, and we're taking care of her."

That word, "diplomat," was an important one, conveying strong notions of diplomatic immunity and at the same time carrying strong risk—because if the PSO wanted to make an issue of the event, they could just get the Ministry of Foreign Affairs to declare us, any of us or all of us, persona non grata (PNG). That's actually a technical term, and it requires the embassy to immediately withdraw a person so designated from the country. No one wanted that. It could be a scandal. Certainly it would be bad for that person individually. It's never a good thing to have to explain to headquarters why you've been forced to leave an embassy assignment.

Being declared PNG was one option. But these services could be subtler and still make things difficult. They could just whisper to some of our superiors, not even at the ambassadorial level. This was more of a veiled threat and maybe did not carry the same stigma as getting PNG'd, but it could still make our lives harder. Or they could mess around with inspections—paying visits to our villas, checking cargo we shipped in, asking for documents in triplicate, just generally making things difficult. We didn't want any of that.

I knew all this. And I'd already staked our position by using the "diplomat" word. So I softened our approach a bit, saying, "We're all diplomats, and she's our maid. You're welcome to interview her but not any of these guys. I'm the senior officer here, so you can talk to me."

The girl, thankfully, remained soundly passed out.

And the PSO let the matter drop (probably yet another benefit of my having chewed a few bundles of qat with some of them in other, less anxious times).

The MRI came back okay, no fractures. And the doctors, taking off her bandage, admired the stitches in the girl's head—which I explained by telling them that one of the SOF guys worked as an orderly in our embassy health clinic, a bit of a stretch but not too far from the truth. We'd done the stitching ourselves but just wanted to bring her into the ER to make sure she did not have more serious injuries, like a concussion.

This seemed to satisfy everyone.

The PSO departed.

Some of the Ethiopian girl's friends came to pick her up.

And the SOF guys owed me big time, which never hurts, especially in a country like Yemen. We Marines can fight. But it's always good to have the most lethal people on the battlefield squarely in your corner, even if they're only there as trainers.

■ ■ ■

THAT INITIAL TWO-MONTH TEMPORARY set of orders quickly turned into two years, then three. I came home about every three or four months for a few days of leave. But the deployment, the pace of it, and the very different life I lived in Yemen compared to Dearborn made a wreck of my marriage with Zainab.

Sometime in 2003, having come back on a long series of flights, layovers, more flights, and a stop in DC for outbriefs, I arrived home tired. I'd had no hot food for several days, so Zainab and I went out to dinner.

She looked at me, like a different person from the woman I remembered and loved, and said, "I've already talked to a lawyer. She's drawing up the papers. I want a divorce. It's not working out between us. This life isn't working out for me."

I was hurt. I wanted to keep the family. I knew I was gone too much, and we had started to develop different views on life. Zainab was independent; she wanted to be more independent and pursue what she wanted to pursue, so taking care of four kids and running our shared family businesses was taking a toll on her. She didn't want to do it anymore.

I considered not going back to Yemen then, but the orders kept coming back, that same presidential recall to fight in the War on Terror, and I didn't have a real choice in the matter.

It was my duty.

And my duty was, more and more, my identity.

CHAPTER 6

CONTRACTOR

ONE THING I prided myself on most during my years working for DIA in Yemen was the ability to form lasting relationships with important people there. These relationships proved, time and again, to be important, mission critical, and even lifesaving. I truly enjoyed the social aspect of my duties, even though every relationship, no matter how genuine, had to be viewed as a point of potential future leverage to make things happen for our embassy and our country. Among the relationships that combined both business and social aspects, I include my friendships with Abdulghani Jamil, Ahmed Yafa'i, and many others. I first met these Yemeni power players while I served in an official government capacity, but they proved key to my transition into a civilian career too.

Yemen, like most Arab countries, does business based on personal relationships. In American professional situations, while personal relationships are always important, there's an understanding that business contracts are formed between entities, whereas in an Arab context the personal relationship retains primacy, and the contract is often viewed as between not two entities but the people themselves. As a result, it's the time, understanding, and friendship—dear and constantly nourished friendship—that get the work and the deals done.

Although I recall using my relationships to some advantage or another in scores and scores of incidents, big and small, one of the most important happened just before the start of the Second Gulf War, when Vice President Dick Cheney came out to the Middle East on his tour of all the Arab countries, frantically drumming up support for the coalition's plan to invade Iraq.

Yemen had been the one Arab country to support Saddam Hussein during the First Gulf War under George H. W. Bush, so the importance of Cheney's visit to Yemen wasn't lost on anyone. The White House wanted the visit to be a success. Our embassy wanted it to be a success. Even Yemen knew it was a big deal. President Ali Abdullah Saleh wanted to be on the right side this time.

I ended up facilitating the security for the visit, calling in favors from numerous close Yemeni contacts in order to bring the Yemeni security up to the (somewhat unrealistic) standard the Secret Service expected. I had to call one of Saleh's nephews, a general at that time, to ask for additional security at the airport. Saleh's threats and bribes to the local sheiks increased safety much more than any troop deployments would.

In the end Cheney's visit lasted no more than a half hour, but it was critical. And it would not have happened—with the Secret Service threatening to cancel the visit over additional security requirements—had it not been for these local military and political contacts I'd developed.

This type of thing happened repeatedly, and not just with VIP visits. Shipments of armored vehicles would be impossible to get out of port, not allowed into the country or held up with red tape, requiring payment of some sort of bribe, or they'd just get detained under murky circumstances. Our office would get them through, leveraging these same contacts and trust. For the State Department, even for the agency, it was tough to get vehicles or even communication, or "commo," gear through the ports. But we could get it done because we'd taken time to develop our friendships. For many of these shipments during my time working at the embassy, the deputy for customs was Abdulghani Jamil. Abdulghani earned big points with us for getting such things done—and quickly. One day after being asked for help, he would often have the shipment complete and the containers or vehicles lined up in the embassy courtyard!

Even after successes like this, the fun—and the work I was doing—couldn't last forever.

■ ■ ■

IN 2004 I FINALLY fell through the cracks with DIA, my string of consecutive ongoing mobilizations in support of embassy work in Yemen and elsewhere coming to an end. DIA didn't renew my orders, so I went back into the Reserves. I returned to Dearborn for a couple weeks, but it wasn't the same without Zainab. And the jobs I returned to there, at my family businesses, just didn't compare with the meaningful work I had been doing in Yemen. That feeling of hollowness because of the split with Zainab, combined with the difference in value I felt between the everyday world and the work I had been doing in the Middle East, meant that I was ripe when British

American Tobacco (BAT) contacted me to be its security manager in Saudi Arabia.

I accepted right away.

My family stayed in Dearborn, just as if this new job were another military deployment overseas.

I worked in Jeddah, Saudi Arabia, during my first assignment with British American Tobacco. And I also worked out a deal to continue drilling as a reservist, using the time allotted for drill weekends and my two-week summer training to help embassy personnel in Riyadh, Saudi Arabia's capital, familiarize themselves with Jeddah, hosting them and taking them around to meet the right friends. It was a good arrangement, since the contacts I made in Jeddah for British American Tobacco both facilitated the security BAT needed and also were good people for our embassy to know. Basically, I continued my role as a problem solver and relationship manager, all with a security focus, doing it full-time for my civilian employer and part-time for the embassy in fulfillment of my Reserve obligation.

This went on for almost two more years.

During my time in Saudi Arabia, I was able to watch—and participate in—the ebb and flow of pilgrims to Mecca, completing the Umra, or minor pilgrimage, almost every weekend myself. There was excellent snorkeling in Jeddah too, with the shores of the Red Sea really a pristine wonderland. I didn't partake in that much though, remembering my near-drowning experience in that Dearborn gym class all too well!

At one point in 2005, I just happened to call up the regional security officer (RSO) for our consulate in Jeddah to have our periodic coffee catch-up meeting. We'd do this every other month or so, with me coming to the consulate just to shoot the breeze, meeting him at the Marine House, or maybe going with him somewhere out on the town. I remember on this particular day, as I went through the gate of the consulate, thinking to myself how easy it would be to breach the compound there, for when the gate opened up, nothing prevented a second car from ramming its way inside after a first car entered legitimately. The only real protection was the bar of the gate and then a couple half-asleep Saudi guards in a Dushka truck outside.

We had our coffee, focusing our talk on some of the really bad security things going on back then: a couple of bombings had just happened in Riyadh and also in Dammam at one of Saudi Aramco's entrances. I think I also mentioned the gate to my friend, the security officer. And then I went on my merry way back to the British American Tobacco office.

Within minutes of reaching my desk, I got a call from one of my BAT trade marketing representatives in the field. "Mr. Sam," he said, "the American embassy"—which is what they called the consulate—"is under attack." He reported shooting inside. "They're going wild."

The consulate had been breached, right at that gate, just as I imagined.

I ran back to my car and sped to the consulate, or as close as I could get, but the whole area was blockaded by the Saudi police and military forces. Smoke rose from behind the consulate walls, a block or so away from the nearest spot I could approach. All I could do was watch.

Needless to say, the attack on the consulate changed the posture for all our work in Jeddah and Saudi Arabia. Things got a lot stricter.

People became a lot more careful. Though I'd made good contacts and maintained great relationships, my employers wanted to button things up, and I wasn't interested in working that way.

At about that same time, I received a call from an old friend, Ali Soufan, the FBI agent who'd pursued Osama bin Laden before 9/11.* By this point Ali had left the FBI to begin his own consultancy, initially working in part with Giuliani Safety & Security, out of the Giuliani Partners. He'd cut ties with the FBI after disagreeing with the George W. Bush administration's use of enhanced interrogation techniques, water boarding, and other practices. Ali was one of the first to stand up against those policies, and he did so on the grounds that information obtained through such means was not reliable, in addition to the techniques themselves going against our values as Americans. He'd made enough of a name for himself that he leveraged his reputation and connections to start his private practice under the umbrella of Rudy Giuliani. I'd met Ali when he was in Yemen working as one of the leads on the FBI's investigation of the *Cole* bombing, and we'd hit it off pretty well since we both spent our youth in Lebanon and then came to America to grow up and live the American Dream. I was excited that he called me.

"Come out to Qatar," Ali said. "I want you to check something out with me."

This was 2006, early in the year. Giuliani Safety & Security had begun working in Qatar to train the Qatar government personnel, and Ali himself was serving as the Giuliani Group's director of international operations, managing the project and the relationships on the ground.

---

* The 2018 HBO series *The Looming Tower* tells much of Ali's story.

When I got to Qatar, Ali took me around, showing me his training programs.

"This is your line of work, Sam," he said, "coordinating training like you used to do in Yemen for the Special Forces and the Internal Security."

"Well, I know it sounds like a good job."

I was thrilled already. But Ali hadn't got to the best part of his pitch yet. When he told me where the training would be held and whom I would be training, I went through the roof with excitement.

"As icing on the cake, brother, it's not here that I need you."

"No?"

"No."

"Then where?"

"Lebanon."

"Hell, yes," I said, unable to contain my enthusiasm for a job that would take me home.

Ali was planning to expand the training program as a gift to the Lebanese Internal Security Forces (ISF), the policing side of Lebanon's divided security sector—parts of which are primarily Christian-led and run, parts more Sunni, and parts more Shi'a. Ali and I went together to Lebanon and started setting it all up, getting firing ranges and training areas in Dibaye booked for our courses, getting everything set. The Lebanese concept was to train a first counterterrorism unit cohort all the way from A to Z, fresh from the very beginning of the trainees' enlistment to the very end, over a three-month period. Ali's guys, under my supervision, were going to be the instructors.

The plan we put together involved me being on-site through the whole first summer, hands on for the first three-month training rotation and potentially for much longer if the program turned out to be a success. As a result of this plan, I took the opportunity to fly my daughter Amira to Lebanon, thinking it would be a great time to have her with me and let her get to know her (not so distantly) ancestral country and some of her (not too distant) relatives there.

Once all the groundwork was in place, I went back to Jeddah to clean out my desk and complete my handover of responsibilities for British American Tobacco. I then circled back to Doha for two days to check in with Ali and finalize plans before the start of the training program. I left Amira with her aunt at her house in a neighborhood called Khalda, just south of the airport in Beirut.

Crazy as it sounds, right then, at the very moment I went to Doha to put the finishing touches on our training program with Ali and his group, the 2006 Israel-Hezbollah War started.

Our program with the ISF was put on hold.

Everyone thought this flare-up of tension between Hezbollah and Israel would last for two or maybe three days, a week tops. Conflagrations of that sort began and ended all the time, not just on the Lebanon border but between the Israelis and the Palestinians in Gaza, the West Bank, and Jerusalem and, in the not-too-distant past, also with Egypt, Jordan, and Syria, not to mention other flare-ups inside Lebanon itself, which also tended to involve Syria. The Israelis would come and do their thing, conduct a few air raids, root out some Hezbollah cells, and it would be over. All of us had gotten pretty used to it over a lifetime, even a lifetime like mine, half spent in the United States. Israel's incursions and Syrian occupations were always present in our minds, only a little bit more troubling than a thunderstorm might be on the Great Plains or a hurricane in Florida.

But this time, when the ground troops really started flowing en masse, we knew it was going to get bad.

And of greatest concern to me, Amira had remained in Lebanon, and I was stuck outside the country, unable to return for her.

Khalda, the neighborhood where her aunt lived and where Amira had her refuge, abutted the airport along its southern edge. Of course, in war airports tend to be one of the most targeted places, and pretty much the first thing, the Israelis started hitting this one with their planes.

I wanted to get Amira out of there.

She'd phone, crying, from the bunkers at the side of her aunt's apartment building. These bunkers had a long history, actually starting as bunkers, then being converted into a parking garage for the complex, then being hastily remade, right as this bombing started, into makeshift bunkers again.

"Dad, the whole building shakes," she'd say, as the Israeli strafing and bombing rose to a crescendo a rock's throw from where she hid. "Come and get me out of here."

Just as frequently as Amira phoned, a worried Zainab would call too, yelling at me to do something, even though I was as stuck as anyone else, trapped in Doha with all the air traffic into and out of Lebanon absolutely halted, the runways cratered by bombs, and shooting and troop movements escalating all throughout the south. The eastern border with Syria had backed up too, crammed with caravans of people trying to flee from the southern and western parts of Lebanon where the Israeli troops began making their push north toward Beirut.

Amira was only twelve years old then.

My mother lived just down the road in a safer neighborhood, but the aunt wouldn't chance exiting the bomb shelter to drop Amira off. They wouldn't leave that bunker for the better part of the first, and most difficult, three or four days, except to sneak back into the apartment to use the bathroom.

Finally, after realizing the thing was going to last longer than a week and would be more devastating than most such events, I called our defense attaché in Lebanon and said, "Hey, my daughter is there. She's an American citizen."

"Sam, get her as close as possible to the US Embassy. As soon as we have the means to get the citizens out of here, we will. Drop her off here, and I'll take care of it."

But getting Amira out of southern Beirut, all the way through downtown and then to the northern suburbs where the US Embassy had been relocated after the Marine barracks bombing in 1979, formed yet another a problem. After exhausting all my own family as a resource in trying to get Amira to the embassy, I remembered that my friend Assaf Maakaroun had a property in the northern parts of Beirut. I called him, and he quickly sent someone south to pick Amira up.

Assaf is a Christian, hailing from the swath of mountains and impenetrable regions around Wadi Qadisha, the Holy Valley north of Beirut, around the Maronite Christian heartland centers. His heritage and affiliations in the north made it easier by far for him to come and go through the Maronite territories of northern Beirut around the embassy and also down south near the airport—since everyone needed access to the airport.

It had been ten days of constant bombardment, and Assaf's emissary found Amira in a real state of shock. Just imagine, a young

American girl who has spent her life to date in the safe haven of Dearborn, Michigan, all of a sudden finds herself living in a bunker! Assaf got Amira situated in an apartment he owned right outside the US Embassy. He made sure she was cared for, looked after, and comforted. But he couldn't get her out of Lebanon entirely.

Amira's escape from southern Beirut to the relatively safer northern part of the city made me much less nervous, but I could still hear the shock in Amira's voice every time we spoke on the phone. I'd call her, and then I'd call my friend the attaché, and I'd call Assaf, and still nothing seemed to be happening. No one seemed to have a way out—not for civilians, not even for American civilians. In fact, in the end, it took several more weeks for the embassy to get ships in and even evacuate its own staff, which it did while leaving most US citizens to fend for themselves, including Amira.

My attaché friend tipped me off to this, ahead of the embassy's exodus.

"Sam," he said, "between me and you, if you can get her out of here, get her out, any way you can, because right now it doesn't look good for us to even get ourselves out."

After that advice I didn't waste time.

In our line of work, connections are critical, really the only thing to depend on in a time of crisis. I'd already called in one favor from Assaf. But this was a time of crisis indeed. I needed a bigger favor, and I needed it quick.

I called around and found another friend of mine, Farah Nahme. He lived in the far north, in a town called Cheka, which sits on the border between the Maronite and the northern Sunni lands. He had the ability to cross over that area, just as Assaf could get Amira from down by the airport up to the embassy. Farah knew Assaf's house too.

I explained the situation to him, telling him I needed him to get Amira to the Syrian border.

He said, "Tell me when, and I'll have her delivered to you, but not through the regular Musna border because it's been bombed. Instead I will have her taken all the way north to Tariq al-Areeda."

Farah arranged for his aged father to pick Amira up and load her, along with another family, into the back of a pickup truck to take her to the border.

I flew into Syria, though at first the Syrians wouldn't give me a visa. They stopped me in customs, and I had to explain why I was on an American passport despite speaking a Lebanese dialect. I had to tell them the whole story about how I was coming to rescue my daughter.

"I only need two to three days to get my daughter and get out," I said, putting a fifty-dollar bill in the folds of my passport book.

They stamped me with a one-week visa. As crazy as it sounds, Syria wasn't then what it is today. Back then, before the Arab Spring, it was very modern and easy to travel through, especially for someone with language and cultural understanding. I simply rented a car, drove from Damascus to our predesignated spot at the Tariq al-Areeda border crossing, got her, and brought her back to Doha after a couple more days in Syria, which I needed just for her to decompress and realize she was okay now, okay with me. Safe with me.

Perhaps this should have been my warning. Perhaps this should have been the moment I compared life in the United States to the unpredictability of life in the Middle East. But that message didn't sink in. I focused on her, on getting her back to safety. But I didn't reflect on my own safety or how the work I was doing in the region might, at any point, put me in peril.

CHAPTER 7

ARAB SPRING

FOR THE NEXT several years, between roughly 2006 and 2009, I continued working for the Giuliani Partners in Doha as the project manager of its suite of training programs. The idea for training the Lebanese Internal Security Forces (ISF) never got picked up again after the 2006 Israel-Hezbollah conflict. But the work in Qatar proved to be right in my wheelhouse: intelligence, counterintelligence, FBI-type stuff with investigative training and creating role-playing scenarios. We also did more advanced training for the Amiri Guard, which is like our Secret Service, designed to accompany and protect Qatar's ruler, the amir.

Ali Soufan remained my boss as the director of international operations for Giuliani's office. His role included—among many other things—not only supervision of the training programs that I led but also consultation on Qatar's new Industrial Cities. I was in the best shape of my life, running three miles a day, doing meaningful, vigorous work, and loving life.

My family remained in Dearborn except for parts of each summer. Then the kids would come and spend some of their time with me. They were still in high school and didn't want to leave their friends and come to the Middle East, at least not permanently. Visits were fun and gave all of us something to look forward to. The kids had their lives and passions in America. They couldn't uproot themselves, and I didn't expect them to.

We'd just gone through the difficult situation extracting Amira from Lebanon the year before, and things were falling apart for me on the home front. I needed to be home more often. I needed to rest more, I knew that.

But I couldn't leave the Middle East. At first my work there had been somewhat compulsory, those Global War on Terror mobilization orders, the frantic pace of that critical juncture in America's involvement "over there"; then it became a matter of self-worth, of doing work that I felt really made a difference, especially during those years in Yemen. By the time I got into the groove of my contracting role, especially in this new incarnation in Qatar, the value and the inescapability of being "over there" came perhaps from knowing I was helping make a difference on a bigger scale and in a critical place and time. Just as important, though, was the money I made, earnings I couldn't equal by running a gas station or a restaurant in Dearborn. I was really socking it away in a manner I hadn't planned or even really dreamed of. I was not just supporting my immediate family back in America but also helping my family in Lebanon and elsewhere. I felt very fortunate to be in such a position, and I liked giving back where and when I could.

When I came home for Christmas that year, I started feeling really weak. At first I thought it was just exhaustion, that my lifestyle and frenetic activities were catching up with me finally. But when the weakness wouldn't subside after a few days in the Dearborn cold, I went to the doctor for a checkup.

The doctor informed me, after a few tests, that I had significant blockage in my arteries. They shuttled me right to the hospital, and I was put under for what they thought would be a simple stent or balloon clearance procedure. When I woke, though, they told me they had discovered three arteries blocked at 90 percent each and opted to perform immediate triple-bypass surgery.

Everyone was shocked about this, including my boss, Ali Soufan, who pointed out that just the week before I'd been running around with the top young officers, training them and running them ragged, not to mention running for leisure myself, playing kick-ass racquetball a couple times a week, and lifting. I think, truly, had I not been in that level of physical fitness, I might not have survived. I might have had a heart attack long before. I might not have weathered the bypass surgery as well as I did. Any of a million other fates might have befallen me. But here, again, the Marine Corps and the Marine mentality paid big dividends for me. It had taught me the benefits of keeping myself in good physical condition, and even though a genetic trait or maybe a dietary issue had led to this heart condition, I was able to survive it and hardly miss a beat, heading back to Qatar within a couple short weeks to resume my position with the Soufan Group.

■ ■ ■

ON NOVEMBER 1, 2008, exactly thirty years to the day from my first enlistment, I retired from the Marine Corps. So much had happened over those thirty years! It gave me pause, looking back on the family I'd raised and supported, the work I'd done, the crazy twists of life that had led me from Lebanon, through Libya, to America, and then back to the Middle East. I didn't hold a big celebration or party. Usually after thirty years of service, the unit you're in puts on some sort of retirement ceremony, but for me, being in Qatar—although still doing my drills in association with the Defense Intelligence Agency and with various embassies to help new personnel acculturate—I didn't belong to a robust unit. I sort of fell through the cracks. But that's okay. I knew where I was and who I was, and the quiet reflection upon my retirement was as good for me as a larger ceremony would have been.

Once you're a Marine, you're never *not* a Marine. The culture of the corps stays with you. I knew that I'd soon be attending Marine birthday celebrations, balls, and formal events, breaking out my old uniform, and celebrating with brothers in arms I'd known and respected for years or sometimes with newbies who would sop up the stories I had earned the hard, old-fashioned way. The Marine Corps culture doesn't just abandon its members. It lives on. And that would really prove to be a big comfort to me later, when I was taken hostage. Never once during my Marine Corps career did I feel abandoned—perhaps misunderstood and misused a little, as was the case when I first tried to volunteer my language skills—but I was always included and always valued as a Marine among Marines.

■ ■ ■

AROUND THIS SAME TIME, the company in Doha converted from Giuliani Security to Soufan Group. Rudy Giuliani was running for

president in 2008, so he divested himself of his big overseas contracts, knowing the lucrative deals he had with Qatar and elsewhere
might follow him on the campaign trail and cause his opponents to
question whether he could lead without bias. More specifically, with
regard to Qatar, newspapers around this time started accusing Qatar
of sponsoring terrorism, and our firm was working there, so Giuliani
had to choose whether to fight those claims or just step away from
them.

He stepped away.

He could have gone on the air, put out an official statement, or
said something to the effect that the state of Qatar wasn't sponsoring
any terrorism. He could have emphasized that the firm was not involved in such things. He could have clarified that we were training
the Qataris to protect not just themselves but also our American interests on the ground.

But he didn't. He just let the American press badmouth the amir
and gave off the impression that he had bigger fish to fry, that he
could afford not to stick up for his clients or for the work of his team
over in Qatar.

This of course upset many in the Qatari leadership and eventually led
them to cut the ties with Giuliani. As they did this, they simultaneously
had a conversation with Ali Soufan, reassuring him that they liked his
team, the work he and his guys were doing, and wanted him to continue. They offered him the opportunity to start a security academy, the
Qatar International Academy for Security Studies and I continued
working with the Soufan Group in exactly the same capacity as I had for
Giuliani.

I kept working with the Soufan Group for about another year,
until mid-2009, when fate took me back to Yemen once again.

■ ■ ■

IN JUNE 2009 MY FRIEND Steve Gaudin called me from the US Embassy in Sana'a, needing help with a shipment of communication equipment they knew would be intercepted and held up by Yemeni customs for a long time. This was my old role—facilitator, negotiator, problem solver. I agreed to help, but not because the work seemed particularly interesting or difficult: it would probably just require a couple calls to the likes of Abdulghani Jamil or Tariq Saleh, maybe a qat chew or two. Really, the reason I went for what should have been a couple days or maybe a week's worth of work was Steve himself.

Steve had come back to Sana'a on his second tour in the embassy. He was serving as the legal attaché (LEGATT), an FBI role primarily responsible for facilitating domestic US investigations with overseas components, meaning crimes involving US persons or crimes that occurred in America but included an element of foreign involvement.

Steve was one of the finest FBI agents I had ever worked with. He and I had first encountered one another back in 2002 on his initial tour as a LEGATT in Yemen, back when I was working in the attaché shop. Just before New Year's Day, two of my colleagues—the operations coordinator, Henry Grant, and our Force Protection Detachment officer, Nick Butros—were preparing to drive with me to Aden for some needed vacation time. Back then, it was permissible to travel around Yemen by car, without a big security detachment, and to go wherever we wanted really, even to hike or ride horses in the mountains or visit the beach down in Aden on the Indian Ocean. With our bags packed and loaded into the car, we pulled into the embassy to officially sign out on our leave when one of the Marines from Post One—the official guard shack and call center for the embassy—ran up to us.

The young Marine caught my arm as I got out of the car and said, "Hey, Gunner, the ambassador wants to see you and Nick ASAP!"

I looked at Nick and said, "Did you do anything? 'Cause I don't remember doing anything wrong, at least this last week!"

In truth, we were both a little nervous. We'd just had a vehicle confiscated by the Yemeni police. It wasn't a big deal. We'd been through similar issues in the past, since various elements within the Yemeni military and police structures were always jockeying for power and could try to flex their muscles in our direction on occasion. No matter how innocuous, though, it always ended up being a little nerve-wracking because you couldn't quite tell whether the media would get ahold of something like that, or whether the authorities— such as our own ambassador—might believe a bit too much of whatever story the Yemeni contingent had cooked up. We'd need to do some "'splainin'" in that case. And interference, or even awareness and concern from the press or the leadership, would make recovery of the vehicle (and explaining whatever shenanigans surrounded the incident) all the tougher.

The ambassador at that time was Edmund Hull, really a great man and a great statesman. He understood Yemen well, and he and I got along fabulously. On numerous occasions I'd had the opportunity to discuss policy in Yemen with him. Even though things were pretty open for us to travel around Yemen, the State Department had put our embassy—like many others in the Middle East—on "authorized departure." We were still in a post-9/11 security posture, with a lot of people pretty nervous, and the "authorized departure" status meant that any families or embassy workers who didn't want to be there were legally entitled to a flight home, as well as reassignment, no negative evaluations for opting out, and so forth. Whenever Ambassador Hull mentioned this "authorized departure" status at meetings or rallies of our very large embassy staff, I'd raise my hand to volunteer to leave. He knew I was joking, of course, so he'd tell me to put my hand down and say something like, "When you leave, you'll be taking the flag down with you, Sam!" He knew I was addicted to Yemen. And I was happy to play the part of the foil for him, just getting that repeat laugh and helping everyone make light of what was, truly, a pretty stressful environment to work in.

With our vehicle impounded and a hundred other possible issues in mind, I took some comfort in the good relationship I'd established with the ambassador. I knew I wasn't in for an ass chewing. But still, the young Marine from Post One sounded pretty panicked, pretty urgent.

Nick, Henry, and I dropped what we were doing and, in our vacation clothes, went right through security, up to the second floor, and down the hall to the ambassador's office. His assistant led us right into the big corner space where his desk, a lovely grouping of plush chairs and sofas around a coffee table, and a few glorious windows overlooked Sana'a's Old City, down below in the humming, honking, brown-hued valley.

Steve Gaudin was already sitting in one of the ambassador's armchairs. A few other people were in the room, all of them looking worried. The ambassador spoke into a phone, back turned to us. Henry, Nick, and I stood there, just inside the doorway, until he finished.

As he turned to us, we could see sadness in his eyes, not tears, but that special sort of quiet, deeply concerned shadow that creeps into the gaze of someone who has taken on the burden of bad news and now must share it with others. He said, looking right at Nick and me, "Change of plans gentlemen. Your leave is cancelled. You're heading down to Jibla."

(I'll admit it: I drew a breath of relief, knowing now that we weren't in trouble for the confiscated vehicle or any other weird mistake.)

"Jibla?" I said. Though I knew Yemen pretty well, I didn't know where that was. A village most likely. Or a region of some sort.

"On the outskirts of Ibb, down south on the road to Aden," the ambassador said. "That's where you were going anyway, right?"

"Yes . . . basically, though we intended to—"

"Three doctors were just killed there. Shot and killed at the Jibla hospital, which is sponsored and run by missionaries. All three were missionary doctors. All three were Americans."

So we changed course. Henry stayed behind to coordinate the response and some of the notification of the families of these doctors, not to mention recovery and transport of the remains. Steve, being the official FBI investigator, jumped in the car with Nick and me to set off for Jibla to investigate. To make a long story short, the investigation itself went well enough. We got there and soon caught the guy who did the shooting. But it was really extremely sad, both for the loss of life and for the damage it did to this community. The killer confessed his motive was based on a mistaken idea that "these missionaries [were there] to convert Yemenis to Christianity, and he was there to stop it"—basic religious extremism, fueled by al-Qaeda no doubt. But all three of the doctors, as well as an American pharmacist who was wounded, had been working in and around Jibla for over twenty-five years. None of the staff at the hospital had ever heard of anyone converting to Christianity during that time. The doctors were just there to help people.

The three of us spent that New Year's Eve in an empty house waiting to continue our investigation the next day. We did some more investigating. We tied up some loose ends. And we prepared to head back to Sana'a, unable to accomplish much more.

Walking out of the hospital that next morning, on New Year's Day, we confronted the amazing spectacle of something like seven or eight hundred Yemeni women, all of them in *abayas*, black from head to toe, like a sea of ravens flocking together in the square in front of the hospital. All of them were crying, wailing for the doctors. These doctors had been members of the community. More tellingly, one of them, a woman, had been there forever and helped birth over 1,000 children, removing many of the dangers and discomforts of delivery for a generation or more of the region's women.

These ladies in their veils were the mothers, the grandmothers, the aunts, and even some of the children, now grown, whom this doctor helped into the world. The hospital staff told me this woman would go to people's houses in the middle of the night to deliver babies, not just in Jibla but even up in the mountains. The way these people loved her so dearly, as one of their own, across cultures and religions, seemed unbelievable to me.

But the sight of all these women coming out to mourn her affirmed it most strongly, and the image gave me chills; it still does. Unlike the assassin, and unlike many other people nowadays who can't see past the *abaya* or the color of someone's skin, constantly mistaking compassion and religiosity as a virtue belonging only to their own sect or people, the Yemeni women in this crowd didn't care that the doctor had been American. They cared about her humanity, and they loved her for it. They understood and appreciated the sacrifice that she, and the two other slain missionaries, had made for them.

To top it all off, in their wills, this woman doctor and one of the others had requested that they be buried there, in Jibla, rather than transported back to their homes in America. We found this out when Sergeant First Class Henry Grant started to coordinate preparation of the remains for a flight home. And so, according to their wishes, we ended up giving the two bodies over for burial in the Jibla cemetery, two Christians interred amid a hundred generations' worth of Muslim tombstones.

So when Steve Gaudin called in 2009 asking for my help to smooth things out with his commo gear, I couldn't, and wouldn't, say no. We'd been through a harrowing (and poignant) moment together. Brothers like that don't say no to one another.

I asked Ali for a bit of vacation time and jumped on the first plane to Sana'a.

■ ■ ■

MY TRIP TO YEMEN went without a hiccup. And I got right down to business, as I normally did, attending a number of dinners, parties, and social events—how else does business get done? The owner of a company called Griffin Group happened to be my neighbor during one such dinner. Griffin Group specialized in providing local Yemenis as guards for Western facilities and businesses. He asked me to come on board as the general manager for the company. This would be a promotion from my role with the Soufan Group, where I served as the director of training. It would be, more or less, my own show—a good thing. I told Ali of the new opportunity, packed my bags, and was rather suddenly living in Yemen again.

During the first year of that contract, I helped develop Griffin from a local security company into an international establishment by arranging contracts with several other international security firms, such as Olive, Control Risk, and Salamanca, all of them populated with and owned by people I knew and had either trained, or trained with, elsewhere. Bringing the standard of training for Griffin's Yemeni guards up to this international level allowed us to start working and setting up joint ventures with places like the nearly finished Belhaf Oil Terminal, out near Mukalla, as well as with the US Embassy, where Griffin won the contract to provide many of the local guard force personnel who augmented the Yemeni soldiers posted outside and around the embassy gates.

After some disputes with the company managers, I eventually left Griffin and took a job with the larger, truly international firm Control Risk, working as a consultant in business development and security. I took the job with a decent monthly retainer, but most of my earnings would be commission based, and I thought—given my contacts not only in Yemen but also in Qatar, Lebanon, and Morocco—that I was going to really capitalize.

Then, about a month later, the Arab Spring started.

All of my contacts, especially the security managers—all of them personal friends—refocused their efforts on evacuation and totally shelved any notion of business development. None of them were expanding their current programs or launching new ones. This was bad for Control Risk and for me personally, having bet on making most of my money through those fat commissions. I found myself in

Yemen on a much tighter, much less comfortable budget than I'd anticipated, especially as things really started to heat up with the Arab Spring.

■ ■ ■

THE ARAB SPRING STARTED in Tunisia, of course, with the self-immolation of Muhammad Bouazizi in protest of wage stagnation and lack of jobs. It quickly became a more general protest against the tyranny of many of the region's long-standing, autocratic governments. The protests often began on university campuses, among students and the more progressive elements of society in and around those universities, though the working classes and other marginalized groups joined the protests in the hope they might gain new and much-needed liberties either through concessions from their current governments or overthrow of the system. Many of these protests turned violent and did indeed lead to the toppling of several tyrants. The ouster of Hosni Mubarak in Egypt is perhaps most famous, followed by the downfall of Libya's Muamar Qadafi. Yemen did not avoid this fate.

Initiated at and focused around Sana'a University, the Arab Spring in Yemen really heated up when one of the most prominent generals under President Ali Abdullah Saleh—Ali Muhsin al-Ahmar, who had been waging a series of significant campaigns against the nascent Houthi movement in the northern mountains—switched sides from supporting Saleh to opposing him. This divided Sana'a fairly neatly in half. Ali Muhsin controlled the northern and western parts of the city from the strategic location of the 1st Armor Brigade's base and headquarters. He also controlled the university area and the Technology Hospital.

Ali Muhsin was a prominent, founding member of the Muslim Brotherhood–affiliated political group called Islah. At one time he had also been involved in supporting and recruiting for al-Qaeda, and his political party remained ideologically aligned and tacitly supportive of al-Qaeda in Yemen. The powerful sheiks of the al-Ahmar family—who aren't actually related to Ali Muhsin al-Ahmar despite their similar names—supported this opposition as well. Also, strangely, the Houthi rebels—whom Ali Muhsin had been fighting for the past decade—overcame their issues with the very radically Sunni al-Ahmar as well as their issues with Ali Muhsin and joined the opposition, citing a desire to overthrow Saleh.

In Yemen, political and military alliances tend to follow long-term trends—North versus South, Zaydi Shi'a versus outsiders (like the Egyptians, who sent 70,000 troops to Yemen in the 1970s, and the Ottomans), and—more recently—Shi'a versus Sunni. But those long-term trends also have a lot of flexibility, as this cooperation between Houthis and Islah during the Arab Spring demonstrates. Yemenis are opportunistic and put the advantage and survival of their family and their clan ahead of other political or ideological allegiances.

This four-headed opposition—Ali Muhsin, students and liberals, Islah, and the Houthis—together controlled significant parts of the capital and most of the area north of Sana'a. The Saleh family's base of power in Sana'a, however, was located around the headquarters of the internal security forces—not so very far from the 1st Armor Brigade and the defense ministry, skirting the north side of the city along the border between the lands held by the al-Ahmars but just inside the territory of Abdulghani Jamil's clan, where Sana'a International Airport was situated. The airport stayed open, in government control, along with the significant military jet fighter presence. The US Embassy also lay within Abdulghani Jamil's territory on the east shoulder of Jebel Nuqum, the mountain overlooking Sana'a. Hadda, in the south, remained in Saleh's control, but the main route between Hadda and the embassy, called Zubayri Street, also happened to be the on-again, off-again demarcation line between the two sides, a tense standoff zone and often the area where outright fighting started.

Ali Muhsin took control of a strategic hill near the 1st Armor Brigade that held the radio and TV stations. He started giving away government land on the hill to squatters so that they would occupy and defend it, even as protestors—led most conspicuously by Tawakkol Karman, who later won the Nobel Peace Prize for her efforts during this time—congregated in Tahrir Square, or Freedom Square, which just happened to be the name of similar squares in each of the nations where the Arab Spring happened.

The Saleh family and the political party they led, called the General People's Congress (GPC) or Mutamar watched the Arab Spring spread from one country to the next in the Middle East. It came a bit later to Yemen than elsewhere. And they actually understood that Tahrir Square would be significant terrain. So they occupied it before the students and the opposition groups got there.

While the fight and the protests centered on political demands, their very urban nature meant that a lot of civilians ended up accidentally in the crosshairs. For instance, you could often walk down Zubayri Street and see it lined on one side by 1st Armor soldiers or Islah loyalists and on the other by ISF, the police, the Republican Guard, or Special Forces (all loyal to Saleh, largely due to who their commanders were—Saleh's sons and nephews elevated to high rank in the military and security). As a civilian you could switch sides, have lunch in one place and coffee in another, talk to everyone. But you also might get caught in a flare-up at any time. Just north of Zubayri Street, on Hayl Street, about twenty-five to thirty civilians died in a particularly grievous massacre. This incident caused a rift between Islah and the Houthis, breaking their alliance when it looked like they might dethrone Saleh after all.

Things dragged on in this stalemate and only came to a close during Friday prayer, on June 11, 2011, when Saleh was bombed at his own mosque in one of his palaces (not the new mosque that was still being built). The bomb was planted in a personal area and activated by a cell phone, whose signal needed to be in the immediate vicinity to trigger it, so the user had to have been near.* The Political Security Organization, still loyal to Saleh, recovered the sim card from this trigger device and traced its number to the 71-9 prefix, which pointed to one of the two big phone companies in Yemen, Sabaphone. Sabaphone was owned by Hamid al-Ahmar, chief among the al-Ahmar clans.

Saleh survived but was pretty badly wounded. As he was being loaded onto a stretcher, his son, Ahmed Ali Saleh, who had been nearby but was uninjured, began to take charge. He already commanded the Republican Guard and the Special Forces. He was the heir apparent. He jumped on the phone to his subordinate commanders and was about to order an artillery barrage on the Usbahi area of Sana'a, where a good portion of the al-Ahmar family have their city dwellings, intending to wipe it out despite what such an atrocity might cost in collateral damage, in the deaths of innocents

---

* Suspicion fell on the mosque's caretaker, who later disappeared.

who just happened to live nearby, or the fallout in the court of world opinion.

However, as a testament to just how far-sighted and strong Ali Abdullah Saleh could be, even as he still smoldered, bleeding and uncertain of life, he looked ahead toward reconciliation and told Ahmed Ali, "Do not retaliate. Leave it alone. Let them look bad. I'll be back."

Saleh was playing the long game—a much longer game than anyone knew he could. The bombing weakened him and his alliance and basically forced him to accept a UN-negotiated settlement that saw his deputy, Vice President Abdrabbuh Mansur Hadi, take over as interim president while the country submitted to a UN-led constitutional reform process called the National Dialogue.

Perhaps two months after this assassination attempt, I came to the regular monthly meeting of the Overseas Security Advisory Council at the embassy. There I met Elizabeth Richards, the new deputy chief of mission (DCM), whom I would get to know well in the coming years. She is now the US ambassador in Lebanon, but then she was brand-new to Yemen. She and I struck up a conversation, and she told me, "Saleh is in Saudi Arabia getting medical treatment, that's it. He'll never come back." Gently, I corrected her, betting her a cup of coffee that he'd be back by New Year's Day or even sooner.

Even though Saleh stayed nominally behind the scenes, by that January he was indeed back in Sana'a, pulling the strings of his GPC party, reforging his many alliances, and skewing the outcome of the National Dialogue talks in favor of his return. It would take him, and the National Dialogue as a result, several years to solidify enough power so that Hadi could announce new constitutional terms that satisfied no one except the GPC and that basically preserved Saleh and his family and friends in their positions of power.

Hadi's actions pushing through this unbalanced National Dialogue Conference caused two primary rifts: one between the North and the South (a long-standing grievance, as the two had been separate countries, with the South losing and getting what they still see as a seriously raw deal in the merger), and the other between the Houthis and the rest of Yemen, as the newly redrawn regions isolated the Houthis and kept them landlocked.

Saleh came back, way before the New Year. I got my cup of coffee from DCM Richards, but Saleh's continuing political and personal influence spelled bad news for Yemen. He threw his lot in with the Houthis, and that really brought the country into chaos.

CHAPTER 8

NATIONAL DIALOGUE

•

I N LATE NOVEMBER 2011 I decided to start my own security company, which I called Universal Eagles. It was a noble sounding name that combined my history with the Marine Corps (those eagles on every Marine's collar!) with an aspiration to bring greater security and goodness to the world—universally. After parting ways with Griffin Group, and after missing out on a lucrative arrangement when commissions fell through with Control Risk, I decided—if I was going to continue to stick my neck out in Yemen—I might as well call the shots myself and be my own boss.

Universal became my means for doing ongoing security consultation work, often still contracted through the bigger security players, like Control Risk, Pax Mondiale, Pilgrims Group, and a lot of the oil companies. Universal's work focused mostly on Yemen but also took me, and my small but growing body of employees, to places throughout the region—sometimes to Somalia but mostly to the Gulf states and the Arabian Peninsula. For instance, immediately following the Arab Spring, I started to line up great jobs, like with the Australian government, taking its military and diplomatic attachés, perhaps seven or eight of them in total, all over the Gulf. I accompanied them as their security consultant as they traveled because they weren't overly familiar with the region.

Australia does not have embassies everywhere, just a main one in Saudi Arabia to cover all of the Gulf. It had embarked on a major assessment for its citizens living the region in case it needed to evacuate them in another Arab Spring–like situation. Control Risks helped the Australian delegation organize its security in Bahrain, Oman, and Kuwait and helped coordinate joint security agreements with local British and American embassies in the places where the Australians didn't have a robust evacuation capability. It was a perfect gig for me, as the Aussies were super outgoing and fun to travel with, and I liked nothing better than good company in places where I could serve both as a hired gun and as a social and professional networker.

One of the first people I hired for Universal was Yasmine, my goddaughter, who was now in her third year of college after completing the vocational school I had sent her to in record time. She finished her college studies that first year, then immediately launched into an MBA while working for me, first as one of two people in human resources, then after about a year as head of human resources and payroll, which expanded to eight employees—she was an amazingly talented person, my best employee.

Universal—and I, personally, by extension—contributed somewhat to the lead-up to Yemen's National Dialogue period, helping plan and certify the security procedures at the Moevenpick Hotel, where the conference would be located. We also helped provide security for high-level visitors from outside Yemen, who had come to check on and provide expert support for the democratizing ideals of the conference. These visitors needed local expertise as well as security, and Universal proudly supported them.

Part of the National Dialogue involved a much-needed restructuring of the Yemeni army, which had broken into factions based on loyalties to various commanders. Even before the breaking apart of allegiances that occurred during the Arab Spring, the Yemeni army could not reliably and consistently extend its influence into tribal lands, and these areas—in the south and east—had long been supporting and abetting various incarnations of Islamic fundamentalism, most prominently al-Qaeda's most virulent branch, called al-Qaeda in the Arabian Peninsula. The United States, as its contribution to the process of reconciliation and restructuring, committed to leading the reformation of the Yemeni military. In similar fashion the British undertook a program of work to remedy Yemen's various police entities. Both of these efforts moved forward in fits and starts throughout the duration of the National Dialogue but ultimately produced little in the way of true reformation before the Houthis came in and overthrew the government, with large factions of these forces—just like in the Arab Spring—either tacitly or directly supporting various sides in the conflict.

As a good example of the difficulties faced by the Yemenis, not to mention the Western countries attempting to encourage reform, for a long while the main prison in Sana'a had been more or less taken over from the inside by some al-Qaeda members imprisoned there. They couldn't leave the prison due to an agreement between the Yemeni government and their tribes that they would stay there. Tribal influence and shelter carried more weight in their remaining than any punishment the civil authorities could mete out. Therefore, though able to escape whenever they wanted, these prisoners had nowhere to go and would even be subject to active tribal persecution if they didn't uphold the arrangement their elders had come to with the government.

As a result, the al-Qaeda personnel were stuck in a prison, held in not by the walls or the guards or even of the penalties of law but by force of custom. And so they stayed put, but they took over, running the day-to-day life on their floor to such an extent that they even took the doors off the hinges and turned them around so that the handles were on the inside. The guards could not come in and had to knock and ask permission to enter.

While this is an extreme case, the reformation of all sectors of the Yemeni government and military structure entailed situations much like this: tribal issues, graft, corruption, nepotism, and strange alliances that most Western agencies and personnel just weren't prepared to understand, let alone explain to bureaucrats and politicians back home, who were accustomed to and comfortable only with Western notions of the rule of law.

As much as I love Yemen and her people, I noted during these reformation processes how adept the Yemenis proved at turning the efforts of the Western countries into cold, hard cash to line their own pockets. I brought this up at one of the Overseas Security Advisory Council (OSAC) meetings when these efforts kicked off. Deputy Chief of Mission (DCM) Elizabeth Richards was giving the group a briefing about how well the initial military restructuring efforts were going and how everyone was coming to the table and providing their inputs, wish lists, and needs.

I brought to DCM Richards's attention how adept the Yemenis would be at "repurposing" the funds we earmarked for these purposes. While they were coming to the table now with the right words and promises on the tips of their tongues, once the gear and funds arrived in Yemen, how would we ensure their proper employment? How would we ensure that their requests for more wouldn't go on indefinitely?

I went to her afterward and said, "Do you really think the Yemenis are going to spend the money you give them to do the things they're saying?" She remained confident that the embassy's Office of Military Cooperation would be able to review the funded programs and certify that any equipment or dollars were being used appropriately.

I said, "The Yemenis will certainly come to the table now, but they'll find a way to pocket the money. You watch. They'll say all the right things, agree to all the monitoring. They'll give you all the yeses you need to get those dollars flowing. But when it comes to action and execution, they won't be ready for it, and you'll find their requests become a bottomless pit."

The difficulties weren't only financial when it came to forcing change. A societal and status issue also interfered, in which many personnel who obtained rank, power, or any semblance of position assumed that they were untouchable, viewing such positions as sinecures. Of course, dollar signs also attached to any position of authority, as commanders and ministers commonly skimmed from their own budgets. But the concept of *wasta*—the importance of authority for authority's sake—also played a part. When, for instance, attempts at structural change in the Yemeni army were made, the Ministry of Defense sent a new commander to one of the outlying bases. The previous commander—who was being relieved for graft or disloyalty or who knows what—refused to step down. The soldiers under him, to whom he personally doled out pay (often keeping parts of their salaries for himself in the time-honored way), would not let the new commander on base. In fact they fired on him and his retinue, and he had to give up and return to Sana'a. The troops were loyal to the individual, not to the organization or even to the idea of the nation.

This was but one among many such issues, each of which seemed to get only more complicated the deeper the National Dialogue conferees dug into them:

- Redistricting the political divisions
- Reconfiguring wealth and economic issues since certain parts of the country contained oil and others did not, putting the latter at risk of increasing disparity in services and development compared to their neighbors
- Reparations to military members who had been furloughed several decades earlier during the civil wars between the North and the South
- Infiltration by al-Qaeda not just of certain military units but also of whole agencies and departments in the government, which necessitated disentangling the legitimate political party of the radical Sunni Islahi movement from its almost imperceptible blending with and succor of al-Qaeda
- Alignment with other military units and government bodies
- Plain old corruption that spread throughout even the most respected Yemeni institutions, such as the coast guard, which were supplied with new ships, weapons, gear, and training by

the United States in order to interdict smuggling from Somalia and Djibouti and, while demonstrating success via metric tons of interdicted materiel, would thereafter mysteriously lose accountability for the interdicted goods, only to have them show up wholesale down the street in one of a host of nearby semi-legal, grayish-black markets*

The meetings of the National Dialogue Conference (NDC) mirrored the chaos of Yemeni society. Everyone would come and sit down for the regular daily sessions in the big Moevenpick ballroom. Groups from all over Yemen attended: from the South, North, East, and West, all of Hadramawt, Shabwa, various factions and political parties, some wearing *dishdashas*, some in suits, some in more colorful tribal gear. Each came with grievances from the civil wars, from the reunification of the northern and southern parts of Yemen, which had once been separate countries.

Especially potent divides existed in two directions: between the Zaydi-Houthi groups, who are Shi'a and had ruled the northern Yemeni imamate for centuries, and the southern—eastern—coastal Sunni groups, which outnumbered the Shi'a but, until recently under President Ali Abdullah Saleh, had not wielded comparable power or influence. These groups got along remarkably well in peacetime, with many members of one or another sect praying at each other's mosques and most strife focusing on intertribal rather than sectarian disputes. But the increasing partisan and sectarian issues at stake during the

---

* The Coast Guard was a great unit, probably one of the better ones in Yemen, a real success touted by the US Embassy. But it was doing everything it could, just like the rest of Yemen's security sector and really anyone in a position of power in Yemen, to turn whatever advantage it possessed into profit.

National Dialogue, exacerbated by al-Qaeda's propaganda, really began to drive a wedge into Yemen's traditional modes of compromise and habits of tolerance.

A second and even trickier divide existed between the North and South, sometimes accentuated by Shi'a-Sunni cleavages. This divide went back to the North-South unification in the mid-twentieth century. The North not only won the civil wars that resulted in unification of Yemen but did so with the help of a large number of defectors from a previous brief but extremely bloody intra-South civil war between two factions called the Tuqma and Zumra. The Tuqma prevailed, and about 30,000 Zumra fled to the country of North Yemen. The Zumra members then helped the North conquer the South when war between the two Yemens erupted.

Saleh emerged at this time as the driving force in the North. He rewarded Zumra members for their support by granting them high places in government, as well as large tracts of desirable land in the (former) South. Subsequently, the Zumra were seen by their brethren in the South as traitors, as carpetbaggers of a sort. In the North the Zumra did not have an organic tribal support structure, which tended to be critical for any individual leader's political and military aspirations, especially under Saleh, as can be seen by the way Abdulghani Jamil skyrocketed to prominence due to the tribal support his family could muster. More importantly, once the ties of loyalty to Saleh became less important, the Zumra did not have an organic base of power in the North to resort to.

While all this infighting may sound academic, easily relegated to the history books, it was a significant factor during the National Dialogue and during the chaos afterward when the Houthis ran the interim Yemeni government out of town. Both President Abdrabbuh

Mansur Hadi and then defense minister Ali Nasser Muhammad were Zumra, as were many of their key staff. Through some sort of misguided understanding of Yemeni power structures, the United Nations and Gulf Cooperation Council (GCC) pinned their hopes for reconciliation on these particular Zumra-affiliated individuals. This meant that the NDC process was, from the beginning, fraught with one of Yemen's most contentious internal rifts and represented by its living embodiments. It did not require much work for the Houthis to claim that the process of Hadi taking power through the National Dialogue was illegitimate and that they (or at least the Zaydi minority as represented by more illustrious clans like that of Muhammad Sharafuddin) represented a more time-honored, traditionally successful power structure, one that had lasted for centuries under the imamate.

The National Dialogue Conference faithfully reproduced many of the rifts prevalent in Yemeni society as a whole. The various factions all came armed with their issues. They all wanted old slights and injustices remedied in the most exacting ways.

None of these groups came with solutions.

One time when I was talking to Tawakkol Karman, the recent Nobel Peace laureate, I said, "You always oppose what someone is doing, or saying, but you never come in with a solution or a new idea." And that same thing happened over and over again, day after day. It became, especially at the end, much more about personal or provincial grievances than about national reconstruction and unity.

I remember talking to one of the delegates, asking him how he felt about the progress they were making. He said, "Yeah, I go every day, but only because they pay me a per diem stipend to be there and they feed me free lunch." That's where things stood after the first few months.

The Saudi and Qatari embassies wielded the most influence at the National Dialogue Conference. After all, they had signed up to pay not just for the conference itself but also for massive investment and rebuilding plans. The entire GCC was involved, and so were the Western embassies. But the interesting and somewhat damning aspect of Saudi and Qatari participation was that they chose to back different sides, both of which were deeply flawed.

The Saudis wanted to see Hadi stay in power, and—a point of contention with the official US perspective here—Hadi had aligned himself, through Ali Muhsin, more and more strongly with Islah and other radical Sunni elements. Hadi didn't have a powerbase of his own (being Zumra and alienated from his own tribal structure in the South), so he didn't have much choice. Islah was the only group who accepted him with open arms.

The Qataris, on the other hand, while elsewhere supporting the Muslim Brotherhood, also a deeply radicalized Sunni movement, changed tactics in Yemen and started out by throwing their support behind the Houthis and the General People's Congress, which was Saleh's group. Qatar, I believe, did this mostly to counter Saudi influence.

All of this jockeying played out publicly in the Moevenpick ball-room, but the decisions and alliances were forged privately, at qat chews and dinners, down in Hadda and at the key players' walled mansion compounds—places where, increasingly, US diplomats could not go. The security situation put the Americans behind walls of their own making, leaving them to understand Yemen only through the talking points of the elites they met in formal settings or through the eyes of the few people like me who still lived and worked out in town.

■ ■ ■

THE GENERAL, OMNIPRESENT THREAT of al-Qaeda, of lawlessness, kidnappings, and bombings, certainly contributed to the gradual retraction of the Western diplomatic presence. But also, at this time, a few specific events began to weaken the security situation.

Just before the National Dialogue Conference kicked off, one of the main heads of the Zaydi clans, Yahya al-Mutawakkil, was assassinated. Then, during the conference itself, another big Zaydi clan leader, Muhammad Sharafuddin, was assassinated as well. Those murders eroded much of the main Zaydi power dynamic and unbalanced the more conservative and cautious wing of the Zaydi elites. We heard rumors that Saleh's guys were behind it, not wanting a return of traditional Zaydi influence. We also heard rumors that Islah ordered the assassinations, as the Zaydi-Sunni tensions had begun to flare up. Most intriguingly, we heard some speculation that the Houthis themselves got rid of Sharafuddin as he was one of the few strategically minded leaders with enough gravitas to have overcome their movement. He'd been starting to eclipse Abd el-Malik al-Houthi, the head of the Houthi movement, as a figurehead for Zaydi political ambitions, and that couldn't be tolerated.

Another event that really shocked Sana'a was the suicide bombing in May 2012 during the graduation parade for the Yemeni military academy. The parade field was located right on the periphery of Hadda, very near diplomatic quarters, and the bombing occurred in a most brazen and destructive manner, with the bomber walking into the middle of the rigid parade formation and detonating, killing more than seventy young Yemeni cadets just as they were about to cross the parade stand to officially begin their careers as officers. Traces of this bombing could be seen for years afterward, not just in the blast marks and blood on the parade field but also in posters of the dead shellacked to the wall of the parade ground, right on the main street between Saleh's new mosque and the Hadda neighborhood.

While this bombing was the bloodiest event, another incident likely contributed even more to the withdrawal of the Western diplomatic community behind the barricades of their embassies. On September 13, 2012, two days after the 9/11 anniversary, the Houthis staged a protest in front of the US Embassy. This protest swelled in size, and the crowd spilled up the street toward the newly barbed-wire-surrounded Sheraton, which had been rented in its entirety to house American embassy personnel. I was at the embassy at this time, participating in one of those monthly OSAC meetings.

Suddenly the protest, which had begun peacefully enough, took a weird turn as all the Yemeni military personnel posted around the embassy abandoned their positions. (Later information I obtained indicated that an Islah-affiliated leader in the chain of command of these troops ordered them to stand down so that the peaceful protest might get out of hand and tarnish the Houthi's reputation with the United States.) Still, the incident wouldn't have gotten too much worse had the first few protestors who approached the US Embassy not shaken the gates, which were loose, basically unhinged, and collapsed inward to give the whole crowd access to the interior embassy grounds.

To the credit of the embassy security staff, all employees managed to get inside secure buildings ahead of the crowd. From there, looking through thick glass windows, the embassy staff watched a few hours of mayhem: cars with their keys left in the ignition being driven like derby mobiles around the manicured embassy grounds, riotous dancing and chanting, smashing and looting of anything moveable, a few halfhearted attempts to break through the windows of the secured buildings. The embassy's chief of security ordered the Marines on the roof of one of the buildings to be prepared to fire a warning shot or two, but they knew the Houthi protestors were unarmed, and not wanting things to escalate, they held back.

The protestors' success on the embassy grounds carried through the crowd, and a few protestors on the opposite end of the crowd began to scale the even-less formidable walls of the Sheraton compound. There another group of the Marines on the Sheraton roof were not only given the order to fire a warning shot but also authorized to use deadly force should anyone get on top of the wall. When the first protestors crested the wall, the Marines received a nod of agreement from their leader and fired several bursts from an M249 machine gun, as well as a handful of M4 rounds. I read in a local newspaper the next day that a nineteen-year-old Yemeni was killed. Not much was made of it afterward, as I suspect the families were paid off by the Yemeni forces, a traditional way of settling a feud, called *diah*, or blood money.

The Islahi sect of the military scored a victory then, a political victory, simply by stepping away. Until that moment the US Embassy had been treating the various factions in Yemen pretty much equally, despite the official Houthi slogan "Death to America, Death to Israel, a Curse on the Jews," which decorated all their flags. This slogan was meant to rally their base and excite their youth, while in reality (at least up until this moment) the Houthi leadership had been very careful not to endanger or harm any foreign person or property: no kidnapping, especially not Americans, no hurting, no killing. They'd committed no criminal acts against foreigners. Now, after the rioting inside the embassy grounds, the American government was going to have a very hard time trusting or negotiating with the Houthi leadership.

The breach of the US Embassy was the tipping point but not the sole factor in the worsening security situation. A somewhat spectacularly unsuccessful suicide bombing happened later outside the gates of the US Embassy, rumored to have been an al-Qaeda operation, leaving just a stain of blood and soot on one of the outer perimeter walls, just to the right of the main entrance gate. Although a failure, this direct attack continued to reinforce the edgy situation all the embassy employees and security personnel faced, never knowing what might happen on any given day.

The Americans weren't the only ones targeted either. Another suicide bomber tried to detonate himself on the motorcade of the British Embassy's delegation, again unsuccessfully. Kidnappings increased in Sana'a itself, mostly of Western individuals for ransom, with Dutch and German personnel often targeted since their embassies were known to negotiate and pay for the release of hostages. Sometimes issues cropped up that didn't involve direct targeting either. Various factions took potshots at each other or staged displays of power, with a lot of firing into the air, even of larger weapons and artillery, but never much killing. Diplomats' houses could be nearby. Their convoys and motorcades might get caught in the middle. All of this added up to a worsening, tense, and restrictive environment.

Toward the end of the National Dialogue Conference, we few expatriates were getting together with our diplomatic friends much less often, with American and British personnel coming down to Hadda for an occasional dinner or event but no longer living with us out there. Still, we saw the diplomats at least every once in a while and were reassured by their continuing presence and commitment to Yemen. Two of the most regular and important gatherings we enjoyed were the semiofficial OSAC meetings—now reconstituted as something of a private affair since many of the attendees didn't want to go through the enhanced security procedures necessary to get onto the grounds of the US Embassy or Sheraton—and also the monthly or bimonthly soirees hosted by my old Lebanese friend Assaf at his villa in Hadda.

I'd become a regular fixture in Sana'a by this time, which didn't help my second marriage at all. Soon it, like my first, ground to an end. I loved—and still love—Zainab dearly. But Yemen had my attention and a big hold on my heart. I'd spent years basically living as a geographical bachelor and started to think I wasn't really fit for family life anymore. The work in Yemen was a passion, but also a distraction, preventing me from really being the husband I could and should have been.

As my marriage with Zainab ended, I began to rekindle a friendship with a Yemeni woman named Abeer, whom I first met back when I worked in the attaché office. Abeer had come to the embassy one day to get a visa, and she had seen me there in my Marine uniform. She asked some of the other Yemenis who worked at the embassy about me and, through them, finagled a meeting. We became acquaintances, and when I left my post in Yemen, we stayed in touch as friends. We grew closer and closer over the next couple years, and the relationship proved to be critical once the Houthis took over.

Like the work, Assaf's parties were a distraction too. At one of these parties I met Ben Buchholz, who has now teamed up with me in writing this book. He was then chief of the attaché office, the same office I'd worked for about a decade earlier. He and I struck up a good friendship, one that has survived these years and even strengthened despite the divergence of our paths after the US Embassy finally shut its doors and evacuated in early 2015. Ben would bring a few other attachés and security personnel, maybe a handful of people who had been authorized to go out on the town, and they'd all arrive together with their bodyguards in a big caravan of armored Land Cruisers. They traveled this way whether going to an official meeting, heading to one of Assaf's parties, or attending the OSAC breakfast meetings now being hosted at Jannah Hunt or one of the other oil-industry compounds.

These parties were full of interesting people with diverse backgrounds and genuine characters. Our expatriate group numbered among its members an ex–Navy SEAL, an ex–Green Beret, an ex–Canadian Mountie, a couple former British Special Air Service guys who now worked for oil concerns, and a few liberal types who worked for NGOs doing humanitarian work like demining, health care, or agricultural and economic support. A French contingent always brought wine and cheese (but drank our beer and liquor first before breaking out what they called the "good stuff"). And the Germans, who won the World Cup in soccer that year, vied with the Dutch and British in their chitchat about sports. At Assaf's parties, the clientele also included movers and shakers from a wider swath of both Yemeni society and the expatriate community: businessmen, relatives of the Saleh family, generals, ministers, underministers, diplomats, general managers of the oil companies, even a few literary types. Assaf thrived at making connections between people. His events tended to take on greater importance the more apparent it became that they were among the only intersections of the diplomatic and expatriate communities.

I'd soon enough have reason to rely on him again, just as I had when Amira was trapped in Lebanon during those beginning days of the Israel-Hezbollah conflict.

CHAPTER 9

THE HOUTHIS COMETH

THE HOUTHIS' BASE of power centered, and still centers, on their tribal lands in the far northern mountains of Yemen, almost on the border of Saudi Arabia, in and around the city of Saadah.

There the leader of the movement, Abd el-Malik al-Houthi, lives in guarded seclusion in the fashion of other rebel leaders: switching houses, video-taping statements to his followers rather than appearing in person, rarely keeping to a schedule or to a pattern of behavior. The Houthis fought six wars against the Yemeni government over the decade between 2004, when the Yemeni government placed a bounty on Abd el-Malik's brother, a rising political star named Hussein Badreddin al-Houthi, and the fall of 2014, when the Houthis marched victoriously into Sana'a.

During these years they engaged off and on in skirmishes with Saudi forces along the border, as well as with Sunni radicals, some of them Wahhabis coming in from Saudi Arabia, some of them homegrown Islahis, who adhered to a similar view on Islam as the al-Qaeda fighters. Hussein Badreddin al-Houthi had been killed in the first war, after the price on his head rose from $55,000 to $75,000. His nascent movement—still officially called by the name he gave it, Ansarallah, or the Victors of Allah—took his name after his martyrdom, while his brother Abd el-Malik ended up running the show.

The Houthis had a chip on their shoulders compared to other Zaydi clans, since they were only the third- or fourth-most prestigious, and since they had suffered much worse than other clans through those six wars. When the other clans moderated their behavior, preferring to work with former president Ali Abdullah Saleh and take whatever assistance (and cold cash) he provided, the Houthis took the road of rebellion and became something of a rallying point for more radical-minded Zaydis throughout Yemen, including a significant population of Zaydis in Sana'a's Old City, right there under the nose of the US Embassy and the Yemeni authorities.

Throughout most of my time in Yemen, the Houthi wars experienced upticks and then calm periods. They became something of a feature of the landscape, just like al-Qaeda's attacks and assassinations. Besides the occasional hot fighting that Ali Muhsin's 1st Armor Brigade (and a few other units of Yemen's army) brought to the mountains north and west of Sana'a, the Houthi problem seemed to be a regional one rather than a national one.

That changed toward the end of 2013.

First, as a gesture of reconciliation, the interim government of President Abdrabbuh Mansur Hadi returned Hussein Badreddin al-Houthi's remains to Saadah for proper burial. Rather than reconciling, though, the Houthis took this as a victory. Some missteps by the government in denying certain people visas to attend the burial further aggravated and emboldened those in the group who were already advocating for increased militarism in the light of the interim government's fragility.

A second, even bigger reason for the change in the Houthi dynamic was the collapse of a school, officially called the Dar al-Hadith, or House of Hadith, in a small village just to the south of Saadah. That village is called Dammaj. And the school itself often would be referred to more colloquially as the Dammaj Institute.

Situating the Dammaj Institute right in the Houthis' backyard was one of President Saleh's more brilliant ploys. This was a staunchly Islahi institution, led by a man with close ties to the Islah party and to al-Qaeda. In fact, rumor had it that the major purpose of the Dammaj Institute was to provide a "forward staging base" and cantonment area for radical Sunni fighters—Wahhabis from Saudi Arabia as well as Islahis—to operate in and around Saadah. While it might seem that situating an institution of this sort so close to the nucleus of rebel power would be a bad idea, in fact it kept the Houthis focused on Dammaj, on protecting their neighborhood, and not on national-level issues or military forays into other provinces. And, from Saleh's point of view, it probably helped keep the radical Sunni fighters focused elsewhere too.

Throughout the earlier parts of 2013, we'd hear reports from Saadah and from the vicinity of Dammaj, mostly coming from Red Crescent or other aid workers who were occasionally permitted to bring medical supplies or other assistance into the area. A virtual no-man's-land developed between the school buildings and the surrounding foothills in Dammaj, with Houthi artillery firing potshots at the school, night raids by fighters venturing out of the walls of the compound, and bodies—mostly those of the Islahis, it was rumored—strewn on the ground between the forces, left to rot.

I believe that the issue of the bodies precipitated the next fateful event: a truce was negotiated. The sides started talking to each other, at least at the political level, mediated by various international aid groups and diplomatic missions in Sana'a with an eye to justice and rightness (understandably possessing much less of Saleh's foxlike consideration for how best to balance and neuter the various forces that could disrupt Yemen). These negotiations resulted not only in a cease-fire to retrieve the remains but in a larger framework for shutting down the institute, relocating its "students" to various Sunni areas (one sticking point was not getting them to leave, but finding new homes for them because not many tribes wanted hardened Islahi fighters coming in to rile up their own youth and disrupt their own tenuous political and sectarian equilibria), and also, somewhat inadvertently, allowing the Houthis to reconsolidate their power.

Had the Houthis stopped at that point, things might be very different in Yemen right now. They'd likely be living in Saadah semi-autonomously, perhaps with some of their grievances unaddressed but with the rest of Yemen still on the road to recovery and perhaps even enjoying some semblance of representative democracy.

However, Abd el-Malik had a problem on his hands: he too had a core of hardened fighters, like the Islahi fighters from the Dammaj Institute, most of them eager youth, flush with what they considered a significant victory. This presented a fork in the road. Either Abd el-Malik would need to work very hard to redirect the energy of these core supporters into productive pastimes—tough to do when, at the same time, the National Dialogue Conference (NDC) was taking measures to restrict the Houthis' power, like redistricting their province so that they had no access to a seaport—or he would have to give

These are the ruins of the house in Tebnine, Lebanon, where Sam Farran's grandfather lived. Sam stood next to these ruins, in the street, on the exact spot where he remembers his grandfather sitting every day, enjoying the rhythm of life in this small, traditional Lebanese village. *(Author collection)*

Sam attended Fordson High School in Dearborn, Michigan, where some of his formative moments as an American occurred, including his first real romance and his burgeoning desire to join the US Marines. *(Photo by Remhermen; CC 4.0 International)*

Sam poses for an official photograph in his full Marine regalia. Despite being a native speaker of Arabic, it took Sam two tries at volunteering—even after 9/11—to put his language skills to use for the Marine Corps. He finally landed just where he was most needed, though, working in the Defense Intelligence Agency (DIA) attaché program in locations across the Middle East. *(Author collection)*

Sam, like many Marines, supports the yearly Toys for Tots donation program around the Christmas holidays. One standard part of the Marine Corps ethos is that no one is ever a "former Marine"— once a Marine, always a Marine. So too for Sam: even after assignments all across the world, ending in Yemen, the Marine Corps has remained a big part of Sam's life. *(Author collection)*

...e port of Aden, on the Indian Ocean in Yemen, bustled with commercial cargo traffic, at least before ...e Houthi uprising and subsequent civil war. Sam was nearly called here in the immediate aftermath of ...e bombing of the USS *Cole*, which occurred here, in Aden. A year later, just after 9/11, Sam arrived in ...men and began working from the embassy in Sana'a. Even then some of the strands of the *Cole* bomb-...g were not fully wrapped up; they affected life and attitudes in the country and in the work Sam was ...ing. *(Photo by Brian Harrington Spier; CC SA-2.0)*

Beautiful traditional buildings of the Old City in Sana'a, seen here before the destruction of the civil war between the Houthis and the Saudi-led coalition attempting to support President Abdrabbu Mansour Hadi, were known for their multistory ...onstruction and for the frosted details around their windows. *(Photo by Jialiang Gao; CC SA-3.0)*

The view of Jibla shows the intensively terraced mountainsides and dense but traditionally built cityscapes of much of Yemen. This is the town where Sam investigated the senseless murder of three Western doctors who had been working in Yemen for over twenty-five years, a sign that the extremism fueled by radical concepts of Islam would soon make Yemen inhospitable for non-Yemenis. *(Photo by Rod Waddington; CC SA-2.0)*

Most Yemeni men, and many wome[n] too, partake in the daily ritual of a q[at] chew, stripping fresh leaves from qat branches and chewing them in a wa[d] in their cheeks. Qat produces a talkative euphoria mixed with calm[e] contemplative periods. It is a social pastime in Yemen, with most chews involving several individuals and oft[en] lasting from the middle part of the afternoon into the evening. *(Photo b[y] Ferdinand Reus; CC SA-2.0)*

Former President Ali Abdullah Saleh served as the ruler of a unified Yemen from May 1990 until stepping down as part of the Arab Spring in February 2012, replaced by an interim government headed by his former deputy, Abdrabbu Mansour Hadi. Before that he was President of North Yemen from 1978 until 1990. *(Kremlin, Presidential Press Office; CC 4.0 International)*

Abdrabbu Mansour Hadi was the head of Yemen's interim government during the National Dialogue process to affect reconciliation after former longtime President Ali Abdullah Saleh stepped down. He remain[s] the head of Yemen's UN and the Saudi-backed government-in-exile, even as the Houthis have effectively controlled the capital of Sana'a and much of the rest of the populated portion of Yemen since late 2014. *(US Department of Defense)*

strikes from the Saudi-led coalition attempting to return Abdrabbu Mansour Hadi to power have
uced much of Yemen's capital city of Sana'a to rubble. Though, for obvious reasons, no photos of Sam in
uthi captivity exist—or at least none that the Houthis have cared to share—Sam's captivity began
ause of the mistaken idea that he might have been contributing to the Saudi targeting at the beginning of
s bombing campaign. *(Photo by Ibrahem Qasim; CC 4.0 International)*

nstruction in Sana'a, and in much of Yemen,
is simple concrete and rebar. It has not borne
he brunt of bombing and blockade well since
e start of the Saudi-led coalition's Operation
)ecisive Storm, which began in 2015. During
is maelstrom of destruction, Sam (and many
other prisoners) could do nothing but listen
rom their cloistered jail cells to the sounds of
ar outside, never quite sure whether the next
bomb might fall on them. *(Photo by Ibrahem
Qasim; CC 4.0 International)*

Shipments of military materiel, like those seen here on the
tarmac at Sana'a's International Airport, require close
coordination from military personnel in roles like Sam's
as attaché so that they meet all the regulations and
inspection requirements of host nation authorities.
Interestingly, when the Houthis first took over Sana'a
International Airport, they did not stop US shipments
outright. They simply observed. This phase only lasted a
few months as they consolidated power. Then the Saudi-
led bombing began and things got more hostile, leading
to the US Embassy withdrawal from the country. *(Author
collection)*

Sana'a sits in a bowl at more than 7,000 feet of elevation, ringed by craggy mountains. Its climate is unex pectedly pleasant for its location in otherwise scorching Arabia. Its tower houses and the minarets of th Old City's mosques, many of which will not have survived this latest war, lend a sense of fairytale othe worldliness and ancient urbanity to the view. Through this landscape, invisible to him as he was near suffocating with a bag drawn tight over his head, Sam's captors drove him from his villa in Hadda on th south side of Sana'a along a twisting route meant to disorient him. Eventually he would end up in prison building to the northeast of the Old City. *(UNESCO; photo by Maria Gropa; CC SA-3.0)*

One of the more famous mosques in the Old City of Sana'a, al-Bakiriyya, was built by the Ottomans in th mid-1500s. It remains a fixture of worship today. NSB Headquarters, where Abeer selflessly ventured da after day to inquire about Sam's whereabouts, is very near this mosque. *(Photo by H. Grobe; CC SA-3.0)*

A 737 jet plane owned by Oman Air, here on the runway in Cairo. Oman's Sultan Qaboos ordered a plane much like this to transport Sam when he was finally released by the Houthis. The Omanis maintain a careful neutrality in the Middle East and therefore were able to serve an instrumental role in helping Sam reach freedom. *(© Raimond Spekking; CC SA 4.0 via Wikipedia Commons; converted to grayscale)*

Sam, thinner and showing the pain of his captivity, emerges onto the tarmac in Muscat, Oman, after being freed from captivity in Sana'a. *(NBC News)*

Sam stands on the ramparts of the old, ruined castle in Tebnine and points across the valley toward the bells of the church towers in the Christian part of town. Although not seen in this photo, the minaret of Tebnine's mosque also rises above the valley—two faith traditions coexisting in the town. Following his ordeal and now in retirement, Sam has returned to rebuild his life, living for much of the year in a house on the outskirts of town. *(Author collection)*

his blessing to further military activity and hope it would lead to a better outcome than a negotiated peace.

Abd el-Malik chose war. But he did so in a very slow, almost unnoticeable way.

Unnoticeable to us in Sana'a at least.

He took plenty of time to reconsolidate, to rebuild his forces. And he could afford to do so because most of the attention of the Yemeni government, of the diplomatic missions, and even of the expatriates like me was still focused on the NDC. What little other attention we had tended to drift toward either al-Qaeda or the new threat in town: the Islamic State in Iraq and Syria (ISIS).

For a while, just as ISIS was making its name in Iraq and Syria and spreading its franchise into other areas like Africa and, yes, Yemen, it looked like the radicalized Sunni elements in Yemen would abandon al-Qaeda and join this new, more radical group.

Al-Qaeda had morphed a bit over the preceding few years. At one point it had conquered and instituted Shari'a governance in several provinces in the east of Yemen: Shabwa, Abyan, and parts of the Hadramawt. But, while at first al-Qaeda's presence might have seemed to the local sheikhs like a relief from the ineffective and corrupt governance of Sana'a, its version of Shari'a didn't sit too well with the average Yemeni. The people at first tried to live with, work with, and help their new black-clad al-Qaeda leaders. They seemed resigned to or even supportive of harsher punishments, with stoning and summary amputation and decapitation reported as common outcomes of Shari'a legal rulings. However, when al-Qaeda tried to impose a block on chewing qat, the Yemeni people had had enough.

Combined with a fairly successful campaign launched around the same time by Yemeni military forces—rumored to have been trained and even assisted by US Special Forces and US drone operations—the populations of these provinces knocked al-Qaeda into hiding, into the background, and put an end to its designs to create a Yemeni caliphate.

At this moment ISIS arrived on the scene.

Unfortunately, this group's methods were more draconian by far than al-Qaeda's: crucifixions, assassinations, condemnations. The Yemeni people had already soured to all of this. They did not want to go back to Shari'a law. They did not want to give up qat or alcohol, which many Yemenis also partook of, albeit on the sly. What's more, al-Qaeda had learned from its mistakes. It came back in a softer, subtler way, advocating for the establishment of a caliphate but willing to let qat as well as most civil administration and judicial functions continue according to tribal and societal norms. Al-Qaeda also responded to some of the more flamboyant attacks launched by ISIS by stepping up its military efforts—it needed to be seen not only as a more moderate governing option but also as a stringent, capable, and winning avenue for military action and for the youths' need to test themselves in battle.

As such, al-Qaeda's new strategy turned out to have two prongs: govern moderately but attack severely. Reports of an uptick in attacks started to come in from the provinces out east: bombings, suicide attacks, complex attacks. Then al-Qaeda took things a bit further, brazenly entering the port city of Mukulla—which it had been kicked out of the previous year—ambushing and taking over the headquarters of Yemen's 3rd Military District, which had responsibility for all of the Hadramawt and Mahrah provinces. Operatives drove a suicide vehicle into the front gate, entered with a score of fighters through the flaming wreckage, and then battled Yemeni forces for more than a day from within the perimeter of the headquarters building. This attack sent notice to the tribes that al-Qaeda was back in charge, that ISIS was a thing of the past, and that whatever happened in the National Dialogue dragging on back in Sana'a, there in the comfort of the Moevenpick, the next government would still be a long time coming to the rural, eastern parts of Yemen.

■ ■ ■

THE HOUTHIS CONTINUED THEIR regrouping efforts and began—ever so slowly—to take the first preparatory steps on their march south from Saadah to Sana'a. Never committing to any major action, and with the government in Sana'a rendered ineffective by dint of its interim status and its focus on the NDC talks, the hardened Houthi fighters, many of whom had been at war for most of their lives, began targeting the houses and compounds of known Islahi members or sympathizers on the margins of their own tribal lands. This meant conflict with the al-Ahmar family, who were the most proximate Islahis. The Houthis would come in, surround a compound, bombard it, kill or cause to flee any of the household servants or fighters housed within, and then—in a brilliant marketing and military ploy—finish the job by razing all the structures to the ground.

This tactic not only prevented the families and fighters from returning to these facilities but also sent a message to any neighboring tribes: you're either with us or you suffer the same fate. Most chose to join the Houthis. Usually Zaydi, most of these neighboring tribes were closely aligned already, to be sure, and became more so when a major confederation of tribes in the north of Yemen decided to throw in their lot with the Houthis rather than with their age-old nemesis, the al-Ahmars. But many of these tribes felt the keen compulsion of the Houthi military presence too, being constantly reminded, any time they passed by one of these homesteads, of the dangers of resistance.

As the first reports of Houthi attacks on the al-Ahmar family started to reach Sana'a, al-Qaeda struck again. It seemed like al-Qaeda didn't want to let the Houthis have the spotlight, and vice versa, the two sides, on opposite edges of the country, almost engaging in a long-distance game of one-upmanship.

■ ■ ■

MUCH LIKE WHEN I was working in Jeddah and had been having a breakfast chat with the RSO, the head security officer at the consulate, on this particular day in Sana'a I was supposed to go to the military hospital, a facility located inside the sweeping, self-contained courtyard grounds of the huge Yemeni Ministry of Defense complex, the headquarters for all of Yemen's military and the office and brain center of the minister of defense himself. I was planning to visit the hospital because a few friends of mine were receiving treatment there. While good care could be had at a number of Western-affiliated commercial hospitals in Sana'a, the best hospital in the land was the military one. All the members of parliament, Saleh's family members, and even visiting dignitaries used it.

Fortunately, I had to cancel my visit. USAID had a new company coming into town and asked me to provide a country-orientation briefing. I was on my way to that briefing when al-Qaeda launched a spectacularly gruesome attack on the entire ministry complex. This attack involved two suicide vehicles, one of which blew down the headquarters' exterior gates and one of which got inside the grounds and turned toward the defense minister's office before blowing up in front of the hospital. A large contingent of al-Qaeda fighters, mostly Saudi nationals, flowed in behind these vehicles. They split in at least two directions, with a couple entering the hospital and killing nurses, doctors, and patients—dragging many of the Filipina nurses into a closet and executing them there. Among those killed was a prominent judge and member of the National Dialogue Conference deliberations, Abdojaleel Noman, who was sedated on the operating table when the al-Qaeda fighters entered. They killed the doctor operating on him, they killed him, and then—as his wife called her daughter in a panic—they killed his wife too, even as she spoke on the phone.

The Yemeni authorities claimed to have recovered control of their ministry buildings later that day, but word got out that three al-Qaeda fighters remained holed up in a room of the complex. The Yemeni military ended up having to drill holes in the roof and drop grenades into the room. Still, one of the fighters managed to approach the Yemenis and detonate his suicide vest, killing a few more.

In all, the attack claimed the lives of fifty-six people, most of them Yemenis but also two German doctors and several Vietnamese and Filipina nurses, and it did so right in the heart of what was supposed to be Yemeni military power.

This brazen attack left people shaken. It also likely precipitated the end of the National Dialogue Conference, which published its results about a month later. Key to those results was the redistricting of Yemeni provinces into seven regions, which ignited complaints from not only the Houthis, who were left without access to a seaport, but also much of the South and East of the country, where people felt like the lines had been drawn specifically to strengthen the North and weaken the South. Throughout this, despite having been appointed to only a two-year term as interim president, which expired in 2013, Hadi was viewed by most Yemenis as trying to consolidate power, which was at odds with the purpose of the NDC and the goal of following through on inclusive, democratic government.

The NDC agreement looked good on paper, and the smiling photos of the delegates resulted in great PR, but I suspected that the Yemenis wouldn't actually do much to implement it. They didn't have the resources. What resources they received from outside sources, like the Saudis, anyone in power would try—through a hundred thousand schemes—to pocket. Those who benefited from the current system had no reason to facilitate a transfer of power. That wasn't the Yemeni way. Hadi's attempts to consolidate power demonstrated as much at the very highest level, and the principle applied to every level of Yemeni government, right down to the soldiers manning desolate checkpoints, who would extort a bag of qat or a few coins from each traveler as the price of passage.

■ ■ ■

THE HOUTHI EXPANSION CONTINUED, ever southward along the spine of mountains toward Sana'a. Still, people were loath to believe the Houthis would ever make an attempt on Sana'a itself. People at the Overseas Security Advisory Council (OSAC) and in other knowledgeable corners of the expat community couldn't believe the Houthis would be so dumb. Or that the Western powers, operating out of the embassies, would allow it, or that the Houthis weren't really interested in a political settlement. We thought everything would settle down, just as it had in the previous several Houthi civil wars.

"That would be dumb," my compatriots at OSAC would say. "They couldn't ever hold Sana'a if they took it."

"The West would resist it," others would say. "The West would never stand for it."

"They're going to make a political settlement. Maybe Hadi will give them a seaport after all, and then they'll go back to Saadah."

We didn't realize how serious the Houthi problem was getting, though, until someone started sending around a map of the "Houthnado"—a funnel-cloud-shaped protuberance stretching from Saadah ever southward, angling in to the east, so that its spear-like tip pointed right at Sana'a. This map showed the progress of the Houthis over time, and it was unmistakable that the Houthi thrust pointed directly at Sana'a.

Just between Sana'a and the tip of this Houthi spear, though, a major town called Amran, with a major military base, sat athwart the only real road southward, blocking the Houthi advance. This would be a serious hurdle—much more of a pitched battle—compared to what the Houthis had been up against in their attacks on individual compounds or in the few skirmishes outside villages or minor military outposts along the way.

As they approached Amran, for just a bit it seemed like the Houthis hesitated and reconsidered whether it was wise to bite off such a huge target. For a month or more, their attacks focused to the west, still pushing southward and still following the spine of mountains but making a detour around Amran and therefore also around Sana'a.

When we realized that the Houthis were doing this not out of fear but as a rather brilliant strategic sleight of hand—whereby they still aimed at Sana'a but were setting the conditions for a successful entrance by first cutting Sana'a's only road to the Red Sea, interdicting its principal lifeline and escape route—all of us in Sana'a began to feel seriously uneasy. The map of the Houthnado now looked less like an unintelligent, if ambitious, wall cloud and more like a guided, perhaps even fated, master plan. The link between Sana'a and its closest port, Hudaydah, would shortly be broken right in the shadow of Yemen's highest mountain, Jebel An-Nabi Shuayb, a 12,000-foot eminence beneath which the road makes several perilous and easily controlled switchbacks: impossible terrain to push the Houthis out of once they seized it. With the cutting of the Hudaydah Road, Sana'a would be stuck like a pig in the cupped valley of its mountain fastness.

As this realization sunk in, a number of other things began to happen all at once:

- The Houthis launched their attack on Amran.
- Hadi, in perhaps his most misguided decision, cut the subsidies for gasoline and some food staples.
- Protests in Sana'a erupted, fueled by many grievances but fired by the gas subsidy change.
- Houthi banners began to fly openly in the Old City, and even in other parts of Sana'a, plastered to walls, to light posts, to the doors of Houthi partisans.
- The attack on Amran, which everyone thought would result in a long stalemate, if not a Houthi loss, turned out to be lightning fast and frighteningly successful.

Suddenly the Houthis, with their numbers swollen by fighters from other tribes along their march south, looked like a much more formidable force, one that might bloody the Yemeni governmental forces and create quite a wreck of Sana'a, even if they did not prove ultimately victorious.*

The Houthi numbers had swollen, but their core remained those hardened bands of fighters who had endured a decade or more of guerrilla war. We expected that these hardened bands would be used at the forefront, and after a defeat, or even after encountering some good resistance, the supporters from other tribes might melt away, leaving the hardened bands exposed and outnumbered. The truck-loads of irregulars from the neighboring tribes looked formidable but had not been tested in battle like the Houthis. They were, however, surprisingly well equipped, both because every tribe in Yemen prided itself on its weaponry and because the victory at Amran resulted in the seizure of masses of small arms, ammunition, artillery pieces, and even tanks.

Worse, unlike their normal tactic of leveling buildings and mov-ing on to the next target, the Houthis occupied the headquarters compound in Amran, taking all the gear as they normally did. They then hauled Hameed al-Qushaibi, the general in charge of the plussed-up Amran Brigade, a longtime ally of the al-Ahmars, out of a shack on the grounds where he had been hiding and executed him with a single shot to the back of the head on the parade field of his own compound. Photos of this execution began filtering from person to person, even appearing in the paper. While the battle resulted in more than four hundred casualties for the Yemeni military, the Houthis did a very smart thing with the majority of the several

---

* Sana'a held a considerable amount of firepower in the city itself, with much more Yemeni strength in the ready to reinforce from bases to the south and east, troops who were US-trained in the fight against al-Qaeda and whose equipment was provided by the US Embassy.

thousand troops they captured. They took all their weapons, all their vehicles, all their equipment, then sent them trudging the twenty-seven short but winding and mountainous miles from Amran to Sana'a. This meant that for days after the battle, the road to Amran, which descends along several highly visible switchbacks out of the mountains above the northwestern suburbs of Sana'a, was clogged with bedraggled, demoralized, dislocated, and disarmed soldiers—a potent message to those in Sana'a who might resist. This also presented, like the leveling of enemy compounds, a potent psychological choice: surrender and be disarmed, or—like Qushaibi—make yourself an enemy and find yourself executed in your own yard.

Sana'a was surrounded, with escape possible into only the impassable wilderness of the Rub al-Khali desert or via the long and treacherous road south to Aden on the Indian Ocean. The road south from Houthi land stood open, with all of us watching the switchbacks for the first sign of the Houthi onslaught.

All kinds of wild rumors percolated throughout the city during these anxious days. Some of them proved to be wildly incorrect—like the one I heard about the Houthis getting ready to shell Sana'a with missiles and artillery from the hillsides, as they had done for so long to the Dammaj Institute. But some of them turned out to be fairly accurate too. For instance, along the Hudaydah Road, which they had cut beneath Jebel an-Nabi Shuayb, the Houthis apparently began to send vehicles loaded with troops eastward, a few first probing maneuvers back along the road toward Sana'a. They couldn't come all the way into Sana'a via that route because the Special Forces headquarters at Asbahi Base, on a cliff right above the ritzy suburb of Hadda with its diplomatic compounds and nice restaurants, blocked the advance there. This was Ahmed Ali Saleh's base, presumably filled with Yemen's best-trained fighters.

What happened next still mystifies most observers of Yemen.

These government troops, with their strategic advantages, their training, and their loyalty to Yemen—or at least to Saleh and Hadi and those considered the ruling elite—all of these troops at Asbahi, at 1st Armor Brigade in the northwest corner of Sana'a and in many other places, all of them just laid down their arms and let the Houthis in. None, or very few of them, fought.

The Houthis came into town in two long columns, one from Amran, one along the Hudaydah Road from Jebel an-Nabi Shuayb, and they met almost no resistance. We watched the tanks the Houthis had captured in Amran as they rumbled down the switchbacks on the mountainsides, sitting ducks if the Yemeni government had wanted to fire on them. The column chugged along, looking like blips on an old Atari video game.

A short skirmish occurred once those tanks got down into Sana'a itself, with some maneuvers on the flanks of TV Station Hill, right near Ali Muhsin's 1st Armor Brigade headquarters. It was tank on tank, each turning, firing, turning again, motoring a few feet, a puff of gun smoke spewing from the muzzle of its cannon. Then one of the tanks went silent. The other one rumbled away. Other than that and a few units holing up in their compounds, the Houthis came in, surrounded the important buildings, took over all the important checkpoints, and began to act like they were in charge.

They didn't molest anyone, though things remained tense. They had obviously been ordered to be polite and win over Sana'a's citizens and diplomats. The only people they seemed to interdict were Islahi fighters or known Islahi politicians, though most of them had gotten out of town ahead of the Houthis like rats fleeing a sinking ship.

When the Houthi forces, many of whom seemed like mere children, child fighters, surrounded the US Embassy, the embassy personnel geared up for another event like the break-in and bumper derby of two years before. However, the Houthis did not disturb the embassy. They set up checkpoints on the streets leading in and out of the main compound and the Sheraton. And they monitored who came and went, only becoming concerned if anyone affiliated with the Islahis tried to approach the embassy. What's more, a really well-trained unit of Houthis rolled up in a vehicle the first or second day, went to an apartment complex just outside the gates of the embassy compound, which friends told me had long been suspected of harboring an al-Qaeda cell that monitored the embassy, and pulled three or four al-Qaeda personnel out of the building, questioning them and then executing them in the street.

It was bloody. And frightening. And eerily calm too.

Most of all, it was effective.

■ ■ ■

THE SECOND NIGHT of the Houthi occupation, Abd el-Malik, who remained in Saadah, put out instructions to light all the fireworks in all the areas controlled by Houthi forces. The Yemenis have a tradition, during marriages, of setting off a cascade of fireworks, each wedding trying to outdo the others. Every night a certain number of weddings would occur in various parts of Sana'a, with not only fireworks but also random celebratory gunfire peppering the air. This could be dangerous, with stray rounds falling, but for the most part, from the windows of the embassy or of the Moevenpick or Sheraton further up on the haunches of Jebel Nuqum, the valley of Sana'a below would be lit with a colorful show, a few splotches here and there, a bouquet of sparkling festivity. But this also meant that Sana'a had warehouses filled with fireworks waiting to be bought and sold to adorn these nightly jubilees.

When Abd el-Malik ordered them all set off at once, we thought he might control perhaps a quarter of the city. He controlled it all—every square inch except for a few scattered military compounds. And he demonstrated this with a fireworks show the likes of which none of us had ever seen. It lasted more than two hours and spread across the entirety of the city, a blanket of fireworks, a multicolored panoply of bursts through which everyone—the embassy personnel up on the flank of the mountain and us down in our houses in Hadda—thought a rain of artillery or mortar shells would come at any moment, as if shielded, disguised from retribution by the omnipresent roar and burst and color. It would be the perfect cover.

But no artillery ever came. No mortar fire. Celebratory rat-a-tat-tats from all corners of the wind, sure, but that was a normal part of Yemeni life, Yemeni celebration. The Houthis did not intend to attack during their display. They gloried in it. And they knew it sent a signal, both of control and mastery and of restraint. After two hours all that remained of this show was a fog, a low sulfurous cloud that trailed like a wounded animal out and down through the city toward the shallow passage north and east between the mountains, out and down into the night and, lower, far lower, into the vastness of the Rub al-Khali, which might still echo with the sounds of that evening.

The Houthi technique, for each of the military bases that remained loyal to Hadi and also for any resisting ministries or government buildings, was not to attack outright but to surround and only let Houthi or Zaydi personnel come and go: house arrest, a bloodless, white-gloved coup. Known Islahi compounds or businesses were more aggressively treated, but the tactic still resembled the way the Houthis surrounded and dealt with the al-Qaeda cell near the US Embassy: they had specific objectives but remained cautious and even courteous to the rest of the population, clearing out the problem individuals and groups but being extra nice to everyone else.

They clearly had an agenda of political reconciliation in mind. Or they wanted to quickly establish legitimacy, and their concern seemed to focus more on the Yemenis than on outsiders. They wanted to demonstrate to the average person in Sana'a that they did not intend reprisals. They would rule well and honestly. It was their platform, part of what Abd el-Malik had been saying in his recorded speeches, contrasting the millennia of (what he suggested was) good Zaydi leadership with the corruption of modern life and modern politicians. As for outsiders, Westerners, the Houthis did a fairly good job too; at least their more senior people demonstrated adequate concern and courtesy. Sometimes the younger Houthi fighters (many of whom were barely teenagers) had swallowed that "Death to Israel, Death to America, a Curse on the Jews" motto too fully. They'd get excited to see a car full of Americans or Brits or Dutch, be they diplomats or aid workers or security and energy personnel. In their zeal these youth would stop, search, accost, even make strange demands of diplomats and expatriates transiting through checkpoints or going about their daily business in whatever fashion they could. But, almost always, the Houthi youngsters making these mistakes were quickly reprimanded, or at least corrected, by more senior

Houthis on-site or with a quick telephone call or two back to their commanders.

Life almost seemed normal. Too normal.

■ ■ ■

FOR THE HOUTHIS TOO, the takeover of Sana'a almost seemed surprising. They didn't seem disappointed, that's not the right word. But they seemed like they had braced for more and could now exhale, collectively, perhaps with a bit too much energy and enthusiasm on occasion but also with a sense of invincibility that bordered on arrogance.

We soon started to hear rumors about why this may have been, why the Houthi takeover of Sana'a had occurred so quickly and easily: Saleh.

The bases led by his sons and nephews and the ministries led by his General People's Congress cronies weren't surrounded and managed as closely by the Houthis as those facilities or institutions adhering to Hadi or Islah or the other fragmentary parties. In fact, many of the bases that the Houthis took over belonged to Saleh-allied commands. We started to hear rumors from lower-level military personnel that all the Saleh-aligned bases had just opened their gates and let the Houthis in, perhaps putting on some sort of face-saving show but mostly just turning over the keys and then working out a deal to appoint a Houthi "minder" as the deputy commander (for a military facility) or deputy vice minister or deputy manager (for a ministry or government facility or even a private concern, like a bank or university department).

As the news of this secret alliance between the Houthis and Saleh began to leak out, things took a turn for the worse.

The Houthis surrounded the presidential palace where Hadi had taken refuge. They began to apply their same constrictor technique, only allowing in or out those persons who were affiliated with their movement. Everything remained relatively bloodless and eerily quiet, but I could tell that the Houthis were preparing to storm the palace and kill Hadi or take him prisoner.

I began to advise my clients to not come to Yemen. I began to tell them to pack up and leave if they were already in the country, no matter how sure they felt of their own personal safety. I began to make preparations for my clients and my employees to continue on with their work even if Yemen had to shut its doors for a while.

The various embassies in Sana'a began to evacuate their nonessential personnel, a task they had all perfected over the previous several years, going into limited shutdown mode when big events happened, like the al-Qaeda takeover of the Ministry of Defense or, earlier, the Arab Spring conflagration. This time, though, rather than just imposing a limited shutdown, one by one the embassies started to close their doors completely.

■ ■ ■

THAT'S WHEN I LEFT—in mid-October 2014.

I flew to Beirut, trusting I could conduct business for my clients and take care of my contracts in Yemen from afar. I didn't think that I'd be gone more than a week or two.

I conceived of my departure as just a little breather to get my feet back under me and let the situation around Hadi's palace calm down. I thought I needed a vacation. I told myself I was just going on a little excursion to get some perspective, to see Yemen from afar, to see it in a new light. But that first week turned into two, three, five, ten.

. . .

FINALLY, IN JANUARY 2015, Hadi escaped his own palace under cover of darkness and fled all the way to Aden far to the south.

With Hadi went his new minister of defense, Mahmoud Subeihi, who had previously been the commander working most closely with US Special Forces against al-Qaeda. Strangely, owing mostly to the lack of other allies Hadi could gather, Ali Muhsin also fled with them. They'd thrown their lots in together, three individuals with odd backgrounds: the Zumra interim president who'd been overthrown, the new defense minister with strong ties to the United States, and the former al-Qaeda recruiter and Houthi nemesis.

Subeihi was taken prisoner by the Houthis in fighting around Aden, but Hadi and Ali Muhsin fled to Saudi Arabia and convinced the Gulf Cooperation Council (GCC) to launch Operation Decisive Storm. This operation had the support of the UN mandate for Yemen, but even so it put the United States in a tough position: though Saudi Arabia, the United Arab Emirates, and seven other GCC and African countries formed the coalition prosecuting the war on Hadi's behalf, much of Hadi's support inside Yemen came through Islah and Ali Muhsin, especially with Subeihi captured. Though the United States would not admit it, and still won't, by helping the Saudis help Hadi, they unwittingly also helped radical Sunni-aligned forces, which were known to incorporate al-Qaeda fighters as shock troops in their front lines. The United States had this choice: support the UN- and GCC-supported effort in Yemen, or negotiate with the Houthis, who had already proven themselves fairly adept at killing al-Qaeda and Islahi fighters. Which was the more pressing US goal in Yemen: eliminate al-Qaeda or prop up Hadi?

In the end Saudi Arabia did a good job of tying the Shi'a (but Zaydi) Houthis to Iran, from whom they took help but to whom they did not want to be beholden due to the differences in the Zaydi and "Twelver" branches of Shi'ism. This false equivalency, which also played on US strategic goals in the Middle East to oppose Iranian influence, tipped the scales and kept US support for Saudi Arabia's coalition intact.

It was a complicated situation, but it's important to understand because it makes a difference in terms of what ended up happening to me, as an American but also as a Shi'a Muslim.

I'd been out of Yemen for three months by the time this all went down. And I wasn't going to go back in during active fighting. By this time the US Embassy was fully evacuated but still manned by local Yemeni guards. The Houthis had not entered the compound or the Sheraton hotel. Some of the embassy guards were still Griffin security guys whom I had trained, so I heard from them pretty regularly. They thought the Houthis would come in anytime and take over the embassy grounds, but it never happened, and it still hasn't happened.

I later heard from the Houthis themselves that they were trying not to invade any foreign embassy so as not to alienate any particular country. They wanted to present themselves as a legitimate government and facilitate the return of the various diplomatic missions to Yemen. Unfortunately, the outside world still viewed the legitimate government as the one certified by the GCC and the National Dialogue Conference, at least until elections could be called. Though the Houthis had the power and were governing by default, international support remained tied to the interim government structure built around Hadi, even if much of that structure had been displaced first to Aden and then abroad, to Saudi Arabia, where Hadi and his ministers tried to hold things together in absentia.

■ ■ ■

AFTER I EVACUATED, I didn't stop my work leading Universal Eagles. I kept managing my contracts from afar, calling, giving direction to, and paying my Yemeni employees for the work in Yemen that we still supported. I also picked up a few more jobs abroad. One of these took me to Somalia just before Christmas 2014. There I completed a security assessment in Mogadishu for a company called Transoceanic Development. From the outside things seemed pretty normal—just another big shipping company that dabbled in security. But soon I began to have concerns. Transoceanic dealt with a lot of strange things: unmarked planes coming in and out, shipping containers that bypassed normal customs and inspections (what normalcy Somali authorities could manage in that regard), groups of Americans on the ground, civilians you could tell were a bit out of place, not real military guys but more like college kids. Of course, with our training you know not to ask too many questions; you just get used to the kind of operations that run all over the world with these kinds of people. I didn't pry too much into the types of equipment or the specific purposes of the logistics Transoceanic was involved in. I just kept my head down and walked through the steps of the security assessment that I'd been hired to do.*

---

* Only later did I learn that their business involved moving things for the Special Ops community. See Adam Goldman and Eric Schmitt, "Aid Coordinator in Yemen Had Secret Job Overseeing U.S. Commando Shipments," *New York Times*, June 6, 2017, https://www.nytimes.com/2017/06/06/world/middleeast/scott-darden-transoceanic-yemen-pentagon.html.

My work there only lasted one week, maybe ten days. But it ended up being important. Somehow the Houthis had tracked this information about my work with Transoceanic, put two and two together, and came to the conclusion that I was spying for someone. This was not a good look for me when I went back to Yemen.

The ten days in Mogadishu went by quickly and uneventfully—if unmarked planes and mystery shipping containers and Ivy League greenhorn kids in a battle area can be considered uneventful. I flew back to Beirut for a bit, then returned to the United States for the Christmas holidays.

■ ■ ■

I SPENT THREE WEEKS in Detroit and elsewhere, seeing and spending time with all my family. These were special holidays for me, having been through a lot in Yemen myself and also—most importantly—because my son had just returned from Germany after two tours in Afghanistan with the US Air Force. Perhaps this period seems really good in my memory because of what was to come next. It was a time of normalcy, of family, of reunion, of togetherness. I clung to the memory of that Christmas during the coming months, even though my marriage had already ended.)

That holiday ended all too soon, and I found myself headed back to Beirut. Almost immediately I took a call from British American Tobacco. They'd heard of my work with Transoceanic in Somalia and wanted me to do a similar security assessment on the ground in Yemen. The assignment was to last just ten days, like the one in Mogadishu. It seemed like good timing. While in Yemen, I thought, maybe I'd use the opportunity to clear up my affairs there and take care of my personal stuff: the apartment, car, furniture, and all the tasks I'd left undone, all the dirty laundry—both actual and metaphorical—that I had so abruptly left behind back in October. The loose ends of my life in Sana'a were in need of some attention.

I wanted to go back, but at first I resisted. Operation Decisive Storm was being planned, and things looked bleak in Yemen.

My sixth sense for safety itched. I knew it wouldn't be wise.

But, also, part of me whispered in the back of my mind, *Who would go back if not me?* What non-Yemeni knew more about Yemen than I did? Who could possibly be a better candidate to help a company like British American Tobacco get its operations back up and running than someone fluent in the language and the culture and, especially, who shared a religion with the Houthi rebels? *Who else but me?*

I maintained my objection to this plan right up until I started to catch word that the Saudis were going to declare an end to Decisive Storm.

The Saudis hadn't won. It didn't look like they were going to win. They'd earned a bit of land back in the non-Zaydi South and East. But the Houthis held Sana'a and all of the old northern Zaydi heartland up in those mountains. They wouldn't be leaving soon. It would take more than bombing and some halfhearted ground assaults to dislodge them. However, I took the rumblings of this Saudi declaration as a means for them to declare a quick victory, save face, and jump to the negotiating table. This would make things a lot safer. It would put Yemen in a pause, one in which I could safely return.

Or so I thought.

The whole history of my life—my childhood in Lebanon, Libya, and Dearborn, Michigan, my maturation as a US Marine and defense attaché, my contracting work in Yemen, my loves and my losses and the near misses that had taught me so much (and made me just a little cocky)—all of this welled up in me so that I had almost no choice but eventually to accept British American Tobacco's request to return to Sana'a.

On March 20, 2015, I found myself stepping aboard a plane, on my way to being one of the first Americans to go into Yemen since Hadi had fled his own country.

CHAPTER 10

BAGGED

I WAS A LITTLE BIT fearless and a little bit dumb that day as I stepped off the Yemenia plane onto Yemeni soil, walked across the tarmac to the waiting bus, and held on to the greasy silver rail as the bus huffed and chugged toward Sana'a's beaten-down 1980s vintage airport terminal, there to hiss to a stop among the milling young soldiers, dapper-but-skinny suited inspectors, lounging watchers, busy errand boys, and harried businessmen. The doors of the bus opened. I stepped into the airport hall, right into the customs line, the start of a journey that seemed—at least at the outset—no different from a hundred other such journeys I'd made.

The inspector stamped my passport. My bag rumbled into view on the carousel. I grabbed it and strode through the rest of the little terminal to the place where a car awaited my arrival. It was driven by contracted guards from the British American Tobacco villa where I would stay for the next week or two.

Everything went according to plan for the first few days.

There were definitely hiccups. There always were. It was Yemen after all: a strange place, armed to the teeth. While this was normal for Yemen, everything also had a bit of an edge. The guards, wearing their same uniforms, now worked for the Houthis. The police now worked for the Houthis. The checkpoints were manned by Houthis too.

I wasn't afraid of this dynamic though. As far as I could tell, the Houthis weren't out to get us, especially not me. They seemed to be acting rationally enough, and I trusted that—even though the official political situation might be in flux—the Houthis would behave as much like good hosts and good rulers as they could.

I hoped—at least for my clients—that my presence and my work might be the first step toward a return to normal operations. I could look at their facilities and make sure nothing had been broken into. I could write up a few reports and advise them when it might be safe for their staff to return, which was important not just for British American Tobacco or Transoceanic or any number of other companies but also for Yemen as a whole. By proving Yemen could be considered safe for Western workers, I felt like I could make a difference for average Yemenis too, because many Yemenis depended on Western aid for food, medicine, and other things. Yemen, then as now, was experiencing the world's worst humanitarian disaster: famine, disease, and war. I knew that much depended on a return to normalcy for Yemen's people.

Even commercial companies bring critical business for Yemen. The flow of dollars through normal commerce, rather than black markets and smuggling, means stability for the average person and engenders more widespread prosperity. Capitalism might have its faults, but without it the whole system collapses, and those people in the shadows, the already-starving people I noticed so keenly this time as I passed through the airport, quickly become skeletons, sacrificed to a world gone nuts.

I awoke on the morning after my arrival to begin a day just like a thousand others I'd spent in Yemen. One of my security guys, Abdulghani, was waiting outside the villa where I was staying. It was in the neighborhood of Bayt Bous, a ritzy enclave near Hadda on the south side of Sana'a, squeezed between the Presidential Palace and the jagged slag-heap mountains that rise in the west.

Abdulghani was a trusted employee. I'd hired and trained him myself through Universal Eagles. He still was moonlighting with me, earning a bit of extra money in his downtime from his day job as a Counterterrorism Unit (CTU) Yemeni Special Forces soldier. He was in his mid-twenties, twenty-four or twenty-five maybe, tall, strongly muscled, friendly, with all his family living in Sana'a. When I hired him for Universal, I'd known he was CTU already because it was on his application, but this didn't cause any alarm. Moonlighting had become common practice in Yemen since military pay came neither regularly nor in large enough quantities for soldiers to make a decent living. Also, since Abdulghani worked for the CTU, and since Yemen's CTU had been trained through the very program I'd helped reconstitute and run while our Special Forces weren't allowed in country, I knew he was professional and had no question about his loyalty. Loyalty was part of his training, and he had been going into battle against al-Qaeda, time after time, with American advisors right alongside him. If I couldn't trust him, whom could I trust? We were on the same side.

A few other escorts and armed guards accompanied us, regular guys. They changed from day to day. I remember the names of more than a few of these guards. One of them was Abdulghani's assistant, Mohammed Jaboh. Another was named Saif al-Abasi. And then there was Tamim. All three were Special Forces—or CTU-trained guys. Abdulghani was the tallest. Tamim clocked in at about my size, a little stockier; Saif was short like Tamim and me but skinnier. None of them spoke a word of English except "Yes, sir," and they only knew this because, when I trained them at Universal, we'd drill, and I'd be yelling and screaming at them along with other instructors before saying, in English, "Do you understand?" They'd have to say, "Yes, sir," loudly in English in reply.

Another thing about these guys, which goes back to the tribal nature of Yemen, is that they were all from the city of Taizz in the South. They'd been recruited into Universal on the recommendation of one of the commanders in the Special Forces, himself from Taizz, there to work for the chairman of Universal, Alwan al-Shaibani, also hailing from Taizz. This meant they were mostly Sunni and mostly lighter skinned, and they were held together not just by bonds of pay or unit esprit but by tribal and familial relationships. These guys were blood. And the blood system operated in, even permeated, all of Yemeni—and most Arab—society this way: you got your guards from your tribes and your city, you got your job through similar patronage, and in turn you were expected to become a patron and benefactor to those around you when and if the opportunity arose.

By Yemeni standards, the first day after my arrival went pretty normally, maybe even lulling me into a false sense of security.

At the BAT villa, I used the kitchen to serve up some food we had ordered and the guards had brought from outside our compound. I spent a couple hours working at a computer to type things up, then went over to the Universal Office for the rest of the morning before finally breaking for lunch.

Abdulghani and his team lounged outside the villa waiting for me, should I need to travel. In order to leave my villa, I had to have Abdulghani's guys with me: they dressed like spies or like characters from a Jason Bourne movie—black sunglasses, handguns concealed under nice suit coats, no long guns visible, earpieces if they could get them—and drove shiny, expensive Land Cruisers.

On the second or third day of this routine, we were stopped by some Houthi tribal militia at a checkpoint just a small distance from our villa, in the diplomatic and high-class neighborhood called Hadda. Three or four child soldiers manned this checkpoint, taking fistfuls of bribes and lifting and lowering the little pipe they'd set up between two barrels as a barrier. One older, more senior guy lounged on the side of the road, chewing qat in the shade. The youngsters harassed us in a very practiced and methodical way. They took us out of our Land Cruisers. They checked me over especially well and found out that I was packing a handgun.

I told them I had a license to carry a weapon.

They said, "Those licenses aren't lawful anymore. Not from the former government."

Things started to escalate.

They were going to take the gun, maybe even arrest me, but Abdulghani pulled the older guard aside and "negotiated" the gun back—without paying for it. We were allowed to go on our merry way. But I noticed that, most strangely, Abdulghani hadn't even bribed the guards with qat money. A bribe would have been the expected thing. It would have been the normal thing in Yemen. It's what I probably would have tried to do if the situation continued to get worse. But he didn't pay anything at all.

The following day two cars followed us home from a similar trip around town. Right before we reached my villa in Bayt Bous, they pulled us over. This was an actual police car, not just some trumped-up jalopy. Blue and red lights flashing, siren going off, just like a police stop in America.

I was thinking right away, *These must be friendlies*, because, first of all, my guards wouldn't stop if they were at all concerned that it could get ugly. They'd just keep going and dare the police, or the militia masquerading as police, to try to shoot us while we drove. Why stop and make yourself an easier target?

This reassured me. Friendlies just want to harass you and extort a few dollars. There are definite signs as to whether someone is friendly or not—and these signs applied both to Yemeni tribesmen in general and to the city's new Houthi overlords, who were, after all, not much more than country folk. First of all, if they're after you and just want to get you, they won't try to pull you over; they'll ambush and just start shooting or bombing. Second, the number of people in the truck or the car makes a big difference too. If the truck is stolen, there'll be twenty people in it, crunched in so that the whole back is just one mass of arms and legs. If a group with twenty people in their truck stops you, they'll likely take your vehicle to ease the pressure. It makes sense. And, in the context of Sana'a at that time, might definitely meant right.

Another thing that made me think these were friendlies was that they turned their lights on to pull us over pretty quickly. If these were another sort of "unfriendly"—say from one of the intelligence organizations or members of an al-Qaeda affiliate—then they'd case us for a while to assess whether they could take us or not. In that situation the follow would have lasted a lot longer; maybe they'd even scope us for a few days.

Real police would be quicker about things, and they'd just have a few men with them, say two in front, two in the backseat, maybe three standing in the back bed of the truck manning the heavier, fifty-caliber weapon if they had one. The two police vehicles involved in this incident weren't even little trucks with big machine guns. They were just sedans. How big of a threat could they pose?

All the signs pointed to a simple police stop.

Indeed, when the doors of the police car opened, uniformed policemen got out. They came up to see us. And they made us get out of our vehicles just like the Houthis had done at the checkpoint the day before. They searched us and took our weapons. But this time they began talking right away about how bad it was that they hadn't gotten their qat allotment, so I knew it was more a matter of extortion than anything. I knew they just wanted qat. I knew Abdulghani wouldn't have to use any special magic to get us away without a bribe: when the system works a certain way, you just pay the bribes and keep things within the range of normal behavior.

So I said, "I'm not paying extortion to you but here's a personal gratitude gift—chew qat today on me."

I slipped the leader of this police unit 5,000 Yemeni riyals, about $25, enough to buy nice qat for both cars of policemen. Prices for qat had fallen substantially since the Houthis took over. No one had money anymore, or what they had, they hoarded, so buying bags for 400 to 500 riyals rather than 1,000 riyals was more normal.

They gave me my gun back, but I knew more incidents like this would happen, likely every time I tried to move around town, because word was getting out that I was a mark.

The fifth day we didn't leave the villa because Saudi Arabia and its coalition started bombing the city. This was the beginning of the Operation Decisive Storm campaign.

I stayed in the villa pretty much the whole time for the next few days. The Saudi bombing began in Faj Attan, a neighborhood near us but also adjacent to a military depot built into the side of the cliff. We could see Saudi jets scream in from the roof of our villa. Antiaircraft fire everywhere made an entrancing but macabre show. Of course the Yemenis shot nothing down, because their antiaircraft systems were so old. But still it made a good show, even as the bombs walked closer and closer to me.

The same day that I holed up in my villa, I got a call from another American—I think the only other American who had come back to Sana'a. The guy's name was Scott Darden. He worked for Transoceanic, and he and I had been in touch over the phone and had met once in Dubai before we came into the country.

I answered the phone, and Scott said, "They're bombing the shit out of the area." At that time he was staying in the Transoceanic guesthouse and office in Hadda. He was nervous. I could hear it in his voice, not just in the expletives but in the way his throat seemed to be constricted, his words pitched a note or two higher than normal. "This is fucking scary. What should we do?"

"We're shit out of luck," I said, because I had just found out that the airport was closed, the runway bombed and potholed, so no flights could come or go. The United Nations was still there, watching, reporting, moderating where it could, trying to calm the two sides down. Just a handful of guys were working in the UN compound though, minimal manning. I was on the phone with them and coordinating through them, hoping they still had a way out.

Al'a, a Jordanian, was my main contact and the guy I was speaking to on the phone just then. I think there were also a few French guys. The rest were native Yemenis, holding down the fort. UN planes would be the only ones allowed to come in or out over the next couple days, taking big risks as they did, but somehow managing to get most of the remaining expats out. In fact, the Saudis issued a warning that any plane in the air, other than those UN planes, would be shot down.

I sent my bodyguards to go get Scott. He came to the BAT villa. The ride across town occurred right during a barrage of shelling, and his face was pale when he arrived. As soon as he got to my place, we received news that a shell had hit near his Transoceanic office and had blown all the glass in, shattering every window.

Scott was a big guy with reddish-blond hair, five foot nine or ten, a couple hundred pounds; he looked a bit like a friendly Grizzly Adams. He also had a good sense of humor, which would be useful over the coming months when we were held in cells adjacent to or near one another. Importantly, Scott had also converted to Islam about ten years earlier—Sunni, I think—and he had studied to make himself nearly fluent in Arabic. Scott's job required him to be in Yemen as the country manager for Transoceanic, at least when he could, but for the most part he lived in Dubai with his family, a situation very like my own.

I had entered Yemen ahead of Scott by two days on this trip. I'd advised Transoceanic that it wouldn't be wise for him to follow me. Even if Scott and I both spoke Arabic and were Muslim, I still had an advantage over him. I looked the part, so things were less risky for me. But Transoceanic stood firm in its insistence that it was essential for Scott to come, even though everyone else had pulled out.

The "fireworks" on Faj Attan continued from that point on. By the second day of the air campaign, the bombings had moved up right behind us on the mountain, so we could feel the earth shake as well as hear the explosions. The Saudis pummeled Faj Attan and Hadda nonstop over the next couple days, destroying everything. These were heavy bombs, and they were dropped with impunity. The planes would come in on a first pass, two planes together, and drop some bombs. The ground would shake. Then four or five minutes later, they'd circle back for another pass, dropping more bombs. Then they'd go home, only to return after a few hours for another flyover. It was like shooting fish in a barrel. All the Yemenis thought this was a very cowardly style of war, and the Saudis made these runs in a ruthlessly leisurely manner because they knew the Yemeni antiaircraft guns couldn't touch them.

Around this time, I got a phone call from one of my operations managers from Universal, who was in Jordan at that time. He wanted to check up on me, and he told me to be careful because he had heard the Saudis would be bombing a lot of Houthi posts, not just the big military bases.

I told him that I knew. I'd heard the same thing. And I was witnessing it. I told him we were taking precautions and hiding, and he emphasized over and over again that I should take care of myself. I knew that my phones were tapped, so this worried me. This sounded a lot like advance warning of attacks, like I was somehow "in the know," and I feared—rightly so—that it would raise some eyebrows among the people listening.

But before that came into play, word got out that we had money and were easy to shake down. The next visit we received involved a crew of Houthis coming to our villa.

We'd just sent Abdulghani out for food. Several of us were sitting upstairs in the *majlis* or *mafraj*, a room with big windows on the top story that is unique to Yemeni architecture, designed ages ago to perch on top of the ancient Yemeni mudbrick skyscrapers, some of which are seven and even ten stories tall, so that qat chewers can relax, enjoy the spectacle of the city below, and watch the daylight recede over the mountain faces.

That day it wasn't just sunset. It wasn't just qat. We smoked the shisha pipe, but we were mainly gathered together to watch the Saudi fireworks, our new pastime. It was Scott, me, a Kuwaiti-Yemeni guy named Ali, and Moataz, my Syrian friend who worked with me as an advance scout for British American Tobacco.*

We finished up in that room and came downstairs to the living room. Scott got out his computer and started working. I went into another room and did the same, sending off a report to my supervisors at British American Tobacco to tell them that all was okay.

A few minutes later I got a call on the intercom from the guards at the front door: "Mr. Sam, we have some officers here. They aren't in uniform. They want to come in and inspect the villa for contraband."

This, we had heard, had become a normal enough thing since the Houthis took over. At the expat offices and villas—manned now almost exclusively by skeleton crews of Yemeni local employees since

---

* Moataz would be bagged by the Houthis a few days after me and would spend seven months in captivity too.

nearly all the expats had left—cops and intelligence personnel would come periodically to check for contraband. In a lot of ways, it was just a more sophisticated checkpoint stop. They looked for alcohol, drugs, potentially pornographic CDs. They'd confiscate a few things, wait for the appropriate bribe to be shuffled under the table, and then leave. Up until that point both Transoceanic and BAT had been lucky or just too obscure to be targeted—even before Scott and I returned, our people reported that the villas had been neither visited nor searched. Maybe we were just due for our shakedown.

I didn't do anything in particular to get the place ready for them. Even if I wanted to, I didn't have time. By the time I said, "Yes, they can come in," they had come through the courtyard to the front door of the villa.

They had three vehicles outside blocking my gate: a Humvee previously donated by the United States to the CTU—Abdulghani's unit—and two Land Cruisers just like the ones we drove around in. A number of men secured the whole area, spreading out around the house. Five of these guys had US-patterned desert Marine camouflage as well as M4s. This told me they were actual CTU guys. Their tactics and full suite of commo gear confirmed it: this was an American-trained and, at least until recently, American-financed unit.

Whether wrong or right to trust them, I saw their gear and relaxed. Just like at the police stop the day before, inwardly I told myself, *Hey, these are the good guys.* I couldn't help it.

Three officers came into the villa itself. They wore slightly more traditional clothes. Rather than suits, they had on long *thobes* with *jambiya* knives in their belts. One wore a Western suit jacket over this. The other two did not. All three were still chewing qat from their evening session.

As soon as they walked in, they said, "We're NSB." I didn't know these guys personally. Their claim of being from the National Security Bureau, though sensical, wasn't ironclad. They could say whatever they wanted. I had no way to know.

Just as expected, they said, "We're here to check the villa for contraband."

I shrugged. "Okay, go right ahead. If you need anything, we'll walk you around."

But then one of the NSB guys must have given a sign, a nod, something we didn't see. Two of the CTU guys grabbed us and took our phones. I had wanted to walk away and make a call, let people outside Yemen, back at headquarters, know what was going on, but they grabbed me and prevented that.

They gave our phones to the officers, turned us around, and led us back through the entry foyer of the villa, past the pool table and couches, over to the dining table at the center of the big open downstairs room.

They sat Scott and me at the dining table facing each other. They took our computers and made us put our hands on the table. They told us to sit still. Every time we wanted to say something, they'd say, "Shut up," and the armed guy behind me would threaten to smack me. Most haunting for me personally, they referred to themselves as "Marines," not knowing that I was an actual Marine. "Just relax," they said, playing it cool. "We're only checking. Don't interfere."

We sat at that table a long time—easily more than an hour. I fumed a bit about the Marine thing. I was thinking, *Do you actually know what it means to be a Marine?* I couldn't say this aloud, because anytime Scott or I tried to talk, they'd jab us with their rifle butts, but I thought to myself about boot camp. *If you only knew the yellow footprints we all have to stand on that first day of Boot... If you'd only walked that path. It's the first thing you do, standing there on the footprints where you get your first good hazing by the drill instructors.*

Of course I couldn't help but dwell on the label of "Marine." And, from there, similar thoughts also crossed my mind. They flooded in, as Scott and I waited and as our minds were left to wander. For instance, Lebanese people are never on time. Ever since the Marines beat it into me that I needed to show up ten minutes early for events, I'm the first one to arrive at any Lebanese event or party by like forty-five minutes. I end up helping set up, helping cook, helping the hosts and the maids and the DJs arrange their gear. So I've had to relearn my Lebanese time management. I laughed about this, but I was also painfully aware that while the show-up-early Marine attitude could be a source of social awkwardness, the Muslim thing could be, and would now almost certainly play out as, a similar strange cultural cross-pollination.

Time passed really slowly at that table.

I wasn't nervous. I was still laughing, in a very dark and quasi-confident way, inside myself. This was just another Yemeni thing. This was just another attempt at extortion. This was just part of the price of being there, of helping get the country restarted. I'd have to deal with this and withstand it and carry on. I'd have to show up early, in good Marine fashion, and then be smooth and stay late, as my Lebanese blood allowed me to do. I'd have to pray a little bit and disguise myself.

The time passed slowly though.

The officers went through every room, upstairs, downstairs, the basement. All of a sudden, we saw them start to bag everything. Grabbing things, putting things in garbage bags, not tagging or separating, just taking it all. No labels on anything. They took computers. They took my gun, a Taurus 9mm. There was a safe in the general manager's office, shoulder high. They said, "Open the safe."

"I don't know the combo," I said, my first lie.

The safe held emergency cash, and I think there was a lot of alcohol in it too, because the whole top of the half wall between the pool table and kitchen was stacked with twenty or twenty-five Johnny Walker Black Label boxes of six bottles each. But there weren't any bottles.

So I added, "There's no alcohol in the villa. Management probably put it all in the safe before they fled."

They nodded. This made sense. I decided to push my luck a bit and asked them to give me my phone so I could call the general manager and get the combo.

They said, "No, you're not talking to anyone." Instead, they brought in a dolly, hoisted the safe onto it, and carted it out. They took the whole damn thing.

They also got my advance pay allowance from Universal, $5,000 in cash, US money, which I'd left in my briefcase at my bedside. I had other Yemeni money squirreled away too. They took it all. Then they took my watch, my ring, my wallet.

"What the hell is going on here?" I said.

"Don't worry. You're going to get everything back," they said.

But I started to get angry. "You went through my stuff, and I want to know what's going on!"

The officers were trying to act nice. "We've just been ordered to check everything."

Everything was taken, even the computer for the security monitors and the internet router. They ripped that stuff right out of the walls of the villa.

I was getting more and more uncertain now. I wanted to believe them. I wanted to believe their good-guy act. But everything was starting to point in a much more dangerous direction. Part of me wanted to fight. The other part wanted to play it cool, just in case this could all be cleared up in a few hours, after I made a few calls, talked to the right people.

They were acting the part of the good guy because they didn't want us to get violent. But the act had slowly started to fall apart.

"Get up," they said. "Walk outside with us."

"What's going on outside?"

"Need you to help us look around the perimeter."

"Okay."

I got up. I really didn't have much choice.

They told Scott to get up.

"Why's he got to get up?" I asked. "It's my villa, my company's villa. He's just a guest."

"Nope," they said, "we need him to look around with us too."

When we walked out the front door, one of the 4 × 4 Land Cruisers had pulled into the driveway inside the compound. As soon as we started down the steps, the guard pushed me toward the vehicle.

"What's going on?" I said.

"Put your hands up."

They brought out heavy-duty metal handcuffs, not chain cuffs but the kind with a solid metal bar connecting either side. I started to get violent then. I started thrashing as they pushed me from behind with their rifles, crosswise, right across my upper shoulders to knock me forward.

I resisted, but two people took my hands. One of the CTU guys came and clamped on those cuffs. I resisted moving forward. Another guy came up from behind and bagged me over my head. I didn't see it coming, but suddenly I was in the dark, and they were cinching the cord of the bag around my neck, not too tight but dark, suffocatingly dark.

Oh shit, this ain't good at all! I thought, as all those videos of ISIS executions played through my head at once.

They pushed me to the door of the Land Cruiser and shoved me in. One person was in the backseat already. Another grabbed me from the front seat, and together they pulled me in, a very professional and practiced bit of teamwork. Scott was put in another 4 x 4. He went through the exact same process, cuffed and bagged and shoved forward at gunpoint. I was wearing a shirt, black jacket, and dockers. I thought about those clothes and how long I might now be forced to wear them as the ride began.

CHAPTER 11

CELL ONE

AFTER THEY HAD the shackles on me, after they'd bagged me
from behind and shoved me into the Land Cruiser, I didn't see
Scott for the next 120 days. I didn't see another American for all that
time. And I didn't see the sun or spend any time outdoors for the first
120 days.

As soon as my captors started driving, I put my mind into gear,
into one of the modes I had learned during various training scenarios
that had been designed and rehearsed and beat into our heads for
exactly this situation. You never think, during such training, that it'll
actually be you wearing the almost-stereotypical noose-like bag over
your head. It's always someone else, a vicarious experience, and the
lessons they learned in surviving their captivity (or not surviving it)
always seem to have some distance from you personally, some sort of
otherworldly dislocation from the matters of day-to-day life that pre-
occupy us in normal times. Our training had been case studies,

PowerPoint presentations, classroom exercises, and then practical exercises—getting followed, evading and escaping, enduring beatings and interrogations, learning ways to stay true to ourselves and our country even during the worst of times. All of that rehearsal and study replayed itself in my head, even as the most immediate part of my mind still said, over and over, *This isn't actually happening to me. I'm just a guy doing my job, a guy with kids and a home, a guy minding my own business.*

As the irony of thinking about a hostage situation while also being in a hostage situation wrapped itself around me, the active part of my mind did the things I had trained it to do. I knew the area around my villa very well. I had wandered and driven around that suburb of Hadda many times, in many situations. I started counting the minutes on straightaways, the time of travel, the turns and corners along the streets and alleyways we followed. These twists and turns were difficult for a while, but they led through my own neighborhood, and I knew pretty well that once we left the neighborhood itself, we would have little choice but to merge onto the oddly named "50 Meter Road," so called because of its width. It formed a belt around and through Hadda and so was almost unavoidable. Despite some disorientation, I felt the Land Cruiser approach it, speed up onto it, and turn to the right, the north. I guessed at our velocity and counted the seconds, expecting a speedbump in the road about five or six hundred meters farther on. We struck that with a gratifying jolt. Then we came to a roundabout I knew, then another roundabout. I was tracking. I hadn't lost hope of knowing my whereabouts.

Northbound we continued on 50 Meter Road, and even as I concentrated on my location, I kept up a steady stream of protests and questions with my captors: "Where the hell are you taking me?" "What the devil is going on?"

I was trying to create chaos. But my abductors didn't let themselves get ruffled. They just said, "Ukhras! La tatukullum"—*shut the hell up.*

"Ishfi," I'd say—*what's going on.*

"L-wain, makhidthni?"—*where are you taking me?*

I kept this up for a minute or two, but they quickly grew tired of hearing from me. Without much overt anger—really, more professionally than I ever would have expected—they started stripping my jacket off, my shirt, and then most of my other clothes as well: belt, pants, socks, shoes. I was left wearing only a T-shirt and underwear. This was done as a punishment for talking, but also as a way to further cow me and, I later figured, also to strip me of any tracking devices. I tried to fight it, but when they got out their knives and started cutting the fabric and tearing it with their hands, I thought better of resisting or even moving too much. They did not hit me. They were getting their way, even though I was struggling, and their professionalism was both somewhat reassuring—as I thought, maybe, just maybe, I was dealing with people who could be reasoned with—and also somewhat chilling. Trained killers. Definitely obeying orders and doing so in a way much more like a butcher practicing his trade than a bunch of kids up to hijinks. For my part, I decided that I must walk a fine line between provoking them and continuing to register some sort of resistance. This meant a lot of screaming back and forth but no further escalation.

They were in control. They knew it. My resistance wasn't so much an attempt to change that fact, in the moment, but to set the stage for later situations—thinking I might get a chance to settle scores or speak to a supervisor and lodge a complaint.

That was, of course, wishful thinking. But it was in my mind. All of this could still be a mix up. It could still be a friend playing a practical joke—though a bad one. It could be over in an hour or two once I provided explanations and proof of my innocence for whatever crime they imagined I had committed. I resisted their stripping away of my clothes as a means of posturing for later, holding out hope that I might, indeed, regain the position of moral and physical authority I once had, back when I likely trained these personnel or their bosses and instructors, back when I had been the one initiating the programs that produced the sort of professional maneuvering and dispassion they now used against me.

When we reached the third roundabout northward along 50 Meter Road, we circled it three or four times. I knew we were at Khawlan Street, but I no longer could be sure which way we faced, which exit we might take.

To make matters worse, they stopped the vehicle and pulled me out, right there in the middle of the circle, in the middle of the night, in my T-shirt and underwear, still with the bag over my head and handcuffs on my wrists. Probably no one was there, but I couldn't get a grip well enough in my disorientation to listen for other voices. I yelled out, but my calls focused on my captors still rather than calling for help. I knew no stranger would try to assist me. That isn't the Yemeni way—or the smart way when dealing with armed professionals.

My yelling did have one definite effect: they started to beat me.

I fought them, trying to break away. But they held me, grabbing me by the back of my T-shirt. The buttstock of a weapon hit me in the high back. A couple more blows followed, one to the lower back, forcing me to get into a different truck, an American Humvee. I knew what it was in an instant. Anyone who has served in the US military over the last thirty years knows a Humvee in a heartbeat: that GMC engine, that gritty industrial paint, the odd shape of the interior. I almost laughed aloud at the incongruity of my having trained these guys—if indeed they were members of Yemen's US-supported Counterterrorism Unit (CTU), as I thought—coupled with the fact, the reinforcing fact, that now I was being transported in a Humvee donated to the CTU by the United States in order to encourage the unit to fight al-Qaeda. Ahhh, the best laid plans of mice and men!

I found that funny. But I also found it reassuring. Part of me had expected a swift end when I had been tossed out of the first Land Cruiser into the middle of the Khawlan roundabout. Part of me had expected to be made to kneel, there in the dirt, in the gutter. Part of me still imagined the feeling of the cold earth, the sounds I would have heard in my bound blindness, as one of them—whoever had been chosen as my executioner—approached and cocked the trigger of his handgun. So being tossed into another vehicle resulted in a big sigh of relief, with a stifled chuckle at the familiarity of the Humvee around me.

Also, definitely and undoubtedly, with my heartbeat racing, I lost all track of which direction we had taken. I found myself fully at their mercy. In just a matter of minutes I'd gone from in control, the occupant of a relatively opulent villa, to a creature wholly disoriented and reduced to weakness and insubstantiality.

Two of the CTU members occupied the backseats of the Humvee on either side of me, while I sat, hunched over, in the raised and cramped center space between them. One of the officers from the National Security Bureau (NSB) occupied the front passenger seat. A fourth person, probably also a CTU soldier, had been behind the wheel the whole time, evidenced by the fact that he started the vehicle moving as soon as the NSB officer settled himself.

Even though it may have been dumb, I still yelled and screamed at them. I still struggled between the two soldiers in the backseat on either side of me. The officer in the front had had enough after a minute or two of this.

He turned and said, "Ukhras, ya kelb!"—*shut your mouth, dog.*

Then he grabbed my face, placing his whole hand over my eyes, mouth, and nose, with the mask there as both a cover and a gag. I could not bite him. But as he shook my head, he both suffocated me and made a terrible sense of claustrophobia descend around me, a further loss of control that struck right down to the basal functions of inhaling and exhaling, of seeing and smelling, and of controlling my own head.

My hands, shackled behind me, kept me stuck in one position, and they began to lose feeling. My shoeless feet felt the cold of the Sana'a night as well as the heat from the Humvee's driveshaft, which rumbled away, oily, industrial, and gruff, just beneath me.

We drove on for ten or twelve more minutes. I started counting my breaths as a way to measure time. It seemed like forever, and I lost count once or twice, having to later re-create the counts and the moments I lost count, having to replay the whole experience (I had time enough to do so over and over again those next 120 days), so that I could better estimate where I had been taken: Was I still in Sana'a? Had they spirited me out of the city and into a nearby village? Had they just circled and brought me back to CTU headquarters, not so far from Hadda? Had more time slipped by than I could recall? Where was I?

Eventually we stopped, and they dragged me out again, walking me across uneven ground. That wasn't much of a clue. All of Yemen, whether a city street or a barnyard, felt much the same way. Rocks, dirt, and garbage brushed against my shoeless toes. It felt like an open area, but they took me quickly into a structure, a fairly substantial structure made of echoing concrete and tile. I was upright, walking between the two men who had been sitting beside me in the back of the Humvee. Each of them held one of my arms. My hands remained shackled. I assumed Scott was there with me, but I didn't hear him or see him, though I was listening.

Immediately on entering the building, they threw me into a room with a few other people inside. None of the others spoke, but I could hear them, their subtle movements. I guessed three or four in total. My captors set me down on the floor and didn't say anything to me. I still wore only underwear, T-shirt, bag, and shackles—nothing else.

In a nearby room the CTU guards started to inventory the stuff they had confiscated from my villa, calling the name of each item out loudly so that their voices drowned out anything else that might have been happening: "Wallet. Four credit cards. Military ID. American driver's license. Passport."

They opened my briefcase and continued to inventory its contents: "Pens, computer, battery. Chargers. Phones. Three phones."

They chatted about the phones for a few minutes. It might have looked suspicious, but I wasn't worried. Two of the phones had Yemeni numbers, and I knew the NSB likely had already monitored them. The third was the phone I used in America, just to call family.

They took some money from the suitcase too, about 75,000 Yemeni riyals. That equated to about $350 in US money. The two men called this out and probably marked it down too: professionals.

Then, all of a sudden, they said, "That's it."

I knew they had the safe, the computers, even the house closed-circuit TV systems somewhere. They didn't bother inventorying those things.

Worse, the sum of money they attributed the briefcase was way, way off.

From the little room where I sat, half naked and still bagged and bound, I yelled out, "No, there's more money in the wallet. Eight or nine hundred dollars of American money. And another wallet has other foreign currency. Also in the briefcase there is five thousand dollars I just picked up as salary from Universal."

This money was gone. I knew it. But I couldn't help myself from protesting it. They'd gotten their hands on it, either these two or their bosses, and they'd just made it disappear. The briefcase had been down in my bedroom in the basement of the villa, and I'd already argued about that because when they brought it up, it had been opened and emptied. I tried to make them inventory it back then, in the villa, and I tried again now, but they pretended they hadn't found anything in the briefcase other than pens and phones and pads of paper. It was bullshit.

They'd found and inventoried my gun earlier at the villa, then denied knowing about it. I brought the gun up again, with the money, and wondered whether I was doing a good thing forcing the issue or making things worse for myself—with the gun and the cell phones and the wads of cash perhaps all adding up to paint me in a bad light, even though those were pretty normal things for a contractor to have.

I'd worked up some courage because of the inventory. It might indicate that they'd merely meant to conduct an inspection and had turned it, by mistake or out of enthusiasm, into a shakedown. I knew it had gotten more serious, but I was clinging to any reason for hope I could find. Perhaps they were preparing to release me. Perhaps they just wanted to ask me a few questions and then give me most, if not all, of my stuff back. I tried to imagine myself walking out of that building later in the evening, wearing my shoes again, wearing my pants, with my gun holstered and my briefcase (albeit a little lighter) under my arm.

One of the other men in the little room with me got up then and took fewer than two steps before stopping. Without saying a word, he fumbled with his clothes a bit, and then I heard a stream of urine hit a metal surface, a small toilet or pan. Calmly, again wordlessly, the man redid his clothing and came back to sit on the floor only a few feet away from me. I knew, then, that I was in a jail cell; I heard the sounds of the guards through the doors, the grates, and the grills of our detention. The men around me remained silent out of caution and unfamiliarity. The sound of our cell door, when it opened a moment later, took on a whole new, ominous undertone, as I could now hear its solid, impregnable construction: steel, concrete, tile underfoot, more concrete, and only the wheezing draft of a few small ventilation holes.

The door opened.

The CTU guards took me by the arms again, lifting me and dragging me down the hallway to another small room.

They sat me on the floor and stood over me.

"Sign this," they said, shoving a paper and pen on my lap and unfastening my cuffs.

I flexed my wrists, letting blood flow again, but said, "I'm not signing anything."

The hood remained cinched over my head. I couldn't see what they'd written, and even if it was an accurate and professional account of what they had listed, they'd definitely left off most of the money, the gun, probably other things too.

"I'm not signing until I see the whole inventory," I said again. "I'm not signing until you bring me my money and I see all my money and see everything that was taken from me. Until then I ain't signing a damn thing."

The guys who were doing the inventory left then, and the three NSB officers replaced them after only a minute.

"Well, you are here now," the first one said.

"There's nobody asking about you," the second added.

The third, coming closer to me, said, "The American Embassy is gone. All your friends in high places took off like dogs, like cowards, and you're all alone, and you belong to us. You can make it easy on yourself or hard. We can be here for one day, one week, a month, a year, ten years, or we can just finish you off and nobody will know about it."

"I don't understand why I'm here. I don't know what I did wrong. What did I do that I'm here?"

"Mr. Sam, you know exactly why you're here. You know why you're here. We know why you're here. If you want to make it easy on yourself, just cooperate, and we'll let you go. If you don't play ball, then we're not going to be very nice to you."

"What is it that you're talking about? I came here to clear my people out from British American Tobacco, to do a security assessment in order to better shut down their work, and to get my stuff. To clear my stuff. My loose ends. And to leave. I have no business here other than that."

I mean, I was there to do a security assessment, but only for BAT. They knew that. I didn't need to hide it. Perhaps they'd gotten their wires crossed. Perhaps they thought it was something it wasn't.

"Mr. Sam, we know exactly what you're doing here. We've been following you for the past week since you've been back, and you've been going around and getting locations for the coalition to strike."

"You've got to be kidding me!" I said "You think the Saudis are waiting on me to give them locations where to hit? You think the Emiratis are taking orders from me?"

One of the guys said, "Let me tell you something, Mr. Sam, I know you. I've been holding your file since you've been back as a civilian. But I've known you for fourteen years since you first came as a defense attaché, and I know what you have done, and what you've been doing, and by the way I want to thank you, because no one has done for Yemen what you have done."

This he said with a silky tone in his voice. It was an obvious transition into the old "good cop / bad cop" routine—except that with three of them in the room, they took on good-cop, bad-cop, and whisperer-of-questions roles. The third guy rarely spoke to me, but I think he was in charge. The other two took turns being brutal and pretending to offer me olive branches.

The good cop continued with his schtick. "I know you've been here for many years and have done things for us. I know you were part of creating NSB. And I know you helped bring a lot of military aid to the country. I know everything about you. All of your file. I have all of it since you've come back. I've been the one keeping an eye on you."

"Alright then, you already know," I said. "You know I'm clean. And I'm an ally. Why are you doing this?"

"I know ninety-five percent," he said. "It's that five percent that you're keeping, you're hiding from us."

"If you already know all of this, then what is that five percent that you're talking about?"

"You know exactly what I'm talking about. Just confess and say it, and we'll call it a night and see what we can do for you."

I didn't say anything. I couldn't.

Their theory, that I was somehow helping the Saudi coalition pick out targets for bombing, had no truth to it whatsoever. What was I supposed to say?

As I sat there, not really looking at them because of the hood, but listening and trying to control my breathing, the bad cop started in again, not by saying anything but by throwing something at me. I don't know what. It whizzed past me. He worked himself into a mild frenzy and began screaming and yelling in my ear. Then, without warning, since I couldn't see him, he struck me with both hands flat over my ears, causing my eardrums to pop and a crazy disorienting dizziness to set in. He did this twice. Two strikes to the head, equal blows simultaneously to each ear so that the pressure of the blows had nowhere to go except into the eardrum. My head felt like it was about to explode. I slumped sideways from my seated position to the ground.

I laid that way for a minute, maybe two, before the good cop started speaking again.

This went back and forth, back and forth. The same question or questions, over and over, phrased differently, approached from different angles. But always: I know what you've been doing. I know, you know, just tell us, you know I know. Over and over for perhaps an hour and a half. Every ten or fifteen minutes, when the good cop grew tired or didn't like my responses, the bad cop would start in again, yelling, screaming, throwing things, punching me in the chest once, smacking me on the ears again, until they thought I might have softened.

"You're doing this to yourself," the good cop said. "We're not responsible for any of this. Get it right, cooperate, and you never know, we could release you tomorrow."

The beating and interrogation didn't go much further than that, not during that first session. The bad cop's last two blows knocked me out completely.

Next thing I knew, I was still handcuffed and bagged, but two guys picked me up and dragged me. I wasn't sure if they were the same two CTU soldiers. I wasn't sure if they were taking me back to the same room. I wasn't sure if I had just passed out or been dragged out to a car and carted around the city again. I just didn't know, not in that delirium.

Barely conscious, I heard them open a cell door. I heard the metal screech as they unlocked it.

They threw me inside and said, "Put him to sleep."

Onto my body they tossed some fabric, which I'd later discover to be a set of strange Bermuda shorts and a shirt. One of the guards said, "That's for him to get dressed."

They took the bag off my head then.

I still couldn't see where I was. I was 90 percent out of it. Bleary-eyed. Hardly conscious. Everything I knew, I sensed through gut instinct, almost like premonition. I did not have mastery over, or memory of, sight, sound, or smell. I didn't know what the hell was going on.

CHAPTER 12

CELL MATES

I WOKE TO the rumbling of a cart across tile floors.

I did not know the sound. I did not recognize it.

I had that feeling of having been asleep forever, which sometimes can be pleasant and luxurious but other times terrifying. This time it started pleasantly enough, but even as I stretched, I felt soreness everywhere—from lying on a hard floor, from my bruises, and from the cold of that cell.

I shivered.

The cart approached. Clankity-clank, down the hall, nearer, stopping, starting again. The scrape and tumbler clamor of guarded little windows opening, of pots being lifted somewhat carelessly and shamelessly and handed inward to the waiting grasp of hungry prisoners. The cart stopped four times. Four times I heard the unmistakable sound of metal windows opening and shutting. Four times the cart started moving again before reaching our cell.

I saw a man rise from the floor beside me and go to the opening in our door. The steel window was drawn back from the outside. Through it my cell mate received a pot, a single moderate-sized bowl. The steel hatch slammed shut again after him. Through the blinking darkness he approached the center of the room, where I lay on my side, and he squatted in front of me.

Two other prisoners rose from the floor and joined him. All of them circled around my prostrate form.

One of the men shook me to wake me. They didn't yet know my name.

"Friend," he said, "breakfast has come."

One of the others added, "We have a tradition that the new person must eat first, when it is his first meal."

These men were hungry, but by the rules of their own prison etiquette, they were being immensely polite. The new member was required to break bread with them. Only problem for me, I couldn't get up. I was too sore, too broken.

"I will eat," I said, not wanting to lose this first possibility of obtaining an ally. I knew they hadn't actually decided if they liked me; they were just obeying their code.

No utensils had come with the food. None ever would. Nothing to scrape the slick concrete walls with. Nothing to hone into a weapon. Even fingernail clippers, when needed, were handed in for no more than five minutes, then promptly returned and inspected to make sure all the blades and metal parts came back. The only items they allowed in our cell were the clothes we wore, our sponge-like sleeping mats, a single pair of slippers to share when using the open-pit, Eastern-style toilet, a blanket each, a prayer rug, and a single copy of the Quran for use in our prayers.

I motioned to the bowl with one finger.

"I can't reach it," I said. "Will you feed me?"

My stomach felt queasy. I could taste bile in my mouth. But when one of them scooped three fingers together and used them to ladle into my mouth a bit of *ful mudummis*, the traditional Arab breakfast, I accepted it, chewed it, and swallowed it. Then I motioned for them to finish the rest of the bowl, which they eagerly undertook in only a few moments. I weighed about 190 pounds then, carrying a little extra on my frame ever since I officially retired from the Marines. So I could afford to skip a meal. With the beans came several hard little loaves of army bread, called *qudum*, little round things like scones but drier and plainer. The bowl of beans came in, plus the bread, three or four per person, about a cup of beans for each if shared equally. The food was warm, but not hot, not after making its way down that long hallway on the cart.

As I looked about me, my eyes adjusting to the unlit room, I found that these cell mates had dressed me in the Bermuda shorts and shirt and covered me, as best they could, with a blanket. The shorts and shirt were probably taken from the villa; they were not my clothes but looked like they belonged to a guy who was a manager from British American Tobacco. Fortunately the clothes fit, at least when I first wore them.

The bed that I slept on was a one-inch-thick sponge mattress, two meters by ninety centimeters in its other dimensions. Each of us had the exact same mattress, thrown down on the concrete/tile floor, the exact same blanket. This, fortunately, during the cold nights was thick enough, not unlike one you might buy in any market, a throw with a pattern of regular but unattractive design, probably the cheapest thing they could find. The walls, the tiled floor, and the bare ceiling were all white, giving the place a feeling like a pharmacy or a madhouse. We slept two mats down each side, which is how I know the width of the cell was 180 centimeters: adjacent mattresses fit perfectly next to each other. The length of the cell was five meters exactly, also measured by the fit of our mattresses longways. The room slept four people, with a semiprivate bathroom in the corner, about one meter by one meter, shielded by a half wall about one meter high. The ceiling was pretty high, about ten feet up. One light above the door, tucked into a crevice that we couldn't access (for fear, again, that we'd somehow make weapons), shed some meager illumination. No lights were in the ceiling, no wiring anywhere. Two ventilation cells, or holes, one above the door (which had that light in it) and then one that was just a hole in the wall, three or four inches in diameter through the outside-facing wall's thick ten- or twelve-inch casing, without cover or anything to keep the elements out, high above us. In case anyone misbehaved, the guards could turn the light out from the outside. We could not see out the ventilation holes or the food hatch. My cell mates used to climb on each other's backs sometimes to try to see, but the ventilation hole was like a deep well into the concrete, right up against the ceiling, so even trying to look through it, you could barely see anything below or to the left or the right. The light we did get was orangish and dim, not the harsh light of single-bulb interrogation rooms like you see in the movies.

There was no way to dig through the concrete, not even starting with the ventilation hole, since our guards so carefully kept all utensils from us. We only had our fingernails, and those were useless on concrete.

By counting the stops of the food cart and the clanking of the opening and shutting food windows, I guessed a total of twelve to fourteen such cells lined our hallway. The cell next to mine, to the right when facing the cell door, served as the inventory room. Every time our captors checked a person in or out of the prison, they'd put his stuff in there and repeat the routine of calling out and documenting the list of that poor soul's possessions.

This prison—which wasn't just some remodeled house or store or government building, not with all these purpose-built, methodical, well-thought-out features, like the food windows and the way the ventilation and light shafts were situated so as not to allow us to exploit them, not to mention that thick, reinforced concrete—I later learned was built and paid for by the US government for the Yemenis to confine al-Qaeda operatives captured on the battlefield in Yemen. I also found out later that this prison was indeed located, as I had suspected, on the same base where our Special Forces trained the Yemeni Counterterrorism Unit (CTU). Not only had we funded the construction of this prison, but we—the US government—had planned, funded, and developed the whole base, as well as leading and funding most of the important elements of training conducted there.

Imagine the irony: I had been kidnapped by members of the Yemeni National Security Bureau (NSB), which I helped create, being present even at that first formative meeting between Francis Townsend, then the national security advisor to President George W. Bush, and President Ali Abdullah Saleh. I was then escorted and beat up by team members of the Yemeni CTU for whom I'd conducted liaison duties to establish their first official training preparatory to combatting al-Qaeda, during that critical time when our US Special Forces had yet to rebuild their presence in Yemen post-Saddam. I was then loaded into an American-gifted Humvee and taken to an

American-built jail on an American-funded base built to combat al-Qaeda. To top it all off, as I was soon to find out, at least one of my cell mates was an al-Qaeda member.

I sat with these three guys while they ate, even though I remained half-dazed. I didn't have much choice, the room being small, with nowhere to go and me in no shape to leave or to move even if I could have. Yet I remained in their circle, close to the pot of beans. I did this as a courtesy but also because I needed to know who these guys were and whether I could trust them.

Once the three of them had finished off the food, they started in with questions. But I waved a hand, pointing at my face, my head. I shook my head a little and croaked out half a word, meaning to tell them I couldn't talk. Not well enough. Not quite yet.

They understood.

That was a good thing about the people you shared a cell with. Al-Qaeda or not, whether we shared the same creed, the same background, or not, we all faced the same difficulties and tended to unite against our tormentors.

They gave me space to say nothing, which was critical because I needed to learn about them.

The first one to speak sat cross-legged next to me in the semidarkness. He introduced himself as Ahmed. I believe that was actually his name, not just a nom de guerre. I don't remember his last name. He was something of a normal guy and had been there for about six months, since even before the Houthi takeover. He had been captured by elements of President Hadi's interim government for counterfeiting personal stamps of government officials—governors, notaries, ministers—and using them to forge government papers. That made him more of a white-collar criminal. He hailed from

Sana'a and was perhaps about twenty-seven or twenty-eight years old, married with two kids. He didn't linger there as my cell mate for long, maybe only for the first two weeks, before they moved him out of the prison. I never found out whether he was released or taken to a regular jail.

When the first man stopped speaking, the second began. He called himself Omar and was younger, perhaps only nineteen years old. He had leaned his slim body back, legs outstretched on his thin foam sleeping mat, so that his back rested against the concrete wall. That's how we sat most of the time, back against the proverbial wall, each of us taking up our own space or perhaps using one of the corners to sit at a different angle. The room's small size meant that we didn't need to speak up. Even whispering we could hear each other.

Omar was a nice kid from a Houthi family that claimed descent from the Prophet, making him one of that special class of people called *Sayed*. However, in true rebellious teenage spirit, Omar didn't like his Houthi roots, so he had started several years earlier researching what he called the "true religion" or "true path"—the *at-tariq as-sahh*. Through that research, he openly proclaimed that he had come to know and follow al-Qaeda—a bold and dangerous statement to make there, in a prison where we assumed we were being held by Houthis or by parts of the government that sympathized with the Houthis.

Omar told us about how he had left his home in the Houthi "capital" of Saadah and journeyed down to the al-Qaeda stronghold of Abyan, spending two months there being treated very well and receiving honors from the townsfolk and the al-Qaeda leaders, basically being brainwashed, spending money, and eating good food.

They had decided to give him a role as a medic, though immediately I found myself wondering why al-Qaeda wouldn't have used him as propaganda: what a story—a Houthi Sayed son deciding to leave his tribe's cause and join al-Qaeda! After those first two months of indoctrination, he did a month of paramilitary training—very tough he said: military-style shooting, drilling, working on tactics. At one time later he even diagrammed some of those tactics in the air, explaining with broad hand motions how he had been trained to go after various targets, mostly telling me about regular al-Qaeda methods like coming in and shooting up a place or throwing a bomb, then sending a second wave to get the gathering innocent onlookers or the emergency vehicles.

He did all this and then, after three months, was sent back to his family in Saadah, back to the Houthi center of power. All along he had lied to his family, telling them that he was working in Sana'a. But somehow his father caught wind of Omar's untruths and began trying to talk sense into the boy. The father proved at least mildly successful. When Omar came back to Sana'a to meet with his al-Qaeda contacts, he was no longer so sure of himself. He didn't want to disobey his father, but he was still convinced that al-Qaeda was the correct path, so he found himself in a personal struggle.

That struggle hadn't stopped for him. Even in the cell he remained convinced that al-Qaeda was in the right. He even told me, in the cell, that once I got out, I should research it and know for myself. Unlike Ahmed, who was moved out of the cell pretty quickly, Omar spent about two months in the same cell as me, and he tried on several occasions during those months to convince me. Also, interestingly, one reason Omar not only stayed committed to al-Qaeda but became even more committed to its doctrine was the torture and treatment he received while in jail. Every beating by the NSB or the CTU, which were now working for the Houthis, just reinforced his belief and alienated him further from his father's righteous admonitions.

Omar had arrived in the CTU prison shortly before me but had spent the previous four months of the Houthi invasion of Sana'a under house arrest, held in the basement of 1st Armor Division and Salafi-aligned Ali Muhsin al-Ahmar's compound in Hadda, which the Houthis had turned into a makeshift jail after they forced Ali Muhsin out and started to use his huge compound as a headquarters.

Just like Ahmed and Omar, the third of my cell mates had the almost skeletal body type of most Yemeni men—at least of those not rich enough to gorge themselves on *bint as-sahin* and Western-style food. This third man introduced himself as Haitham, which made me almost chuckle through my bruised delirium, as Haitham is my given name. Everyone just calls me Sam since the *th* sound is often pronounced as an *s* in dialect.

Even there, in the prison, people knew me as Mr. Sam. My cell mates only found out my name midway through my incarceration when a guard came looking, confusedly, for "Haitham Farran."

"Who is Haitham Farran?" he asked. And I had to raise my hand and admit it was my name.

Of these first cell mates, the only last name I remember is Haitham's: Zaytari.

Haitham had been there the longest and had the most stories, so I kind of befriended him more. He was ever so slightly older than the others, somewhere around twenty-four or twenty-five years of age. So that made me the old man, by far. In fact, out of all the prisoners in the compound, I think I was easily the oldest. They even used to call me that, Old Man, when not calling me Mr. Sam.

Haitham had been there for one and a half, maybe almost two years by the time I joined him in that cell. Like Omar he had signed up to become an al-Qaeda medic. Unlike Omar, he had followed through. He was real al-Qaeda. When he joined, he had already begun training as a medical student in Sana'a. He too then claimed to have found "the right path." He lived on Hayl Street near the old Sana'a University, a pretty good demonstration of how al-Qaeda recruited from and maintained personnel everywhere, even among those who would be less likely to lead ambushes and more likely to help tend the sick and wounded.

Overall, I think I got lucky, with two al-Qaeda medics.

The hardcore al-Qaeda guys, including one whom the United States had designated a high-value target, occupied the cell next above us—more about them in a while.

Haitham had been captured by the CTU and then put on trial. But he never got a chance to appear in court or defend himself (not that I agreed he should have been afforded such a chance). Instead he received an in absentia judgment rewarding him with eight years in prison for being an al-Qaeda member.

Of course later we all asked him about those two years, trying to understand what might be in store for us. That ended up being one of our most discussed topics. And Haitham always seemed to have a story ready. When he described the conditions before the Houthis took over running the jail, we were surprised to find out it was much worse—horrible solitary confinement of only one person in each cell, never leaving, shitting in the corner bowl, showering there, eating, sleeping, meditating, having no family contact, no phone calls, not even speaking to anyone or even to themselves. *God help whoever broke the rules.* The Houthis were forced to put more people in each cell because of all the arrests they were making. But still, I found it a little hard to believe—even in the face of testimony from one who had lived through it and didn't have much reason to lie—that a base with so much US involvement, and a prison funded with US money, wouldn't adhere more closely to Western standards.

Maybe that was the goal. Maybe by making a jail in Yemen, we'd sneakily set up a system that wasn't accountable to US morality. But, if so, it disgusted me. One reason I love America and have fought for it for so long is that we are usually better than that. I certainly didn't try to defend America—not to that audience—but that fact lodged itself in my mind, much like the debacles of Abu Ghraib or of water boarding at Guantánamo. Somewhere our government had set aside the torch of liberty that we had carried so long and so well. I hoped it was only temporary and that abuses like these, on the margins of what is fair and right and legal, would no longer be supportable for our culture, even if we were only turning a blind eye, rather than actively pushing doctrines and practices antithetical to Lady Liberty. (This also brings to mind a particular irony I noted in the cell I occupied in Yemen: waiting for food to arrive each day, I couldn't help but read a sticker plastered on the back of the cell door that explained all of our rights as prisoners, in both Arabic and English. How weird to have the Houthis give a nod toward righteousness in that way!)

Poor Haitham—the al-Qaeda medic—hadn't seen or heard from his family in over two years. Even when he was convicted in absentia, the family wasn't allowed to speak, raise their voice at his trial, or do anything to defend him, and he wasn't there to defend himself.

Haitham explained that it had been over a year since he had seen the sun or stepped outside to get some exercise.

And he shared the name that all the prisoners had for that place, that prison: "The Grave."

CHAPTER 13

INTO A TERRIBLE RHYTHM

F OR THE NEXT TWO DAYS I slept, and ate, and slept some more. Always in the background, the threat that they might come and get me for my next session hung like a storm cloud, though one I couldn't see from within the dim room or from my barely moving fetal position.

I couldn't get up to walk. My ears still rang, keeping me dizzy, lightheaded, disoriented. For those two days the only time I stood involved my stumbling, staggering walk behind the half wall to the back corner to use the toilet. Each time one of the three men who now existed as my best friends, my only companions, helped me out, lending an arm, coaxing me, encouraging me. I wasn't bruised, at least not that I could see, because most of the hitting the interrogators had done focused on my head. I couldn't see my head. And it hadn't been punching, the sort of treatment that would leave bruises, only those disorienting slaps to the ears, messing with my eardrums and my equilibrium.

My cell mates warned me, during those first two days when I laid there, doing nothing but sleeping and listening, that the time spent anticipating our interrogators' arrival tended to be the worst, with the rest just boredom on top of boredom. The interrogator's approach, though, that, they said, always caught a person's attention, always made the heart race: "When you start hearing the clanking, the unlocking of the doors, that's when your adrenaline surges, your fingers tense up, the blood comes to the face. Someone is being picked to be taken to interrogation and torture. You know it, and you can't help it at all. You can't run away if it is you. If it is someone else, you can't assist or defend. You're just stuck."

A few days later, when the scraping sound of metal against metal emanated from our door once again, unlocking from the outside and letting someone in, all four of us just looked at each other, wondering, *Who is going to be taken?*

Me.

For the next couple months, every time, the answer stayed the same: me.

They came for me.

■ ■ ■

THREE DAYS HAD PASSED, maybe four, before they came for me again.

I heard those noises.

I heard the footsteps in the hallway, without the creaking wheels of the food cart. I heard the hard-soled shoes clattering. I heard them stop at our door. All four of us heard that. And we heard that ominous groan of metal on metal when the key turned and the door unlocked.

My mind started racing. Right away it turned to my family: *What do they know? Are they aware of my situation? Has someone contacted them? Has anyone noticed my disappearance?*

I thought of my mother, brother, and sister in the United States.

I thought of my aunts and uncles and cousins and nephews.

I thought of my ex-wives, of my children and grandchildren, of course. *What did they know? What could they know?*

The NSB interrogators had told me that no one knew anything, that no one was coming for me, that no one cared.

I knew that last part to be untrue. I had a wide circle of friends and family who loved me. My certainty of that could not be so easily shaken. But the interrogator's suggestions that no one knew and no one could come for me resonated with an element of truth.

As the door unlocked and I lay there on the ground, preparing myself to go back in for another round of questioning, my mind filled with these thoughts. I turned over all the scenarios, all the possibilities that I had already thought through, and reminded myself of the conclusions I had drawn.

For one, reassuringly, I had formed a good habit of talking to my daughter Amira every day. When I didn't answer for two days in a row, I imagined—no, I *knew*—that she would start worrying. What she would do with that worry, I wasn't so sure about. She'd been connected with my friend Assaf in Lebanon, through her own rescue during the Israel-Hezbollah conflict, and she had at least a passing acquaintance with a few of my military and embassy friends. So perhaps she'd call one of them and ask for advice. The quicker she did that, and the quicker she contacted someone official from the US government or even from British American Tobacco, the better. They were the ones who would sound the real alarms and start the diplomatic processes working—what limited diplomatic processes existed between the West and the Houthis—to find me and work on my release.

Likewise for British American Tobacco: they would miss me. How quickly, I couldn't be sure—though I had scheduled calls with them, both with leadership and with my peers and employees. My missing a certain number of those would start to raise eyebrows and signal that something had gone wrong.

A third avenue existed through two of my female acquaintances from Yemen.

The first was Yasmine. In the first few years of working for me at Universal, she had completed her MBA and risen from clerk to my go-to person and office manager. She brought so much energy and such a high degree of awareness to everything she did that it comes as no surprise that she was the first to realize I had gone missing. In fact, the day after my bagging, she went to the British American Tobacco company villa to see why I hadn't shown up at the office and quickly realized from the shape of the ransacked villa what had happened. She asked my villa guards what had happened, and they explained it as well, confirming her suspicions. After that she started right away communicating with my family back home and serving as a link for the US government in their pursuit of me.

Likewise, and perhaps even more vigorously, Abeer got involved in a big way too. Abeer and I had been friends since I had been an attaché, back when she first saw me in my uniform and asked for an introduction. Back then it was just a long-term friendship, staying in touch, having coffee now and again, though we grew closer and closer as I divorced Zainab and spent more of my time in Yemen. When I left Yemen after the Houthis took over, leaving Abeer was one of the harder things I did. And coming back to conduct my literal and figurative house cleaning, I also felt some urgency to see her again, to figure things out, to determine whether our relationship was such that she would be willing to leave with me and start a life abroad. While British American Tobacco paid me to come back, my love of Yemen and this new love I was developing for Abeer were really the things that drew me to return. (Abeer and I eventually married, and we live together in Tebnine now.)

These were my bulwarks against the idea that, as the NSB interrogators had said, I was all alone, with no one trying to locate me, no one caring about me, no one giving a shit. I thought about them, imagined them sounding the alarm, and began to quietly fantasize about what rescue might look like: teams of SEALs bursting through the prison doors, secret communications smuggled in on the food cart, that sort of thing.

■ ■ ■

NONE OF THAT HAPPENED though, none of the spy-like rescue scenarios. I thought about them, but that didn't make them real. The only real thing, the only thing that mattered and caught my attention, was the sound of my prison door clanking open, the sound of the guards coming for me. That interrupted me from what pleasant thoughts I could muster: daydreams and long soliloquys in the quiet of the jail cell, thinking about reuniting with Abeer, thinking about whether Yasmine's career was still on an upward trajectory, reminiscing about home, my many different iterations of home, not just Dearborn but also Lebanon and even Yemen. Yemen had become part of my concept of home, though in a different day and age and circumstance.

All that dissolved from my mind's eye as the door to the cell rattled. I lay there, heart racing. All of our hearts raced. Together we began to say a prayer, the opening sura of one of the verses of the Quran, Surat al-Buqara.

Allah does not burden any soul beyond its capacity. To its credit is what it earns, and against it is what it commits. Our Lord, do not condemn us if we forget or make a mistake. Our Lord, do not burden us as You have burdened those before us. Our Lord, do not burden us with more than we have strength to bear; and pardon us, and forgive us, and have mercy on us. You are our Lord and Master, so help us against the disbelieving people.

We chose that sura because it gives you faith in God and has been used by those in dire straits since first the words were uttered by the Prophet. The first phrase specifically states that God does not burden a person more than he (or she) can handle, so it is perfect in trying times. We recited this verse to steel ourselves, to calm ourselves, and to focus on truth and the comfort of truth during that darkest of dark times.

The door opened.

All four of us cell mates stared at each other rather than at the guards who came in. The odds seemed simple: a one-in-four chance that they'd take you. You don't want to be that one, but you don't want it to be any of the others either, since you've struck up a bond together. A one-in-four chance seemed likely, at least at first, though as the weeks and months wore on, I came to realize that the others were rarely taken out: Haitham was serving a long sentence; they had no need to question him. The others proved less interesting than me, both of them also sentenced and simply being held there. The only person they came and got, regularly, once or twice or three times a week, ended up being me.

Even now, as I think about it and talk through what that time was like, I return in my mind to the clanking of the steel door. It just reverberates in me, like the opening of a death row cell when a prisoner is about to be led to their execution. Truly, death row is the right comparison. I never knew, I couldn't know, whether any of those walks to the interrogation room would be my last walk of all. Haitham and the others filled our days with stories of people never coming back, of how they—the remaining prisoners—could not know whether the disappeared person had been released, or taken somewhere else, or killed. Especially if they took you out at night, Haitham insisted, there would be a higher possibility of them doing something to you and then dumping you on the side of the road. In Sana'a you don't find a soul on the road after 10 p.m., except criminals or people in government or security. The Houthis, and the NSB whom they had co-opted, completely controlled those nighttime streets, so no one could question them. No one could find you, or if they did, if they found you—a dead thing among rags and rats and garbage in the gutter—no one would likely lift a hand to do anything about you. Dogs would just scatter your bones, and children would be warned not to play in the area, your last purpose in the world being simply to dissolve away, to rot, and to serve as a reminder to anyone in the area of what happens to those who don't obey the Houthis' desires.

The guards came in.

I still hoped, against hope and betting against my cell mates, that I wouldn't be the one chosen.

But, of course, they called my name. "Mr. Sam, let's go."

My heart dropped. I didn't want to get up. But there was no escaping it.

I saw relief on the faces of my cell mates.

For Haitham it didn't matter. He'd been sentenced and was just serving his time. But the other two weren't as certain. They'd been called out, taken down the hall, interrogated. The wave, the exhalation of relief that coursed through their bodies, made me as nervous as anything else. I'd had a taste of interrogation, of ear slapping and being bagged and questioned, but had I experienced the worst of it yet?

The guards lifted me to my feet. They forced my hands out and shackled me in big steel cuffs from which no Houdini-like escape was possible. Instead of putting a bag over my head, they blindfolded me, tightening it really well so that I couldn't see anything. They took all the precautions, even though the jail itself gave nothing away, no windows, no identification, just a place that seemed dislocated from time and space.

The guards each took one of my arms and helped me out the door, turning me down the wide hallway. We walked perhaps a minute or so, some twists and turns, though we stayed on the same floor. Later, when I was moved to a cell on the second floor, I learned they had an interrogation room on each floor, which kept them from ever having to lead a blindfolded man like me up or down stairs.

We came to another room, and they led me in, leaving me standing in the middle.

That room wasn't too bad. In fact, the time spent standing there, the moments between the guards leaving and the beginning of the interrogation, stays with me as one of the most enjoyable aspects of the prison. The interrogation room had windows. Or at least one window. So I often felt a breeze from it, so nice, such a change from the cloistered and stuffy atmosphere in the jail cell room. Even though I stood there shackled, waiting for my interrogators to enter, each time I came to that spot and that moment, I let the gentle wind and the freshness of the outdoor air carry me away.

■ ■ ■

WHILE THE BREEZE IN that room took me different places at different times, often I fantasized that it had wafted me to the Corniche in Beirut, that long luxurious walk along the Mediterranean Sea, with the teeming, pulsing city on one side and the blue of the water on the other. I'd place myself, in my memory, somewhere along that strand, next to the lighthouse or the famous arched Raouché Rocks in the sea. At those places, and a hundred more along the walkway, a similar wind blows inward from the sea, bringing with it the sound of laughter from children playing on the barnacled rocks, swimming in the crystal waters, diving for shells, among fishermen with long cane poles and baskets of mullet.

Even though I knew what might be coming next in that interrogation room, the breeze allowed me a sense of escape, of disappearing, of being somewhere else even for a little while. Standing there (not being allowed to sit), my mind nevertheless escaped to imagine and remember a better place for the whole fifteen or twenty minutes they'd delay, thinking they were toying with me, some of them coming and going from the room, getting themselves organized, watching me. I didn't mind. Let them do what they want. They'd say, "Don't move," and they'd make me stand at semi-attention. But even as my brain raced and my heart beat through my shirt, part of me journeyed far away, imagining the Corniche.

I'd think about sunsets at a little café right by the rocks by the lighthouse. Visiting there, I'd go to that place and sit for long periods, watching and listening to the waves, smoking shisha and saying nothing, or joking with friends if I felt more social.

The place has a timelessness to it, having endured conquests and empires. The Phoenicians probably sat there, enjoying that same breeze, then the Egyptians when they came and the Greeks under Alexander. The Romans. The Byzantines. Saladin retook the area from the Crusaders. Then the Ottomans came. All these people, all these cultures, one by one had experienced moments like that of intense peace and satisfaction—perhaps even sometimes, individuals like me, who would later be imprisoned and tortured, would remember Beirut and the way the breeze came from the sea. That gave me comfort. It made me feel not alone, at least until the door slammed and my three interrogators came in, giving me the rudest of rude awakenings.

■ ■ ■

JUST LIKE THE FIRST TIME and like most such sessions from there on out, my opponents numbered three. Only one or two did the talking. Always the third remained in the background, sitting, asking whispered questions, directing the work. The two talkers would play good cop and bad cop. The whisperer either outranked the other two or served as some sort of monitor.

The first of them started out the session by introducing himself. "I'm Abu Saleem," he said, using a *kunya*, the traditional Arabic means of identifying oneself as the father of one's firstborn son, in this case, "father of Saleem." It made a good nom de guerre. It prevented me from knowing too much about him, like his tribe or his identity, though I could be reasonably sure that he was a father, even if Saleem were a stand-in name for his son.

This man told me about himself, reintroducing himself from our first session on my arrival in the jail. He did this to soften me up, to humanize himself, and to try a little bit to win me over. "I am with the NSB. I've had your file ever since you came back to Yemen."

"I know. I understand who you are."

"Look, I don't want you to go through any of this. I don't want any of us to go through any of this. I don't care about having you here. Just tell me what your mission is from the United States government and I'm going to make you a deal to forget about it and let you go."

I didn't have an answer for this, anything different to say than I had said before. All I could do was protest: "What mission are you talking about? You say you know ninety-five percent, but the other five percent is nothing. There is no mission. I'm here for the specific reason to clear up my personal situation, get my people out, and leave."

No second question came. I could feel something like a current of electricity pass through the room, a charged look exchanged among the three men. Then, bam, totally without warning, a stick slapped across my shoulder, like a cane or a branch, the feeling of it like a hundred beestings at once.

"See! That's your fault," the bad cop said. "You're doing this to yourself. You cooperate, we're not going to do anything to you."

The good cop, more softly, stated his earlier proposition again: "Tell us what you're doing, and we'll let you go. We'll even guarantee you transportation from here to the borders of Saudi Arabia and release you to the Saudis. Just admit to what you're doing here."

"Again, what are you talking about?" I said.

"We know you're getting specific instructions and getting warnings from the American Embassy in Jordan," he said. "Right here, on this date [he mentioned the same date that the bombings had started] right on this date you received a call from..."

Indeed I had gotten a call from a friend, a Jordanian who had been my operations director in Yemen and had gone to Jordan for medical attention. When the bombings started, he called just to check on me. These bastards had intercepted that phone call and had somehow come to the conclusion that it equaled some sort of warning.

"You know very well this call is from the American Embassy in Jordan."

This was pure fantasy. I had a hard time not laughing, not making fun of them. If it weren't for the stickman behind me, ready to swing again, I probably would have.

"It's not," I said. "It's not from the embassy or from anyone else associated with the bombings. This guy worked for me. He was one of my employees. His name is Ismail al-Kaylani. He was calling just to check up on me. He was just worried."

"No, he's not. We intercepted the call. He's telling you to take shelter because the coalition is going to bomb here and here and here."

"No, he was just telling me to be cautious, like any concerned friend might do."

"You were sleeping in the basement when we found you. They were giving you the places they were going to bomb. You were sleeping in the basement because you were worried and because you had advance warning."

"No, Ismail was just telling me to be cautious, in general, nothing specific, telling me to be cautious because the coalition is bombing everywhere and just be careful."

"We traced it to the US Embassy..."

The conversation went back and forth like this. I thought, for the briefest while, that I might make some headway, that I might clear the whole situation up, prove to them that Ismail's call was innocent, just a normal call, just what a friend might do. But whenever I protested, I'd get whacked with the stick. The fourth time the stick broke; I heard it crack and break, and they went and got another one.

Every time I'd say no, every time I'd tell them that I had no advanced warning about the bombings, they'd whack me again.

They tried a new line of questioning: "Where'd you get the information that there are ten thousand Pakistani troops coming to the border of Saudi Arabia to invade Yemen?"

"Where'd you get that?"

"It's right here, on the recording of you."

This was news to me. I suspected they were listening to my calls. I suspected that they were recording my conversations. But now they'd given me proof.

I thought about this claim for a few minutes, thought through why—if at all—I had been talking about Pakistani troops. Then, ah-ha, I remembered—and hoped once again that I might convince them of my utter, stupid innocence, that all this was just terrible coincidence and that I wished, truly wished, that the Saudis had never started bombing them.

I said, "If you notice what time the call is, I was watching Al Arabiya news, and just happened to be reading the ticker tape that scrolls along the bottom of the newscast. I was just reading it aloud from the TV, and telling someone that on the phone, and anyway, if I remember right, those troops weren't being put there to invade Yemen but just to protect the Haramayn, the Two Holy Mosques in Mecca and Medina. Go back and watch Al Arabiya. It was public information at that time. I had no special information, and that will prove it."

"No, it's not public. It wasn't public. It was secret info."

"You seem too dumb to realize what's on the news," I said, my temper getting the better of me.

(This resulted in a good whack from the stick.)

"I can't believe you're asking me something stupid like that. It looks like we failed."

(A whack from the stick again.)

"What?"

"Us Americans, we failed. I was sure we trained you guys better than that."

That one cost me not just a whack but two whole sticks, two sticks broken across my legs, back, and front, buckling me to the ground from my standing position.

■ ■ ■

THROUGH THE PAIN of the beatings, I thought about Ismail al-Kaylani.

I'd taken him under my wing, much like Yasmine, first meeting him when he was a young, bright kid of twenty-three or twenty-four years old.

I brought him into Universal Eagles as an assistant trainer for the Canadian Nexen security contract. Then I saw his potential; I noticed that he was a really sharp guy, so had him join in some State Department–sponsored training through ITI, which I had brought to Yemen to help train the CTU, the same guys who had snatched and bagged me. I'd arranged to put Ismail and one other good civilian colleague named Muataz al-Sari through the driving and shooting portions of the ITI training, right alongside the CTU. Muataz al-Sari was bagged by the CTU three days after I was just because of his affiliation with me. He ended up staying seven months in the same jail.

Ismail worked for me in Yemen but had ended up in Jordan the previous week, the circumstances working out well for him so that he didn't also get taken. The previous week, on a day off, he had come to the office to pick up something. He was heading to a wedding, I believe, and a fight broke out between two guards. Ismail, being one of the supervisors by then, tried to break up the fight. He got pushed, twisting as he went down, and landed awkwardly, breaking his leg. We had to fly him to Jordan to get medical attention.

Although he timed things perfectly to avoid the Houthi raid on our compound, he watched from his convalescent hospital room as the Saudi bombing started and so placed that fateful call to me, concerned about me and Muataz. He did nothing more than a normal friend and good employee might do, but the timing made it look like I was receiving these "advanced warning" calls from Jordan—at least in the eyes of the paranoid NSB agents who had been tasked by the Houthis to find out anything, anything at all, that might be useful to defend themselves from the Saudi planes that circled with impunity over Sana'a's skies.

■ ■ ■

THE BEATING ENDED AFTER about two hours, when, half-conscious, I couldn't be forced back onto my feet anymore.

They knew they could get nothing more from me, not in that session. They continued talking to me. They continued asking all the same questions, again and again, but I had lost the ability to respond.

They dragged me back to my cell.

They threw me in.

Just like on my first arrival, I couldn't stand up.

The guys—Haitham and the other two—looked at me and saw how much pain I was in. I told them what had happened. They struggled to help me take off the silly Bermuda shorts and found that both of my legs were black and blue, with wicked red lines showing where more bruises would emerge.

For the next week, I "relaxed" as they let me recover a bit. No more beatings. No more interrogations for a little while. I was their new toy, and they had all the time in the world with me. That grating steel door never opened, no one came in or out, only the food hatch moved, morning, noon, and night.

CHAPTER 14

RESCUE EFFORTS

T HE WATER FOR our prison cells, for the whole building—as with most buildings in Yemen—came from a tank mounted on the roof of the facility. Water isn't a public resource, as in most of America, but gets provided privately. This worked to our advantage, because the Houthis, in establishing themselves as the ruling power in Sana'a, couldn't—couldn't really be expected to—figure out all the systems: how to keep the electricity running, the roads clean, the government functioning, the gas and food rations intact, the airport open, and every water tank adorning the roof of every government building filled.

How was this to our advantage? Wouldn't a lack of water be a bad thing, resulting in some thirsty hours or lengthy times without the ability to flush our toilets or clean ourselves?

Those deprivations—even the lack of drinking water—ended up being well worth it. Because when the tank on the roof ran out of water, the pipes between the jail cells dried out and became our only method of communication with one another.

Haitham, having been prisoner longest, first demonstrated this on a day not too long after my arrival.

The toilet in our bathroom gurgled.

The faucet in the bathroom belched and gave off a foul odor.

Haitham stood, and with a quick check of the door and a nod to one of our other cell mates—I was still incapacitated from my most recent beating—he moved over to our bathroom corner. There he leaned forward to the mouth of the faucet, cupped his hand over the spigot, and began to speak, then twisted his head to place his ear against the faucet, listening for responses.

This went on for a few minutes, in a strange, muted tone—not quite a whisper, because whispering wouldn't reverberate strongly enough throughout the plumbing, but not quite a speaking voice either. Almost a growl.

Al-Qaeda had trained its members how to use one-way radios, so operating the "pipes" came naturally to them. In quasi-military fashion they would start and stop their questions and answers with *Huw-wal*, "over" or "okay," as when using those radios, relaying messages from cell to cell, to the cells above, below, left, and right. Haitham seemed adept at this, as he passed messages through the chain and waited for his turn to ask questions of the network. They all knew they had only limited time, a few minutes or hours, depending on when the tank got refilled—though the guards never seemed to catch on or take any steps to shorten or stop the news and rumor relay.

At one point, after ten or fifteen minutes of this first session, Haitham straightened up and looked at me. "There's another new guy on the floor above us," he said.

My ears perked up.

"What is his name?" I asked.

"Shhhh," the others said, looking to the door and then to Haitham.

"He's your friend," Haitham said. "You came in together, same night. His name is Scott."

This struck me like a ray of light. Scott was here still. I simultaneously felt terrible for him and also hopeful. They hadn't killed him. They hadn't killed me. They were keeping us together. Perhaps they had a plan in mind for us. Perhaps efforts were being made—by the embassy, by the United Nations, by the diplomatic community, by our families or our governments—to negotiate our release. Even if nothing of the sort was happening, his presence made me feel much less alone. I could almost sense him, an ally, nearby.

"Ask how he is doing," I said.

After a moment of speaking and a longer moment of listening, Haitham replied, "Good. He is good. Okay at least. Though he eats a lot, they say."

This made me laugh. Scott had the figure of a full-bodied Midwestern American, and the diet here, in this Yemeni jail, probably already was putting him into starvation mode. I hoped he was making friends with his cell mates, as I had done, even if they were mostly all, to some degree or another, linked to al-Qaeda. The alternative would be not only unpleasant for him but perhaps also deadly.

Scott spoke Arabic fairly well. He'd been in the region for a while and had even converted to Sunni Islam, so I had to think that he would be accepted fairly well among the al-Qaeda prisoner groups. Not that all Sunnis are al-Qaeda of course, but in some ways it would be more dangerous for me, being Shi'a, than it might be for him, as a Sunni, even though he was obviously a white American man and probably—they would suspect—tied somehow to the US government. Just like Scott, I prayed with my cell mates, five times a day, every day. Most of the time I would follow rather than lead. The choice of leader for prayer just depends on who stands up. Normally a praying group allows the eldest, or the most experienced, to lead. Among my cell mates that would have been me, by at least two decades, but I usually refused because by taking over the prayer, I feared I would also assume a de facto leadership role for the group, as well as responsibility if anything went wrong, if anyone were involved in any sort of wrongdoing. I didn't want that, not for these guys. Sunni and Shi'a prayers are the same; there's absolutely no difference between them in performance or intent. The two branches of Islam just believe in a different line of authority from the Prophet Muhammad. My objections were not religious so much as they were practical. I wanted to keep myself somewhat at a distance from these guys. I needed their community, but I didn't want to accidentally become a leader of that community.

Scott—I had to believe—would pray with them regularly too, both for his own spiritual benefit and to be better accepted as part of the group. Perhaps he would even find himself confronting the same sort of leadership dilemma I did—whether to accept invitations to lead the prayer, since he would be the oldest among them just as I was. I didn't know if he experienced that or not—though as I thought about it while biding my time in that prison cell, I imagined he might not feel the same pressures I did due to his status as a white, new convert.

Either way, I chose my course clearly. I prayed with my cell mates but continued for the most part to abstain from leading prayer. This created tension but also drew a clear line. I participated as one of them, but I would not lead them, spiritually or in any other way.

■ ■ ■

A WEEK PASSED BEFORE the guards came and got me again.

Exactly the same process transpired. The door unlocked with the same bone-chilling screech of metal on metal and creaked open. The same guards handcuffed me and blindfolded me, picking me up off the floor of the cell and leading me out the door, each of them taking one of my elbows. They brought me to the same interrogation room. All of this went down just as before.

But one big difference permeated the air, as if everything were tinged with a bitter taste or the expectation that something truly terrible and painful was soon to happen: two days earlier, through the empty-water-tank-pipe communication network, I had heard that the interrogators had broken Scott. This didn't surprise me. Not that I thought Scott was weak. I thought just the opposite—that he had been, and would be, very strong. However, all of our training makes it clear to us that everyone has their breaking point. Everyone breaks at some time, unless they're pushed past the point of endurance and either choose death or lose consciousness. The Houthis and their National Security Bureau (NSB) allies had found a way to push Scott over the edge without him passing out (like I had done) and without killing him.

The message through the pipes told me that he had gone down yelling and screaming, telling the authorities, the interrogators, whomever he was facing at that moment, that he had something to confess to.

But I didn't know what that *something* was.

And so, as I was led into the interrogation cell this time, my mind was filled with uncertainty: *What has Scott said? How will this change their attitude toward me and their questions of me? How should I best respond, both to keep myself alive and also to not endanger Scott any further?*

■ ■ ■

IN THE WORLD OUTSIDE, unbeknownst to me but as I certainly hoped and prayed, the efforts to find me and, perhaps, rescue me continued. After Yasmine and Abeer found out I was missing, they called the authorities, American and Lebanese. This set in motion all the government efforts and also the grim and difficult work of informing the rest of my family. The FBI and State Department traditionally perform this role—unless the individual held in captivity is active military, in which case an officer in uniform comes to the family's front door. It's a scene played out in a million movies, one that you think about in this line of work, one that you sometimes talk about with your family—what it means, what they should do, how they should expect to react and interact with the various authorities, and what assistance they can expect from those authorities.

In this case, the FBI and State Department began the task of contacting my family, my mother, my kids, my ex-wife, showing up in conservative, staid, solemn suits, the classic men in black, women in black, waiting on the doorsteps of the houses to be shown in and made as comfortable as they could be, given this uncomfortable task, in seats and on sofas in the very same living rooms where I had spent at least part of my life raising children, being a brother or an uncle or a husband, being a normal dad—though one who had been absent, serving overseas, for many months and years.

These FBI and State Department personnel did not call beforehand. They did not send warning. My ex allowed them in, made them tea, and got them situated before they gave my family the news that I had disappeared and was presumed to be in captivity, perhaps imprisoned or held hostage, in Yemen.

My mother took the news the hardest. She was in the States staying with my sister at the time, so she found out pretty quickly.

My brother Hisham—her middle child—had died a few years back of a heart attack. I happened to be with her in Lebanon at the time, visiting from Qatar, when we got the news. I was driving her down to Tyre from our village, Tebnine, to have lunch. It was very early in the morning stateside, mid-afternoon in Beirut.

My nephew Matthew called. "We're rushing my dad to the hospital," he said. "He's got a blockage in the arteries, taking him in to have surgery right away,"

To try to reassure Matthew, as I drove down the mountain toward Tyre, I said, "Hey, look, look what happened to me. I had the same sort of blockage, triple-bypass surgery, and here I am, alive and well. They're going to do the same thing for your father, and it'll be alright."

But as soon as they started prepping Hisham for the operation, with the line still open between Matthew and me, I heard in the background my sister screaming, "NO, no no no."

My mother knew right away what was happening. Right away she knew what those repeated words must signify. She heard it and knew. And she started crying and screaming beside me in the car.

Now, only a few years later, she was faced with this new tragedy: me, her oldest son, missing, and dead for all she knew. This didn't go well for her. She experienced a nervous breakdown and wouldn't talk to anyone. For the next six months she couldn't stop crying. Not one day went by without her crying. She stayed in the States throughout that period, living with my sister, so she had some support, and they didn't have to track her down in Tebnine. But it must have been grueling to see her that way. It must have been a nightmare for my sister, having to not only deal with her own grief and uncertainty about my situation but also provide comfort and care for our mother.

My daughters were told by my ex. My oldest son was living with his wife. My younger son already had been stationed out at Hill Air Force Base in Utah. My ex and daughters told them, both of them over the phone. They called up and spread the news to our family, sparing them the visit by the black-clad FBI and State Department personnel. Other than that, the FBI asked our family not to speak to the media or to anyone outside the family as it might interfere with the investigation and perhaps, if all went well, with negotiations or rescue efforts.

No one wants a media circus or the frenzied attention, not while grieving, and especially not while negotiations are ongoing or while there exists the possibility of escape or rescue. Only if and when the government efforts failed would my family consider going out wider. Only then would it make sense to ensure the world knew about my plight and that of Scott Darden, just so we wouldn't be forgotten, just so that the Houthis might know that we could not be made to disappear silently, without notice. In that way media attention could be good. But, as part of our training and our family discussions ahead of time, we'd reviewed some of this scenario, and we'd decided to heed the advice of the experts—at least until their efforts proved ineffective in obtaining my release.

These are scary conversations to have and hypothetical when you're still safe and sound at home. But those talks proved to be a big reassurance to my family: they knew what to do. And they knew what my expectations and wishes would be. They knew they must trust the authorities and let the process work before taking any last-ditch measures like publicizing things through the media.

■ ■ ■

ON THAT DAY OF questioning after Scott cracked, I was led to the same little interrogation room, the one with the window open and the breeze, the lovely breeze, blowing in across my face, filling up my nostrils with that tempting scent of freedom, the outside world. They left me standing there longer even than usual—perhaps for forty-five minutes—beautiful and calming but also unnerving. I knew an extra dose of tension filled the air. I knew the experience of this bout of interrogation wasn't going to be pleasant.

When they came in, they started right away with a new line of questioning. They didn't mess around with good cop / bad cop. They went right to the heart of the matter: "What is your relationship to Scott Darden?"

I stuck with the truth, explaining for what felt like the umpteenth time that I was just a security consultant for the same company Scott worked for, Transoceanic. No lies in that. But the answer didn't satisfy my interrogators, not that day it didn't. Scott had broken down. I knew from the pipe-line communication system that he had asked to confess, but I didn't know what the subject of that confession would have been. I had my suspicions from my work with

Transoceanic in Somalia—all those unmarked planes and unmarked containers of matériel—that the work Scott did involved shipping and transporting goods for certain other intelligence agencies. But all that was just a guess on my part.

And all I could rightly and truly tell them was that I had been hired to help Transoceanic assess the safety of restarting its operations in Yemen: my role had nothing to do with classified work, not on my end, and it certainly had nothing to do with tipping off or informing any of the coalition bombing activities, as the Houthi and NSB interrogators still seemed to think. If Scott had started to tell them stuff that put me on worse footing, that made my activities look more suspicious, then all the information I'd previously told them—truthful information—would look false. The last thing I wanted was for these men who had already beat me unconscious several times to think that I had been playing with them, telling them half truths, hiding things.

At the time, I didn't know with certainty the extent or the purpose of Transoceanic's work in Yemen, although I had my suspicions. And, worse, I didn't know what Scott had told them either, so I couldn't even begin to imagine how my interrogators now viewed me. Or what they expected me to say.

Truth be told, they probably didn't know either. But after Scott's confession, they sure as hell meant to have another go at me and see if I would also crack and tell them interesting things.

When I continued to say what I had always said, they got angrier and angrier: "You're lying. You work with him. You work with them. You know what he's doing."

"I don't know what he's doing. All I know is that he's a logistics manager for the company and that he previously worked in Afghanistan."

"You're lying!"

"I met him a month ago for the first time in Dubai. We've been exchanging emails for three or four months about the security situation in Yemen, just getting prepared. I only met him and his boss that one time in Dubai, a month ago."

The breeze from the window blew across my face, like an exhalation. I stood my ground. Anything more than that, I didn't know. I wasn't going to start making stuff up to appease them.

But they didn't believe me.

And they wanted to hear more and different answers.

All of a sudden, the sticks came out and the beatings started. We were going at it, back and forth, the same questions, the same answers, the same beatings. It lasted like that for an hour, maybe longer. They'd yell and scream. I'd yell and scream in response. And they'd hit me.

But that wasn't the worst.

For the first time during all of this, one of them chambered a round and pressed the muzzle of a handgun to my head, right above my eye, right at the soft spot at my temple.

"That's it," they said. "We're done with you. We know who you're working for, and if you're not going to confess, then fuck it, we're done with you."

■ ■ ■

AGAINST ALL THAT I had said to my family about letting the official government processes work, my mother reached out to friends in Lebanon to see if anyone from the Lebanese government could help. Hassan Hammoud, a cousin of mine in Lebanon, my mother's nephew, thought he could make some things happen. He was able to get in contact, through another relative—this is how it works in Lebanon; everything depends on whom you know and whom you are related to—with the nephew of Nabih Berri, the speaker of Parliament and the most powerful politician in Lebanon. He reached out to Hadi Jaber, the Lebanese ambassador to Yemen.

Interestingly, I knew the ambassador well and had even been in touch with him the same day that I was taken. The ambassador and I were trying to figure out a way to extricate Scott and me from Sanʿaʾa on the UN plane that he was getting out on. He boarded that flight. I did not, as the NSB had bagged me that very night. So the ambassador, now working from Lebanon, knew my situation and offered his help. He did not have good access to the Houthis, so the efforts failed through these official government channels. However, this approach bore fruit in an unexpected way. While official diplomatic channels on the Lebanese side failed, the unofficial channels—through Hezbollah's shadow government—had stronger ties to the Houthis. Someone from their camp reached out, made some calls, and told my cousins and the Nabih Berri camp that they could get me out very easily. But they—Hezbollah!—were worried about what the consequences would be for me. They are, of course, a Shiʾa group. But, to their credit, they understood my role as a US Marine and my role as an attaché. They were concerned about the optics for me if they ended up being the ones to rescue me and ferry me somewhat illicitly out of Yemen and back to Lebanon. From the outside, helping rescue an American might seem like a win for Hezbollah, because they could use that to score points in any negotiations with the West. But, internally, their chief concern was their power base, a population that had grown up on a steady diet of anti-Western rhetoric. Helping me, if it got out, would be bad for them politically. And I think, to save face, they billed this as them "being conscientious" about my reputation, lest I be soiled in US governmental circles as having too close ties to Hezbollah.

I wasn't aware of any of this, of course, and I probably wouldn't have—no, I'm certain I wouldn't have—given a fig for the optics at the time. But now, looking back at it, I am amazed at the complexity involved and how Hezbollah's leadership was able to both offer help and then delicately back away.

■ ■ ■

WITH THE MUZZLE of the handgun pressing against my head, I wouldn't have cared whether Hezbollah or Santa Claus came to my rescue right then.

I thought that was it.

They've got nothing to lose. They don't have to report to anyone. They don't have to affirm anything. I could just disappear. They're going to do it. They're going to shoot me right here, in this room, and it'll all be over.

I started to recite the Shahada, or profession of faith: There is no God but God, and Muhammad is his Prophet.

That was it—I was ready to die.

But instead of shooting, the interrogator holding that gun smacked me on the backside of my head with its heavy metal butt. It sent a searing pain through me, right at the base of my skull. I fell forward, to the ground, hard onto my knees.

They kept beating me with the sticks, two times, three times. Then they launched back into the questions again. Someone from behind clapped both of his hands over my ears again, their favorite move, disorienting me, making me woozy and nauseated.

Then, not suddenly but suddenly enough—maybe I had blacked out—I was being dragged back to the cell.

I knew I had lived. I was aware enough to realize that much.

And even then I found it amusing, as the guards propped me up, gripping me under both of my arms, to think that I had never once walked back from that interrogation room to my prison cell under my own power. They'd always beat enough of the stuffing out of me that I couldn't manage it. Every time I had to be supported, like a mannequin, like a ragdoll.

■ ■ ■

ONE DAY WHEN WE were praying in the cell, the four of us cell mates together, I fell. I dropped to my knees. I couldn't complete my prayers or stand up for the *rukaa'a*.

The guys revived me, brought me water, started asking me what was the matter.

I croaked out a word or two, pointing to my heart: chest pains.

They took off my T-shirt and saw for the first time the scar from my triple bypass.

The Houthis, in their inventory of my goods from the villa, hadn't found or bothered with my medicine. I'd mentioned it to them, along with the money, the guns, the other things they hadn't bothered to list on their sheet, but they'd ignored me. Frankly, I was surprised to some extent that, through all the beatings, I'd managed not to have another attack. But it had just been a matter of time.

This one wasn't bad. It wasn't like the first attacks, more like a faintness, a weakness in my breast and in my breath.

However, Haitham—with all his experience and cunning—seized on the moment and said, "Hey, if you do it like this, just mildly, they're not going to do anything to help you, so we have to fake a massive heart attack. I've seen it happen before. Heart attacks or other issues. If they're bad enough, then they'll take you to the hospital."

I wasn't sure about that, thinking they might just kill me instead. But Haitham knew all the ropes. His eyes gleamed as he said, "I know what will happen if you fake it fully: they'll take you to the hospital to get your meds, and then they'll also stop beating you. They'll stop beating you, do you hear me?"

I was still having minor pains, enough that faking it wasn't too much of an issue. I just increased my groaning, worked on my acting skills a little, letting it all come out each time another throb of weakness or constriction seized me. It caught the attention of our guards, just as Haitham had said it would. And Haitham and my other cell mates made sure they came by banging on the doors as I laid there on the ground moaning and gasping.

"The American is dying," they yelled. "The American is dying, and we don't want to be responsible for him."

The guards told me to shut up, but my cell mates continued their hammering at the door: "He's had a triple bypass, and you're not giving him his meds."

The guards left but not before saying that they'd see what they could do.

Five hours later—five hours of me acting and moaning and writhing on the floor of that prison cell—they finally came back, having gotten permission from their superiors to take me in the middle of the night, maybe midnight or even 1 a.m. They put me on a stretcher, bagged my head again, and handcuffed me just like usual. I was still having heart pain but also still faking it, groaning as they eased me into another SUV and drove me to the hospital.

The beatings stopped after the heart attack. They also moved me to the second floor, perhaps worried that my cell mates, Haitham and that whole crew, had grown too accustomed and friendly with me. The next four or five months continued with interrogations every week or two, though the beatings stopped.

The advice of my al-Qaeda cell mates had worked.

Here I was, being protected at this moment by al-Qaeda and—if Hezbollah's line about protecting my image rather than playing to their base was indeed the truth—by Hezbollah too, as they delicately continued to negotiate for my release.

CHAPTER 15

CAPTIVITY'S FINALE

URING MY CAPTIVITY I helped the other inmates figure out where our prison was located. The pipe system of communication proved helpful in getting information from old hands like Haitham and anyone else who had anything relevant. I figured that if our facility were abandoned or blown up or taken over in another military action and we had the opportunity to flee, we would be armed with the knowledge of our location and could form a plan on which direction to head. Talking to the other prisoners and gathering information, I put together a few facts: the facility had been built by the United States; Haitham and the other old hands testified to the fact that, prior to the Houthi takeover, someone from the US Embassy had been coming every week to check on their status, and that guy would say he was an American. He'd ask questions through the food gate: who else was kept here, how many upstairs, how many downstairs, those sorts of things.

This narrowed the list to about three or four facilities that the US regularly inspected. I pieced that information together with my recollection of the amount of time and general direction we traveled on the night Scott and I were bagged.

This was, almost certainly, the Counterterrorism Unit (CTU) compound on the outskirts of Sana'a, just to the northeast of the airport, about two miles outside the city itself. The CTU had another place in town on the northern edge of Hadda, its headquarters. But the prison or jail there was smaller and older, and I think I would have seen and heard the city around us—the call to prayer from the big new Saleh Mosque, the bustle on the streets outside one of Sana'a's awesome peculiarities: a yummy little Baskin-Robbins store that seemed just like every Baskin-Robbins in America—except, if you knew anything about it, you knew that its owners were al-Qaeda members. From the al-Ahmar family. This oddity, one among many such, was so truly Yemeni—I'd decided for sure we were being held in one of these two facilities, the one in town next to the mosque and the al-Qaeda Baskin-Robbins or the one just out of town that had been built and funded by my own country's government.

■ ■ ■

AT SOME POINT in my captivity, I was moved to my second cell, up on the second floor of the prison. It was slightly larger: 2.8 rather than 1.8 meters wide. But I still had four cell mates, as before.

But this time, one of them, Imad, hated me.

For good reason. He knew I was American. And he knew that I knew him—a somewhat famous al-Qaeda operative who openly boasted of having killed sixty-three individuals, mostly civilians and Yemeni security personnel. Though Imad was his given name, everyone called him the Prince of Ibb. (Ibb is a city in southern Yemen, close the al-Qaeda hotspot of Abyan.)

I feared Imad like no other person in this prison. I worried that when I went to sleep, I just wouldn't wake the next morning. I worried, at least for a while, that he might turn the other three guys in the room against me, though he didn't really need to. Imad was bigger than me. He could have cornered me and finished me off on his own.

But the other guys banded together to protect me. And they did that because of the bombing.

Our facility, for quite a lengthy stretch, was getting bombed once or twice a day by Saudi and coalition warplanes. This provided yet another clue that our prison was located in an important military installation, helping me narrow it down to the CTU compound.

When those bombing runs happened, the guards would often come by, perhaps thinking they'd stir up trouble for me, and casually tell my cell mates and everyone else on that floor of the prison not to worry.

"The coalition won't bomb here," they'd say. "Mr. Sam protects us. He was giving them grid coordinates for their strikes. They won't ever blow up a place where an American Marine is being held."

"See," they'd say, winking at me through the food hatch, "everyone should be grateful for you, since you're protecting us so well."

Their strategy backfired.

Maybe my cell mates were just plain dumb, but for whatever reason they took this all literally. And they banded together to protect me, as if I were their good luck charm, from Imad.

■ ■ ■

I OWE ABEER a lifetime of gratitude for the faith, the hustle, and the bravery she displayed in first trying to find me and then trying to get me freed from the Houthis. In fact, the life that I live now, with her as my wife, is basically a second life, a second start, because without her work and diligence, without her efforts to get me out of that jail, I might not have any of this additional time and space to give gratitude to anyone or anything at all. It could all have very well ended then and there, in the National Security Bureau (NSB) prison.

When the Houthis took me, Abeer and I had been dating a little bit but not seriously. She had a crush on me, or so she's told me. Ever since she first saw me in my Marine uniform at the US Embassy in Sana'a, she'd had that crush. Still, her going to the lengths she did for a man who wasn't even really a boyfriend, just a friendly acquaintance with whom romance and love might eventually bloom, such devotion and sacrifice, seemed almost unbelievable and turned out to be a big part of my salvation.

Abeer is a willowy woman, moderately tall for a Yemeni at five foot five but probably no more than a hundred pounds soaking wet. Her family hails from a village called Nihm to the east and north of Sana'a, straddling an important intersection on the road between the cities of Sana'a and Marib, right where that road descends from the mountains into the Rub al-Khali desert on its way down to Marib. It's very close to the spot where the biblical Queen of Sheba—whom we call Saba in Arabic and Quranic sources—had built her famous dam, the remains of which are still an archaeological and historical site. Nihm's position in this valley, on the main road, means that it has unfortunately become one of the key battlegrounds in the ongoing war between the Houthis and the Saudi coalition, with the

Saudis and Emiratis in control of Marib and the Houthis holding the highlands and Sana'a since September 2014.

This has made things very difficult for Abeer's family: coming and going from the village is dangerous, relatives are in constant danger, and family lands and structures have suffered in even greater proportion than the rest of Yemen, which itself has endured warfare, famine, and terrible outbreaks of cholera and other disease ever since the Houthi takeover.

Abeer's family also didn't fare well in Sana'a itself, since their property in the city—a grand villa—shared a wall with former president Ali Abdullah Saleh's home. This wasn't Saleh's Presidential Palace but his original family residence—just as Abeer's clan hails from Nihm, Saleh's calls the village of Sanhan south and east of Sana'a home, with both clans, like so many other Yemeni families of note, maintaining separate city and village dwellings.

Because of the extreme proximity of these two city residences, every time the Saudi coalition (or, later, the Houthis) targeted Saleh, the windows or doors of Abeer's family's house would also get blown out. They'd have to run and hide, then return, over and over again for those several months. Her family would have the unenviable task of rebuilding their house about four or five times over the first years of the Houthi uprising.

They couldn't just leave either, as the property had been in the family long enough that it held not just commercial but also really deep, long-standing sentimental value. Her grandfather had owned the land initially and had been one of the major businessmen in Yemen. With their roots in Nihm, her father and uncles spread their wings in Sana'a, becoming agents for Emirates Air and Saudi Arabian

Airlines in Yemen, as well as venturing into flying—as pilots for Yemenia and Qatar Airways. One of these uncles owns the Sana'a expo-
sition center. The family had been blessed with well-to-do status, for
sure, but they were also tied to that wealth, trying to weather the
storm and be there as part of the new Yemen, whenever the new Yemen might arise from the rubble and ashes of the war.

Family, especially the connections of a family of the sort Abeer
was blessed to have, is critical to getting business done in any Arab
country. Abeer enjoyed the knowledge that her moderately prominent uncles and father could provide some protection for her. But
still, as she started asking around about what had happened to me,
she knew she was putting not just herself but her whole clan at risk.
The Houthis had demonstrated time and again that if you crossed
them, they would blow everything up. They might let you flee with
your life—as they had even done for some of the al-Ahmar family as
their initial push progressed southward from Saadah to Sana'a—but
they would also not hesitate to take over your home or even blow up
and level the buildings, just as a warning to anyone who might consider similar resistance. It all depended on how they felt about you:
Would you behave? Would you come around to support them? Or
would you become a thorn in their side?

Abeer asked and asked about me. She asked everyone she knew.
She asked in social situations. She asked in official situations.

She met with her uncles and explained what was happening, seeking their advice and assistance, their networking support.

In short, over those first days and weeks of my captivity, she made
enough of a nuisance of herself that one of her girlfriends finally admitted she knew a person who could perhaps help in the NSB. The
girlfriend arranged a meeting with this NSB officer and, reluctantly,

because he felt bad for Abeer (and perhaps because Abeer's friend also used her leverage on him), he agreed to bring Abeer to NSB headquarters.

The NSB headquarters building hunkers in a shadow between the Ghamdan Old Palace, the Al-Bakiriya Mosque, and the wall of the Old City. It's made, at least on the outside, of imposing heavy blocks of gray stone. Inside that gray stone facade, a cluster of mid-1980s office buildings surround a courtyard, and several narrow lanes divide the buildings; all of this, like almost every other official Yemeni building or unofficial villa, is surrounded by walls. It's a strange place for an intelligence agency, being much more reminiscent of the semi-official palace it had been before the NSB was created as a counterweight to the Political Security Organization back in the 1990s. The Ghamdan Fort used to fire its two antique cannons at night during Ramadan to signal the start of the Iftar feast. The place was, and is, without a doubt, part of the ancient heart of Sana'a. And Abeer, in going there and making a nuisance of herself on my behalf, both challenged the patriarchal underpinnings of Yemeni society and upheld the best traditions of Arab women, who have been known, time out of mind, to be tough and fearless and ready to take matters into their own hands.

On the appointed day for the visit to NSB, Abeer's girlfriend's acquaintance, along with another man who worked at NSB, picked Abeer up and took her in, where she was made to wait in one of those semiofficial parlors that reek of administrivia and interminable delay. After perhaps half an hour, they ushered her into an even smaller "interview room" and pretty much dispensed, right away, with any niceties: the questioning began, and she found herself much more under interrogation than ever she expected she would be.

"Why do you know Mr. Sam Farran?"

"What's your relationship to him?"

"Why are you concerned about him? We've heard you've been asking everyone in town."

Abeer held up a bottle of medicine, which she'd gotten from the maid in my villa. "He has a heart condition. He needs these pills," she said.

The men took the pills, looked at them, shook them in their bottle, and gave them back to her, promising nothing.

They showed her out of the headquarters building, perhaps thinking they were done with her. Maybe they weren't satisfied with her answers, and having given nothing away, nothing at all about my status or location, not even confirming or denying that they were holding me in one of their prisons, they thought she would lose interest and give up.

But they did not know Abeer.

The next day she showed up at the gates of the headquarters building again.

And the day after that.

On the third day they brought her back into the same waiting room, and after a nervous pause, some official fluttering of hands, they ushered her into the same tiny interrogation room again.

They asked her the same sorts of questions, almost as if trying to verify her story.

This got them nowhere. She gave them the same answers. She tried to provide them with my heart medicine. After a fruitless back-and-forth, with both sides feeling somewhat exasperated, they sent her home again.

She kept coming back.

After what must have been the fourth time they brought her into the building, things went a little differently. One of the uncles of Sayyid Abd el-Malik al-Houthi himself entered the room. He asked all the same questions. He looked at the heart pills. And he seemed unexpectedly sympathetic. Abeer thought she might be getting somewhere. She thought she might have found a person who could assist in finding me—if he didn't already know where I was—and perhaps could also help in getting me released.

Abeer says that after some surprisingly pleasant conversation, this uncle of Abd el-Malik al-Houthi went to pick up his phone, as if he were going to make some calls or perhaps issue the magic order to free me. But the phone rang right then, right in his hand, even as he was dialing it, and everything seemed to stop in the room.

Abd el-Malik's uncle looked at Abeer, his eyes narrowing to slits.

"No," he said, still holding the receiver of the phone to his mouth. "No, we can't release your friend Mr. Sam. We still need to interrogate him."

That was the first and only confirmation that Abeer received about my location, my captors, or even the fact that I was alive. But it was crucial.

She knew who had me.

She knew that I was alive.

With my mother's efforts having stalled—after such a promising start through Nabih Berri to the leadership of Hezbollah—I believe my family felt a breath of fresh air, relief just to know I was alive and had been located, and that someone had the keys to let me go, even if they—the Houthis—were still unwilling to do so. Abeer had discovered a starting place, a piece of information that could be sent back through official channels in order to lend oomph to whatever negotiations were under way for my release.

Abeer says she doesn't know whom that call came from, but she guesses it must have been someone high up, perhaps even Abd el-Malik himself, since the uncle's opinion and stance changed so much, and since, other than the Houthi leader himself, probably only a few people would be willing to countermand that uncle.

But I have a different theory. Looking back on it, I think this all occurred exactly at the same time that Scott made his confession, exactly at the same time that I was getting my worst grilling about Scott and about Transoceanic. I think the call came from the interrogators at the prison and that renewed suspicions based on Scott's confession may have ruined an early opening for a release.

What's more, from this point forward, the Houthis and their partners in the NSB started treating Abeer more like a hostile player.

"What's in the bottle?" one of them asked. "Is it really medicine?"

Abeer tried to point to the label, clearly stating that it was, indeed, critical heart medicine, showing them and explaining the contents and my need for the medicine for what felt like the twentieth time. But they didn't care. Now they let their suspicions and imaginations run wild.

"Is it poison? Cyanide pills? Are you trying to smuggle this in to Mr. Sam so he will be silenced, so that he can kill himself and not spill American secrets? Are you working for the CIA?"

They took the pills (and never gave them to me, as evidenced by the heart attack I had a few weeks later!). From that point on, the Houthis blacklisted Abeer as well. When she showed up at the head-quarters building, they wouldn't see her. Sometimes they'd let her into the waiting rooms (such was the treatment of a woman and especially the daughter and niece of powerful men), but if anyone saw her, it was either for another round of interrogation or just to placate her. Never again did she have the chance to meet and plead with the sort of senior leadership who could have done something for me.

But she kept coming back, over and over, all throughout my time in prison.

And, in fact, even after I was let go, they still held a grudge against her, planning to pick her up and take her to prison the day after I was at last freed. Fortunately for her (and us), she had snuck away—heading first to Amman, then to Egypt, on the pretense of seeking medical treatment for her grandmother, going along as her grandmother's nurse and helper. Hers was the very last commercial flight that left Sana'a before the Saudi coalition grounded Yemenia. From that day on, no one could get in or out of Sana'a, as all the air carriers had ceased operating or were prevented from flying by the coalition, and the ports and harbors were blockaded.

■ ■ ■

ON THE 120TH DAY since I'd been thrown into the NSB prison, a new thing happened. Our guards came, opened up the cell door, and instead of taking one of us for questioning (and beating), they handcuffed us altogether, blindfolded us, led us from the room, and—with more chains and locks—cuffed us together en masse with a larger group lined up against a wall in the hallway. This made us nervous. Everyone felt it, that nervousness. New and different didn't mean—in fact seemed highly unlikely to mean—anything good.

Are they transporting us to a new facility?

Has something happened to this prison?

Is an attack on Sana'a imminent?

Are they ridding themselves of us, like the Nazis did as American and Soviet forces seized their concentration camps? Will we be shot with these chains binding us all together? Dumped in a mass grave, unknown and unknowable, made to disappear?

But none of that happened. (Later we learned that they had decided, for whatever reason, to check the cells for contraband, all at once, with all us prisoners vacated from the premises.)

They simply took us outside, into the sunshine, and made us sit with our backs against a courtyard wall. Then they instructed us to take off our blindfolds.

Sunshine and fresh air for the first time in 120 days!

At first the brightness, and also the freshness, hurt the eyes and seemed to scour the nose after our confinement in the dank concrete darkness for so long. Thrust out there, suddenly, with no warning, no preparation, you see the sun, but your brain takes time to adjust, time to see straight again, and even more time—after that—to believe and not fear what you are seeing and sensing.

As my eyes adjusted, I looked around and drank in my surroundings—hoping for but not finding a clue as to where we were. The place looked like the totally nondescript, moderately large courtyard of a moderately large building, just like a hundred or even a thousand other government buildings in and around Sana'a. On one side, where we propped our backs, the wall formed an L-shaped protrusion, perhaps fifteen by twenty meters. On the other side, a hill, or a cut in a hillside, or even perhaps a manmade berm, twenty-five or thirty feet high, created a barrier and prevented us from seeing anything beyond the building and the sky directly above that little enclosed space.

The building was three stories tall, without too many windows, just a couple looking down into the courtyard. The door we came out of remained the only one I could see, though I was sure a couple more must exist on the other side, as it appeared we had been given this bit of freedom at the back, enclosed, hidden end of the building. The ground beneath us was composed of cement for a certain distance around the building, a first few feet, then became gravel. I did not see a fence, though it would have been tough to climb the berm and impossible to escape the five or six armed guards who watched us, even if we weren't still chained together.

The idea of escape flitted through my mind, sure, just as it probably did for all of us. But no one acted on it. We all seemed content enough to admire the patch of sky above us, a truly beautiful blue. No clouds marred it, just a blue brightness almost frightful in its radiance.

As I lowered my eyes from the heavens, I saw Haitham and the others from my first cell. I nodded to them in recognition and smiled.

More importantly by far, though, for the first time in 120 days I saw Scott Darden.

He sat against the opposite side of the L-shaped wall. Almost without thinking of possible repercussions, I asked the guard, "Is it okay if I go sit next to him and talk to him?"

The guard thought for a moment but then said okay and uncuffed me from the chain-gang mass. He guided me to a spot next to Scott and rechained me back to the main line of grouped men. By that time I was so weak that I presented absolutely no threat to the guards. I think that made it easier for them to grant my request. I'd also been interrogated so much that they had gotten what they wanted out of me, out of Scott too, and I don't think they felt overly concerned that we might collude in our stories or hatch any sort of plan.

As I was led over to him, and as I sat and looked at Scott and he looked at me, we started crying, hugging, then crying more, hugging more, a sort of affection I never would have expected to share with him 120 days previously, when we were both simply employees of the same company.

We started talking all at once, both of us at the same time: *What's going on? What happened? What will the future hold? What's the possibility of being released?*

After a moment Scott's pale face took on a serious expression, and he held me at arm's length, both of his hands on my shoulders, looking me in the eyes. "I don't know, Sam," he said. "I don't know if we'll ever get released. I think they know too much about me. I don't think they'll ever let me go."

■ ■ ■

I DIDN'T KNOW THIS at the time, but more third-party attempts to obtain my release were being made by various groups. The Defense Intelligence Agency and the US Embassy didn't do much, at least not officially. It was the Omanis who began negotiating with the Houthis for my release on behalf of the US government, though the US government couldn't say they were doing anything, even through a proxy.

The US government didn't, and still doesn't, officially recognize the Houthis, making it hard for them to negotiate. How do you negotiate without first recognizing the other party's authority? Or how do you negotiate without accidentally recognizing that authority? Additionally, US policy with regard to hostages is never to negotiate or pay for release, because to do so tends only to encourage the act of hostage taking. From what I understand, the Omanis volunteered to serve as a go-between, just as they often do between the United States and Iran, and it was their efforts—especially now that the authorities knew I was in the custody of the NSB—that started to gain traction.

Hezbollah, as mentioned previously, wouldn't get involved because of my American citizenship. They had also found out I was a retired military officer. They didn't want anything to do with the situation on those grounds, in addition to actually having a pretty valid and empathetic concern about what it would look like for me if they got involved. They are Shi'a. I am Shi'a. We share a Lebanese connection. But they'd opted out for good reason. Still, they had opened some channels for communication and were willing, if all else failed, to try to get me released, even if that created political problems.

All of this was going down in the background, of course. I didn't know anything about it. But one release scenario did play out in my mind as I was being held; it played out in Scott's, too, it turns out. This involved mind games our captors liked to play with us, telling us the United Nations was negotiating our release, or the Red Cross, or Russia, or Denmark, or whoever. They did this to many of the international prisoners. I remember one specific guy from Rwanda detained there with us. They took him and told him he was being released, but a few hours later they just brought him back, and the prison cell—as I know from my own experience of being told similar things—seemed only smaller and bleaker to him because of it. They did the same to a guy from Syria, Abdel-azziz Azzou, telling him his release was happening and even putting him in a vehicle and driving him around Sana'a for a while before bringing him back to the same old cell.

Of course, even after I spoke with Scott in the courtyard about the futility of release, scenarios like this played on a constant loop in the forefront of my mind. I felt just as skeptical as Scott, but not quite as worried as he was about my connection to Transoceanic; he worked directly for them and had admitted to something onerous. I had admitted nothing, had nothing to admit, and only worked as a consultant. Still, I felt that my chances for a release were almost nothing and that if they decided to kill Scott, they'd most likely do away with me too. One less witness.

■ ■ ■

A WEEK AFTER THAT DAY in the courtyard, the guards brought me to the interrogation room again.

As well as the cessation of the beatings, due to my heart condition, another change had occurred over the last month in terms of the tone and content of the questions posed, as well as the time of day. Now they came for me in the evenings, during qat time, and they even permitted me to chew it with them. They were trying to play nice, of course, trying to make me more comfortable in the hope that I might slip and say something. Qat naturally makes you talkative. It stimulates conversation. And I think my questioners were somewhat bored, using me as a way to liven up their evenings, and they held on to a slim hope that they could get me to loosen up and admit to things I hadn't yet. Part of this new attitude involved a willingness to let me sit, though still handcuffed and blindfolded. I was able to get much more comfortable and could even use my hands to pick qat branches from the communal pile and feed the leaves to myself, my hands shackled together in the front, almost like a penitent praying.

During this session and several more similar, semifriendly "conversations" that followed (I hesitate to call them interrogations, since the tone and technique were so different), they would ask me things like "What would you do still for Yemen? Would you help work with us to make Yemen a better country, just as you used to do? Would you negotiate on our behalf?"

This put me in a spot. "Of course," I'd say, "I'll do anything to help the country. You know I've been helping Yemen for a long time, bringing aid, doing business, helping introduce people to each other and bridge cultures. Anything that is legal, I'm willing to do it. If you want me to be a conduit, to talk to whomever you like, I'll do it."

This type of accommodating and open response encouraged them. "Would you be willing to work for us?" they even asked.

"No, not willing," I'd say (over and over, drawing this fine distinction between help and co-optation).

This angered them somewhat. They were trying to recruit me, no doubt. Gently but definitely, they wanted me to join them. They were dangling the potential for my release and doing so with a condition attached to it, which is something we had studied and trained for—never to allow ourselves to be compromised by favors, favoritism, or deals of this sort.

Still, having sensed some openness on my part, they kept trying, using leverage from a similar but—they thought—deeper angle: "Your heritage, you're from southern Lebanon. We believe in the Twelve Imams. You believe in the Twelve Imams. We're both Shi'a."

This struck me as incredible. Though I kept my tongue and my patience, as I listened to this—still blindfolded and handcuffed—memories flashed through my mind of all the things they'd done to me, from stealing my money and my gun to the beatings and this unending imprisonment, even accusing me during those beatings of not being a good Shi'a. I couldn't believe that they'd now try to forget all of that, pretend it hadn't happened, pretend everything was and had been normal, and hope for me to play nice.

Being a Shi'a means being truthful and honest with yourself about your beliefs. The whole concept of Shi'ism started with and remains founded on the actions of Imam Hussein, *alayhi as-salaam*, remembering and acting on the reasons why he was sacrificed, why he was killed, dying for his belief in what was right. He didn't give in. He didn't give in to the nonbelievers—even if they still were Muslims—and he died a martyr's death for his principles.

So when they said, "You're Shi'a. We're Shi'a," it came through loaded with five months of mistreatment and a lifetime of me working to understand who I was. This made my response clear to me, maybe not an easy response, not with the threat of beatings still there, not with my body so very much weakened during the preceding months of torture, but still the response came to my mind and my tongue with perfect clarity.

"Yes," I said. "Yes, I'm Shi'a. But I'm also a US Marine."

CHAPTER 16

HOMECOMING

O NE NIGHT, a few days later, the guards came around to my cell— the third cell of my time in captivity—passing out new clothes, the traditional *dishdasha* robes. Many of the early prisoners, those with al-Qaeda backgrounds who had been caught and (sometimes) tried in a court of law, thereafter to be imprisoned by the previous government, wore these uniform *dishdashas* already. They were a strange sky-blue color (most *dishdashas* are white, gray, or brown) and included matching overalls or medical pants, like scrubs, under-neath. Because this uniform remained so strongly associated with long-term imprisonment *and* with al-Qaeda, I refused to exchange my clothes for the new ones. I didn't want to be marked as part of the institution. I didn't want that deeper level of association. It would have taken away a last bit of hope, making me more permanently part of the situation, somehow legitimizing my incarceration as if I were a common criminal or a terrorist rather than someone who had been taken hostage and detained illegally by what amounted to an unauthorized, unelected, coup-based government.

The two other prisoners with me in this new cell took their *dishdashas* without much protest. Their spirits had been broken. But I refused. In fact, getting just a little crazy, I screamed at the guards. I really made it a big thing, a big moment for me. It felt like it might perhaps be a last stand, at least for my psyche. In the end the guards just threw my *dishdasha* into the cell with those of the others and told us all to hand our civilian clothes out to them the next day.

When morning came, I hadn't touched the *dishdasha*.

The guards made their morning rounds.

They saw me in my civilian clothes: that same set of Bermuda shorts and that same collared shirt I'd been forced to wear since the very first day.

I ignored them as they opened the food hatch.

I knelt on the prayer rug, reading the Quran by the light that came in through the ventilation hole above the door, and I did not move or acknowledge the guards.

Speaking through the food hatch, the first guard somewhat calmly said, "Mr. Sam, what's your pant size? What's your shirt size?"

"No," I said, ready to fight him, them, all of them, again. "No, I'm not changing clothes. I'm not giving up these clothes. I'm not wearing that *dishdasha* or anything else."

"I need your pant size and shirt size."

"No, no, no," I said.

I put the Quran down, got up from the prayer rug, and walked all the way back to the corner where the little bathroom's half wall provided some shelter. I was still very upset, and I think I went into that corner as a physical sign of resistance, making a statement that I wouldn't cooperate.

"I'm not changing into the *dishdasha*. I'm not giving you my clothes sizes. I'm not surrendering these clothes I'm wearing now."

"Please, Mr. Sam," the guard said, almost pleading with me, "I need your shirt and pants sizes *and* your shoe size."

When he said those words, asking not just for the shirt and pants sizes but also for the shoe size, the whole conversation changed. All of us knew the guards only asked for your shoe size when you were getting out. It had long served as something of a magic word. The few fellow prisoners we'd seen released had been asked for their shoe size and shortly thereafter given shoes or at least a pair of *shibshib*, which is what we called the prison slippers. Between the three of us in that cell, just as between me and Haitham and the cell mates in my first cell and between those in my second cell, we'd shared but a single pair of *shibshib*, using them to keep our feet out of the filth around the edges of the open pit toilet, but then going barefoot at all other times.

Shoes represented not just a luxury but a link to freedom.

As soon as this guard told me he needed my shoe size, the guys in the cell looked at me and jumped up and said, "You're getting out. You're getting out."

I dropped to my knees, right there in the bathroom corner, and just broke down in tears—keeping the guard waiting uncomfortably at the door.

"I'm a nine," I said at last, after I caught my breath and my heart slowed a little.

Yet even as I said this, I started having misgivings. I'd seen similar things happen quite a few times in cells next to us, all the signals and hints and steps being taken to make it look like one of my fellow inmates might be released, only to see them brought back, with negotiations having failed or the guards having finished whatever psychological torture, whatever mind games they'd concocted in their boredom and sadism. I cried at being asked for my shoe size, sure. And this made me feel like they'd gotten me, like they'd gotten *to* me, which immediately brought to mind all the feelings and doubts and worries about how tenuous this could be, about how much it depended on chance and might only be the beginning of an elaborate ruse.

Nevertheless, I had only one course before me, and that course I knew I must follow to the end, wherever it might lead: I had to cooperate. I started praying, thanking God. The guys in that cell demonstrated genuine happiness for me—despite our different backgrounds and situations. They danced around, held hands, helped me to my feet, and slapped me on my shoulders. Those in the cells next door could hear what was going on and joined in the celebration, banging on the doors, shouting, "Farah, farah!"—*enjoy, enjoy.*

The guards of course immediately told us all to be quiet, but no one listened to them. I remember doing this for others, the dancing, the shouting, the celebration—a way to mark time and keep our chins up. We'd wish joy to the departing person, and peace, and tell them not to forget us. We'd tell them not to forget to pray for us from the outside, once they got there. We'd say, "Ma'salama, ala ameena"—*go in peace and righteousness.*

We'd tell each other one other important thing: that getting out of "The Grave," as we called that prison, needed to be looked upon as something akin to a miracle. In fact, to those lucky enough to get asked for their shoe size, we said, "You've got a new birth. Use it wisely."

I gave the guard all my sizes, all my sizes as I remembered them before coming to the prison and losing many, many pounds. He wrote them down and departed, and I remained behind, just where I had been for all those unending days, except now I sat in joyous expectation. This made time dilate, seeming to slow down. The guard had only been gone for about an hour before returning, but it seemed like an entire day.

They didn't bring clothes, not quite yet. Instead, two guards opened the cell, just like always, and called for me. But they didn't blindfold me. Nor did they shackle me. They just led me out the door and set me down in the hallway next to a bathroom that had all along been intended for use by the inmates. Up until that moment, though, I hadn't even seen its doorway, let alone used it. The door was propped open. From where I sat, I could see inside: rows of sinks and a communal shower space. One of the guards entered, took a leak in one of the stalls, and looked over his shoulder at me, smiling. I tried not to watch him, but my mind—so long deprived of new information of any kind—frantically grasped at even this bit of trivia, a communal bathroom with hot water right there under our noses, never used! It made the place seem brand-new, foreign, and even amazing after such a long time of sensory deprivation in the three utterly bleak and similar cells that had been my nearly exclusive habitat for the previous six months.

I was left in the hallway, sitting alone against the wall, for about five or ten minutes.

Then they brought Scott.

They let us talk to each other, which we started to do as soon as he took his seat beside me, whispering, embracing. I hadn't seen him for a month and a half since we'd met in the sunshine of the courtyard on our one trip outdoors.

We looked at each other, and we were like, *Is this for real?*

Tears came to his eyes and to mine. Both of us spoke, all at once, asking and answering questions as rapidly as we could, garbling everything.

"I don't know. I don't know," I remember saying. We were guessing who might have been conducting the negotiations for our release. We were examining the signs of our imminent potential freedom, trying to decide whether each of them might be real—the lack of blindfolds, the lack of shackles, the fact we could just make a run for it right at that moment if we wanted, the promised newly sized clothes the guards were bringing.

Then one of the guards returned with an electric razor and told us to shave our beards, which had grown to eight or ten inches, unruly, unkempt.

Another guard came with the new clothes, one pile for me, one for Scott. He handed each of us a bag within which we found a T-shirt, underwear, belt, socks, shoes, pants, and a button-down shirt, all of it brand-new, smelling of the market and the outdoors.

We clutched the bags to our chests as they took us downstairs, leading us into a regular office room, three or four desks in it, chairs, kind of a spare room of sorts, not used for too much. In one corner two of those Chinese privacy screens cordoned off private spaces. We stepped behind them, one of us behind each, and put on the new clothes: draping, baggy, enormous because of the pre-confinement clothing sizes I had provided. But I couldn't have cared less. They

were the visible badge of an impending departure—of a future different from the weeks and months I had just endured. They represented
home, sunshine, outdoors, family, and the freedom of self-
determination. They represented a definite end to the possibility of
more beatings. They represented life.

Or, as our cell mates reminded us, just before we left them, they
represented a new birth.

Of the items they inventoried at the beginning of my captivity,
the guards returned only my computer bag, two rings, one of which
was my Marine Corps ring, and my watch. All the rest, the money,
my handgun, the electronic components and cameras from the
house, my cell phones, my computer, all of that was gone. Also they
took my Mont Blanc pen, an expensive pen, which had been a gift.
It was a diamond edition, with a real diamond up top, and I bet they
didn't even know what it meant. It seems like a trifling thing, but it
poured a little salt in the wound, and it points to the mercenary and
thievish quality of all of this. The money amounted to about $6,000,
gone, never to be seen again.

The Marine Corps ring presented some consolation. It meant a lot
to me because I'd had it for thirty-six years at that time, and this experience of captivity had only solidified the Marine Corps as part of my
identity. I went into captivity a retired Marine. I came out feeling like
I'd endured, and endured well enough, the most frightening thing that
the Marines had ever tried to prepare me for, this hostage situation.

Still, I couldn't help thinking about the missing inventory items.
Though it amounted to pushing my luck, I asked, "Where's the rest
of our stuff?"

They said, "It's on its way. We're going to give you everything
back."

But we never saw it again. Frankly, although it irritated me not to get my things back, it did not diminish my joy at being set free.

After we changed, they brought out written documents and made us sign them with thumbprints. "Here you go. If you want to leave, you've got to sign these."

"What are these?"

"Confessions."

I knew we weren't supposed to sign confessions, but they didn't let us read them, and frankly, with release so close at hand and the captivity so patently illegal, I didn't really care. Nor did Scott.

We signed. To this day I still don't know what my "confession" said or what sort of words they put into my mouth, even though I didn't actually confess to anything. Whatever they made up, they made up. Mine wasn't a short document. It extended a full seven or eight pages in total, crammed with lines of script. I put my thumb on their inkpad and pressed it down next to my name, and that was that.

Scott went through a slightly more arduous process. They took him outside the room and videotaped him saying something, probably some sort of propaganda or something related to what he'd already told them. I never asked. They didn't video me. When they videoed him, I could see a couple of the interrogators pointing their fingers right in his face in what looked like threats. I thought I would be up next, made to stand in front of the rolling camera, but they didn't require the same from me.

After that, we sat around for another two hours, waiting in the office area. My long military career prepared me well for this, a routine we call "hurry up and wait." I knew things wouldn't move fast. I knew many cogs were turning outside and that patience was really our only choice. Still, the minutes seemed to tick slowly, slowly. We spent the time talking to two of the interrogators, in fact the last two guys who had been trying to "befriend" me via qat chews. They'd begun chewing already, getting out a plastic shopping bag filled with fresh branches and plopping it on one of the tables in that underused office room. They offered some to me, and I accepted it, both to calm my nerves and because I just didn't think it would be right to refuse them at that moment.

The qat kicked in. We became a bit more gregarious. The passage of time didn't matter quite as much. Then things started to happen again.

One of the guards received a call on his phone.

They blindfolded us once again.

It felt weird. With the taste of freedom in our mouths, uncertainty still clung to these actions. Who knew where they were taking us. Perhaps they were still playing with us, carrying out one of their threats to take us up to Saadah. Perhaps they'd just shoot us after all.

The blindfolds awakened memories of trauma, so many moments over the last months of being herded out of the prison cells, down the unseen hallways, past rooms with no known purpose, just gaping voids in our sensory-deprived understanding, gaping voids we could hear and feel but never see. Blindfolds that led us to beatings. Blindfolds that represented our initial bagging and kidnapping. Blindfolds that told us, in no uncertain terms, that we had once again lost control over our destinies and must rely on our captors to lead us, to treat us right, to keep us safe, that we must bear whatever punishment and pain they intended to mete out.

But we had no choice. We had to go along.

The blindfolds were worrisome, but we felt reassured in our new clothes and shoes and by the fact that we wore no shackles. I could bear the blindfold. I'd become an expert in wearing it! I could bear it with all this potential freedom ahead of me.

The guards guided us out. They put us in a vehicle, a smallish SUV, me and Scott and one other guy crammed three across in the backseat. Up front both seats were filled. The driver, strangely enough, seemed to be the guy in charge. This also gave us hope, because if they meant to torture us, kill us, or play some other sort of terrible joke, they'd surely have more people with them for support, and the type of individual who took pleasure in such games wasn't the type to drive his own car. Sadists loved having others do the menial work. Sadists wouldn't be pretending to drive us to our freedom.

About five minutes after we left the facility, they took the blindfolds off us, and we saw the outside world for the first time in months. We were on Airport Road, one of the main arteries in Sana'a, a north-south thoroughfare running along the east side of town, right below the US Embassy and the Sheraton. It was midday by this time. There was an eeriness to the world. Everyone outside the windows was going about their normal day, though Sana'a looked terrible—the buildings bombed, the faces of the people gaunt and haunted, dust and decay everywhere. I was torn between the intense stimulation of having something to look at and the sadness I saw outside.

On the drive, during a lull in the edgy, uncomfortable, nervous conversation, I again mustered the courage (or foolishness?) to ask about the missing items they had taken and inventoried. The driver, the boss of this expedition, turned to me and very politely explained, "It's at another location, at the Old Sana'a location, our headquarters there. If you want your stuff, that's fine. We can go back and wait in a cell until someone can fetch it all."

Those last words had an edge. We understood the threat immediately. Scott looked at me. And I looked at him. And we shook our heads at each other in unison, in a definite "fuck that" expression. I dropped the questions about our missing gear and never brought the subject up again.

When we arrived at the airport, they took us to the VIP lounge, secluded from the main terminal. We sat in overstuffed leather chairs, guards still around us, uncomfortably comfortable for another hour.

As a means of mental resistance and religious strength, I had fasted for five of the six months of this captivity. I was fasting that day, like most days, and so did not avail myself of the cappuccino stand in the corner of the VIP lounge or the snacks. They seemed unreal. Scott did not touch them either. We just sat, on the edge of our seats not in a physical way but certainly in an emotional one.

The Omani plane landed, a huge 737, one of the only civilian planes we'd seen on the runway.

It touched down, and our hearts stirred, as if we could get up right then and run out of the lounge directly onto the tarmac. It was right there. Right in front of us, just a glass door away. We could run out to the big passenger plane and grab hold of the wheels and simply signal to it to fly away, not to linger, not to chance it. We could hold on. We would hold on until we crossed the border with Yemen.

Whatever it might take. We could do that, even in our weakened, emaciated state.

We didn't make a run for it.

We waited.

We gripped the leather armrests.

We watched the seconds tick by on the gaudily ornate clocks in the lounge. We listened to the news, each word as slow and uninteresting as molasses.

We watched the guards finger their weapons, pick at their nails or their noses, look at us, at the plane, at the door, at the ceiling, at their shoes.

Finally, the plane pulled up, almost right up to the door of the VIP lounge.

One of the guards opened the door. The backwash from the jets buffeted the room. They beckoned for us to stand, to approach. A stairway was maneuvered into place alongside the jet. The door opened. We climbed in, and the guards prodded us past the first-class seats and into the front row of the economy class.

It was just the two of us sitting there for perhaps another ten minutes. Then other people started arriving, filling up the seats. Within an hour, the seats had filled completely with people who were injured, going for treatment in Oman, accompanied by their families, doing whatever they could to get the heck out of there. We became something of a ticket to freedom not just for ourselves but for all of the passengers boarding that day. Part of the deal must have been for the Omanis to stay neutral and keep the peace talks going, and by bringing that plane in and taking the injured out, they were doing the Houthis a favor. They also brought a Houthi delegation, including Muhammad Abd as-Salam, the chief negotiator for the Houthis, heading to a round of talks in Muscat.

After the plane filled, when we still sat motionless before the VIP lounge, the Omani pilot came on over the loudspeaker and said, "We're waiting on a third American to take off."

Scott and I looked at each other. We didn't know of another American being held—though of course, we knew nothing of what had happened during the previous six months.

We saw this as a positive though, thinking, *Alright, one more American being freed.*

After another moment of pondering, Scott turned to me and said, "You know what, this is great. I think my mother's birthday is coming up. This is going to be a great surprise for her."

"Really, wow! When's her birthday?"

"September 20."

"Scott, today is September 20."

"Oh, man. I'm going to call her as soon as we get to Muscat. Going to call her on her birthday."

His hopes were sky-high. I could see it in his eyes.

This made me nervous.

I didn't want to see his spirit crushed. But I knew a million things could still go wrong, everything from administrative issues that might ground the plane and force us to remain in the VIP lounge or the terminal or a temporary holding cell for a few more hours to the whole shebang getting called off. Back to prison we might still go.

I didn't say any of this to Scott though. I just smiled at him, patted his hand.

"It'll be okay," I said, as much to myself as to him.

We sat there and waited for what seemed like days, though it likely lasted two hours, perhaps three.

The sinking feeling started to creep in.

Scott kept checking his watch.

The Omani pilot came over the intercom again: "They're not re-leasing the third American."

We both had the same thought: *We're leaving someone behind.* That was a huge taboo in the military. Drummed into our heads. But what could we do?

Our thoughts turned once more toward the reality, the dubious-ness of our situation: *They're going to renege on their word and take us back too now.*

Helpless, hopeful but tense, and never letting ourselves really feel any joy, we sat and sat. Deep in our hearts we knew they'd do it. Ei-ther the American side or the Houthis, one of them would call it off, insist on all three of us hostages or none of us. That formed into both a worry and a sadness, because we wanted to get out of there but also didn't want to leave someone behind. We were totally torn. We heard his name discussed among the stewardesses: Luqman, Waleed Luqman. I knew the name; he was another Marine veteran, but one who had come to Yemen to teach English. He'd been taken off a bus, trying to flee with his family across the border to Saudi Arabia. I suppose, like me, he had thought his religion, and in his case his family, would keep him safe. It did not. They detained him for no cause, just as they had done Scott and me.

Upfront a commotion ensued. The lead Houthi negotiator, Mu-hammad Abd as-Salam, had stood and was taking up a blocking posi-tion in the doorway of the plane. Outside a couple of armed guys argued with him, pointing at Scott and me, insisting that we get off the plane so that they could take us back. The Houthi negotiator stood firm though, saying, "No, it's going to be bad for our negotiations."

This escalated into yelling and screaming, right over the heads of the whole delegation in first class, pointing at us, waving their guns.

In the end Abd as-Salam's argument, or his shouting, prevailed. He got back on the plane. The stewardesses hurried to close the doors. The pilot fired his engines up, and—with Scott and me still in shock, still not believing that we'd managed to stay aboard—the plane plodded out onto the runway, where I knew a few dozen guns mounted on the back of vehicles, tanks, machine guns, and .50cals were all pointed at us and could stop us or drop us like a stone from the sky. Yet the plane rolled on, cornered, and took its stance like a bull pawing at the ground. The engines roared, and we felt the acceleration run down our spines as the plane chugged, then sped, then finally grew weightless as the runway, and Sana'a, and Yemen disappeared below.

Again, for perhaps the tenth time that day, Scott and I broke down in tears and hugged each other, a sense of relief like none other, coupled with the unbearably sad knowledge that we'd left a fellow American behind.

We were served a meal on the plane, and I broke my fast in celebration, just a simple cheese sandwich, but it tasted great after all the prison food. I drank a soda too, for the first time in six months—a 7Up.

After all that waiting, the flight seemed super short, only two and a half hours to Muscat.

We landed.

The senior member of the Omani delegation on the plane, an official from the sultan's office, lined us up, the two Americans, a Somali-UK citizen, and three Saudis still in handcuffs. We would precede the Houthi delegation off the plane. He looked at me, thinner and more pitiful than Scott by far, and said, "You go first, then Scott."

I almost fell down the stairs in my weakness and my utter tearful joy. I couldn't see straight, let alone walk straight. I'm glad I didn't fall though, because thirty or forty people waited below, some of them news crews with cameras. It would have been really embarrassing to have this moment of freedom and release memorialized forever with images of me face down on the tarmac.

We could see the crowd out the window before we disembarked, waiting aboard as the Omani airport workers wheeled the stairs into place. In addition to the news cameras, of which there were seven or eight, the gathered people included a number of personnel from the embassy: the ambassador, Greta Holtz, of course, her deputy chief of mission (DCM), the embassy doctor, and—the first familiar face I had seen in six months—the embassy's legal attaché, or LEGATT, Paul Crutcher, who had served in the same post in Yemen until the embassy was evacuated there.

I don't remember all of the words that were said, not in exact detail. Emotion overwhelmed everything to a great extent. Some of it is captured in video, and I can watch and rewatch it on news clips from the time. But doing that seems like I'm spying on someone completely different. I hardly recognize myself in the photos or the videos. I'm gaunt, pale, haggard despite having shaved for the first time in a long while. My eyes look hollow. I can tell I'm not focusing very well.

The ambassador thanked the sultan and his staff for their work on our release; then we were taken into the Omani VIP lounge. Sultan Qaboos was not there himself, but one of his senior ministers greeted us, along with a few other high-ranking Omanis, all in their traditional ceremonial outfits—*khanjjars, kumah* caps on, long robes—very distinguished and solemn but also happy and understandably proud of the role they'd played in our release. In the lounge we sat for a few minutes for pictures, talking to the ambassador and DCM and doctor. Then the doctor took us into another room and did a quick medical checkup to see whether we needed any urgent treatment. He gave both Scott and me some Tylenol, just in case there was pain, and pronounced us fit enough to make it through the night, until the next day, when he'd conduct a more thorough examination.

We loaded into a car and easily, somewhat majestically, like all the world was frozen in time, sealed away behind glass, completed the last leg of this journey to freedom in an embassy car, letting them take us to the waterfront Sheraton in a nice area of Muscat. The concierge had rooms already set up for us. They just gave us keys and ushered us in. "You're the guest of the sultan. Anything you want, just order it, please."

It seemed weird getting to a hotel room and having that much luxury, a bed, sheets, perfumed towels, a view over the beach and the Indian Ocean. I sat for a moment, collecting myself, sighing. Then I undressed and took the longest and hottest shower of my life, thinking the whole time that running heated water was probably the greatest invention of all time. In the cell we'd barely gotten to take a lukewarm bath, always waiting for the warmest of days and then, in Sana'a's mountain air, hoping the sun at noon or 1 p.m. might warm the rooftop water tanks just enough. Then the guy who went first would be luckiest, and we'd take turns afterward in the lukewarm water. That day, though, in the Sheraton, I luxuriated.

I'd put on a terrycloth bathrobe and soft slippers—no more *shib-shib!*—when a knock on my door stirred me.

The concierge stood there, holding a cell phone on a platter. "Please," he said, "use this and dial whomever you'd like."

I remembered my sister's number. I knew she'd be with my mother, so I called her first. They had some advance warning that I might be set free, but they had not received confirmation yet. Worse, they'd been told once before that an American was being released, but it turned out not to be me. So they were waiting, breath held of course, but also not counting on anything as a certainty. Indeed, three of us were supposed to be released that day, but only we two made it out, so they were wise in guarding against too much optimism.

I picked up the phone and dialed.

"Hello," I said, "it's me."

I could hear my mother inhale, a big sucking noise. But no words came out.

Silence.

Then I heard her weeping.

Connected to my mother like that, through the umbilical cord of modern technology, all the way around the world, I couldn't help but remember the words of my cell mates in the Sana'a prison.

"Yes, Mom, yes. This is my new birthday."

EPILOGUE

WALEED LUQMAN, the Marine who did not get on the plane with Scott Darden and me, boarded a similar plane to freedom later that year.

Scott and I flew to America after a short layover in Oman. We first touched down on American soil in New York City, fitting as the beacon of liberty, even if that stop was simply a layover. From there, I continued onward to Detroit. As I came off the plane in Detroit, personnel from Homeland Security, from immigration, from customs, and from the FBI all met me in the terminal to make sure everything went smoothly. This was necessary, because I didn't have any of my papers—though the embassy had issued me an emergency passport.

All the news channels swarmed me at the airport and even at my house after I arrived. You can see it still in clips on CNN and YouTube—my homecoming, being greeted by my mother, family, and relations.* The best part about it was when my granddaughter ran to me, letting me pick her up, jumping or nearly flying into my arms, as she said, "*Jido*, Grandfather, are you here to take me to Chuckie Cheese?"

This, of course, doesn't end the story of Yemen's troubles, even though it largely ended the story of my troubles there.

The Saudi coalition's war continues amid what is now the world's worst humanitarian disaster: famine exacerbated by blockade and disease, including, of course, COVID-19 (though it is tough to know the numbers) as well as a terrible outbreak of cholera. Qat addiction continues, and arable land that could grow food for many Yemenis is used instead to generate profits and service the national Yemeni pastime. And then there is the war too—people living in the crumbling, bombed-out buildings, people dying in wreckage. The rumor is that all sides want to resolve the conflict. They consider this war their Vietnam. Everyone is tired of it—everyone except the ex-Yemeni government figures who continue to live in five-star hotels in Saudi, Lebanon, Jordan, and elsewhere as they "negotiate."

I've been in Lebanon for most of the time since then, living in a house I built on the outskirts of my village of Tebnine. I'm surrounded there by my family. My granddaughters come to visit in the summer from Dearborn. My sister is there, though most of my childhood friends have emigrated to the United States. Yesterday, as a matter of fact, I walked the same side street that leads up to

---

* See Associated Press and Belinda Robinson, "American Hostage Who Was Freed After Being Imprisoned During Yemen's Raging Civil War Returns Home to the U.S.," *Mail Online*, https://www.dailymail.co.uk/news/article-3246160/Man-2-US-hostages-freed-Yemen-returns-Michigan.html.

the ruin where my grandfather's house once stood. A few doors down, I sat and had coffee with my cousins in the shade of their family house, during that long and golden hour of communal bliss we call the *saha*. The cousins sit there every day. Every day they have their coffee. Every day they have their chitchat. Some things never change.

My family has served forty-three continuous years now in the United States armed forces, beginning with me and my generation, but now with both my son Tech Sergeant Ali Farran and my niece Captain Rowan Latif in the US Air Force. Captain Latif is, in fact, deployed in Kuwait as of the writing of this epilogue.

I believe the experience of my family as immigrants to and faithful warriors and servants of this country is not unique. We are, almost all of us, immigrants to this land. These last years have been divisive in many ways, not the least of which involve changing perceptions of the value of immigration. As such, I'd like to leave you with this excerpt from President Ronald Reagan's final farewell speech, a speech that talked about the immigrant strength of our nation:

I've spoken of the shining city all my political life, but I don't know if I ever quite communicated what I saw when I said it. But in my mind, it was a tall, proud city built on rocks stronger than oceans, wind swept, God-blessed, and teeming with people of all kinds living in harmony and peace; a city with free ports that hummed with commerce and creativity, and if there had to be city walls, the walls had doors and the doors were open to anyone with the will and the heart to get here. That's how I saw it, and see it still.

EPILOGUE

And how stands the city on this winter night? More prosperous, more secure, and happier than it was eight years ago. But more than that: After 200 years, two centuries, she still stands strong and true on the granite ridge, and her glow has held steady no matter what storm. And she's still a beacon, still a magnet for all who must have freedom, for all the pilgrims from all the lost places who are hurtling through the darkness, toward home.

ACKNOWLEDGMENTS

S O MANY people have been an important part of my life that to
mention all of them, I would need to write an additional chapter.
This list is necessarily, therefore, incomplete. If you've ever interacted
with me, you know that I have thought of you and you are here, silently acknowledged.

The most influential people in my life have been my father, Mohammed, who always taught me that truth and honesty are the best
ways forward; my mother, Rahme Fawaz, who worked all of her life
to provide a better life for my siblings and me; those siblings themselves, too—Ibtisam, Hisham, and Bassem, who are the backbone of
our family; my late uncle Robert Hamzey, a one-of-a-kind person
who sponsored us to come to America back when my mother decided we must leave the Middle East; my wife and first love, Zeinab,
who held things together for me, a true military wife; my children,
Mohammed, Ali, Marcelle, and Amira, and granddaughters, Sophia
and Samantha, for the big part they've played in fulfilling my life.

Beyond family, I'd like to thank Ben Buchholz, who put this book
together with me; Elise Capron, our agent; and Robert Pigeon, our
very patient editor, who worked hard on getting this book into print.
I'd also like to thank my brothers and sisters in arms, especially my
fellow Marines, who made me the man I am today; as well as all the

fabulous, dedicated diplomats I've served with during times both fun and difficult.

Last but not least, I would like to acknowledge a man who has been my second father and mentor since my father passed away—a man who in every sense exhibited the ultimate in kindness, sincerity, and integrity: my uncle George (Jalil) Saad.

INDEX

Page numbers in *italics* indicate maps.

INDEX

INDEX